Similarity and Symbols in Human Thinking

edited by Steven A. Sloman and Lance J. Rips

A Bradford Book

The MIT Press
Cambridge, Massachusetts
London, England

Reprinted from COGNITION: International Journal of Cognitive Science, Volume 65, Numbers 2–3, 1998. The MIT Press has exclusive license to sell this English-language book edition throughout the world.

Library of Congress Cataloging-in-Publication Data

Similarity and symbols in human thinking / edited by Steven A. Sloman and Lance J. Rips.—1st MIT Press ed.
    p.   cm.—(Cognition special issues)
"Reprinted from Cognition: international journal of cognitive science, volume 65, numbers 2–3, 1998"—T.P. verso.
Includes bibliographical references and index.
ISBN 0-262-69214-7 (pbk. : alk. paper)
    1. Cognition. 2. Human information processing. 3. Psycholinguistics. 4. Symbolism (Psychology). 5. Similarity (Psychology). I. Sloman, Steven A. II. Rips, Lance J. III. Series.
BF311.S5676   1998
153.4'2—dc21   98-7439
                                                                           CIP

Contents

1   Similarity as an explanatory construct   1
Steven A. Sloman and Lance J. Rips

2   Two dogmas of conceptual empiricism: implications for hybrid models of the structure of knowledge   17
Frank C. Keil, W. Carter Smith, Daniel J. Simons, and Daniel T. Levin

3   Similarity-based categorization and fuzziness of natural categories   51
James A. Hampton

4   Alternative strategies of categorization   81
Edward E. Smith, Andrea L. Patalano, and John Jonides

5   Similarity and rules: distinct? exhaustive? empirically distinguishable?   111
Ulrike Hahn and Nick Chater

6   Reuniting perception and conception   145
Robert L. Goldstone and Lawrence W. Barsalou

7   Similarity and the development of rules   177
Dedre Gentner and José Medina

Index   213

Similarity as an explanatory construct

Steven A. Sloman[a,*], Lance J. Rips[b]

[a]*Department of Cognitive and Linguistic Sciences, Brown University, Box 1978, Providence, RI 02912, USA*
[b]*Psychology Department, Northwestern University, 2029 Sheridan Road, Evanston, IL 60208, USA*

Abstract

Theories can be found throughout cognitive science that give an explanatory role to similarity. Such theories can be contrasted with those that model thought using abstract rules. We lay out four possible explanatory roles for similarity. We then review the computational pros and cons of similarity- and rule-based models and outline the empirical work that speaks to the psychological plausibility of the two frameworks. We conclude that an adequate model of human thought must take advantage of both the flexibility of similarity-based inference and the compositionality and certainty associated with rule-based inference. © 1998 Elsevier Science B.V.

Keywords: Similarity; Rule-based inference

1. Introduction

Poor old Aunt Bess has passed away, leaving you some items from her antique collection. There are the fondu forks and the candy dispensers. There's the well-thumbed copy of Hilgard and Marquis, and there's a dusty painting of a vase in multiple perspective. One of Uncle Herbert's better efforts? Or did Aunt Bess have a piece of art on her hands whose value she never realized?

Braque or Uncle Herb? This is a question about categorization: the painting's properties are given to you through perception, and your job is to assign it to a category. But you could also face a somewhat similar question about the inferences you are willing to make on the basis of your knowledge of the new painting. For example, suppose you see that this very painting has rigidium-based paint. The

* Corresponding author. e-mail: Steven_Sloman@brown.edu

question this time is: Do Picassos have rigidium-based paint? Do Whistlers have it? Finally, we can phrase some of the same issues in terms of decision making. Let's say this time that you're shopping for a painting with certain ideal properties, say, having some historical significance, being relatively inexpensive, and fitting the color scheme of your breakfast nook. Would you purchase this painting?

There's a simple theory of how people make all these judgments, a theory that has an enormous appeal to many cognitive scientists. According to this theory, the judgments crucially involve determining the similarity between the specimen and some other relevant entity and then basing the judgment on the resulting degree of similarity. In the case of categorizing, you determine the similarity between the specimen and the prototypes or examples of the categories to which it might belong. For example, you measure the similarity between the new painting and Braque's and between the new painting and Uncle Herbert's. If the similarity to Braque's is sufficiently great, you will call it a Braque; if the similarity to Uncle Herbert's is sufficiently great, you'll call it an Uncle Herbert; and if the similarity falls below the criterion for both categories, you'll place the painting in a new category of its own. In the case of inference-making, similarity may also be the operative principle. If the new painting has rigidium-based paint and if the painting is sufficiently similar to Picassos, then you may be tempted to infer that Picassos have rigidium paint too. And in the decision-making example, if the painting is sufficiently similar to your ideal piece of art, then you'll decide to purchase it.

Part of the appeal of this picture is that it fits so well the traditional world view of experimental psychologists. Explanation in psychology has at its disposal a few key concepts that it wields to account for a host of phenomena. Frequency is one such concept, salience is another, similarity is a third. If we can reduce an effect to a difference in frequency, salience, or similarity, then no more need be said. These three abideth; but the greatest of these is similarity.

Or is it? Although similarity is appealing because of its wide range of application, it strikes many contemporary researchers as a little too easy. For one thing, your judgment of the similarity between two objects can fluctuate with changes in the task you're performing. Your assessment of the similarity between A and B may depend on the set of other objects in the stimulus set, on the direction of the comparison (*How similar is A to B?* versus *How similar is B to A?*), on whether the comparison is based on relational or nonrelational information, and probably on many other factors (Tversky, 1977; Goldstone et al., 1991). For another, explanations based on similarity often look circular. With a little brain storming, we can almost always come up with properties that A shares with B, for any B. With respect to these properties, A and B will be similar, but with respect to some other set of properties dissimilar (Goodman, 1955; Murphy and Medin, 1985). Suppose we want the new painting in our example to be a Braque. If we use similarity to decide the issue, we can rig this outcome by selecting or emphasizing properties that it shares with Braques, but we could have equally well rigged the decision in favor of Uncle Herb.

Because of these problems with similarity, we seem to have a choice. We can preserve similarity as an explanatory principle by tinkering with it to avoid its undesirable properties. Or we can give up on similarity, trying to handle categorization, inference, decision making, and other cognitive skills through different mechanisms. Similarity works best in domains where there is little choice about the properties that determine the outcome. It seems most suspect in domains where the key properties are variable and task dependent. To get similarity to work in these higher-level domains, you need an independent way to select the relevant properties for input to the similarity process, but it often seems that these selection routines are doing all the important work. Why not abandon similarity altogether, then, and elaborate the selection routines?

Here's an example of the difficulty we have in mind (from a thought experiment that Tienson, 1988, has expounded): Take a triangle and remove a tiny piece from one vertex, replacing the piece with a straight line segment, as shown in Fig. 1. The result of this operation, on the right of Fig. 1, looks an awful lot like—we might even say, is awfully similar to—a triangle, but it isn't. It's a quadrilateral. To explain why we classify the figure as a quadrilateral rather than a triangle, we could say that we've computed the similarity of the object to quadrilaterals using the property of having four sides. But the similarity comparison is doing no useful work here. Once we know it has four sides, we have all we need to classify the figure correctly. Moreover, our untutored similarity judgments seem to reach a verdict opposite that of the classification decision. We might very well judge the figure more similar to triangles than to quadrilaterals.

Similarity as an explanation isn't very tempting in cases like that of Fig. 1, where we have theoretical information on which to base our decision. The same is true of the painting example, since whether the thing is a Braque or an Uncle Herbert surely depends on who painted it and not on its similarity to other paintings by these masters. Investigators who are suspicious of the role similarity plays in cognitive science have tried to capitalize on these cases, showing that theory also enters into more everyday instances of classification and reasoning. There are many different cognitive mechanisms we can choose from in order to carry out these theory-based decisions, but for convenience we will lump them under the heading of *rules*.

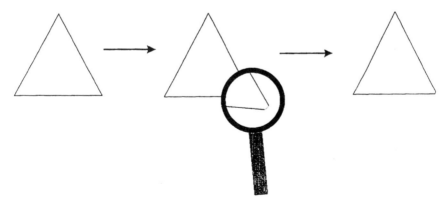

Fig. 1. Steps in Tienson's (1988) thought experiment: a small part of the vertex of the triangle at left is snipped out and replaced by a straight line. The resulting figure at right is a quadrilateral, despite retaining similarity to triangles.

The issue of general interest to cognitive science is whether rules or similarity or both are psychologically plausible ways to explain cognitive processes. Both kinds of systems have specific computational advantages and disadvantages and both kinds of systems find empirical motivation. This special issue considers the issue from several perspectives. Our papers span cognitive and developmental psychology, neuroscience, and theory of computation, and they include new empirical results as well as new efforts at theoretical integration. The papers certainly do not speak with a single voice; rather, they cover the range of problems and issues that animate the rules vs. similarity debate.

2. Four views of similarity

The role of similarity is a matter of debate in most areas of cognitive science that study thinking. Similarity has entered into accounts of concept formation, reasoning, decision making, and many other areas. The term typically refers to the outcome of a comparison among entities, usually a comparison based on many of the entities' properties. Objects are similar to the degree that they have features in common and do not have distinctive features. But not all comparisons produce a measure of similarity. (Consider a computer comparing two bit patterns to decide its next operation). Rather, similarity employs comparison to assess how much the entities depart from identity. Beyond the notions of a comparison and measure of departure from identity, however, similarity is open to competing interpretations, interpretations that ascribe it explanatory roles that differ widely in their strength. Here's a sample of possible positions along this continuum:

2.1. Strong similarity

At one extreme is the 'original sim' view that similarity is primitive in perception and cognition. Although our *judgments* of similarity might be subject to biases, there is a raw feeling of similarity that we have when we confront two objects that is fixed once and for all by our cognitive system. We'd expect similarity of this stripe to be relatively automatic, fast, perceptual, and impenetrable (i.e. unaffected by a person's other beliefs). On this view, similarity is loaded with explanatory power, for similarity relations are fundamental.

2.2. Weak similarity

A less extreme view holds that similarity is not fixed and irreducible, but the algorithm that computes similarity is. According to this view, similarity is a result of a well-defined, highly specialized computation. However, the computation takes place over some more-or-less open and variable set of properties of the to-be-compared entities. Similarity can be context-dependent on this view because the representations that the process uses as input can change. This view gives less explanatory force to similarity than the strong view because it demands analysis of the representations of the objects whose similarity it computes. But similarity remains a force, for people calculate it in a nonarbitrary fashion and can use it explicitly in performing cognitive tasks, such as reasoning and categorization.

2.3. Feeble similarity

Another view holds that similarity is just a short-hand way of talking about property-based cognitive processing. Many kinds of cognitive functions, including those just mentioned, depend on comparison. For example, the system may need to know whether one representation matches another in order to determine whether to perform some further task. There is no need to assume, however, that the comparison processes all use the same fixed algorithm. Instead, they may have only a rough family resemblance because they are all sensitive to the extent of common and distinctive properties between entities. In other respects, the comparison processes might be different and hence some of the seeming utility of similarity may evaporate.

2.4. No-similarity

Finally, at the other end of the scale, is the view that similarity has negligible explanatory power. On this view, cognition operates according to some other set of principles in which similarity has no special place. We always need a way to determine identity—in order to ensure continuity in our relations with things—but similarity is not involved in such determinations. Instead, the direction of explanation is the other way round. Similarity is itself parasitic on identity—for example, identity of common features. We can make similarity judgments, but those judgments, on this view, are so context-dependent, so complex, and so disparate that understanding them would also require understanding whatever we are trying to use similarity to explain.

3. Rules as an alternative to similarity

In specifying the role of similarity in cognition, we should resolve where we stand on the continuum above. But we should also specify what the alternatives are to similarity, and this is an equally open question. We will continue to use *rules* as an umbrella term for possible alternatives, because that term seems to be the most general one capturing the properties of interest. Rules come in a variety of forms (e.g. natural language rules, logical rules) and in a variety of types (e.g. normative rules, descriptive rules, imperatives, formal rules). Our use of *rule* in this article, however, focuses on explicit mental procedures, and when we use the term without a qualifier (*linguistic*, *logical*, etc.), we mean specifically mental rules. Rules take one or more mental representations as input, carry out a finite number of internal steps, and produce one or more representations as output.

This broad use of *rule* is, of course, not incompatible with similarity-based processes, since rules could be sensitive to similarity or could even compute similarity (e.g. by counting the number of properties two objects share). In our initial example, a rule could determine the similarity between the new painting and Braque's. However, rules are not limited to reacting to similarity or to assessing it, and when we talk about rules in what follows what we have in mind are mental procedures that do *not* make essential use of similarity. We're about to see some examples of rules of this sort.

One attribute that many systems employing these rules share is *compositionality*. Rule systems often include a method for deploying rules to build complex representations out of simpler components. Linguistic rules, for example, can build complex sentences, such as (1a), from simpler ones, such as (1b) and (1c):

1. a. Fred left for Chicago, and Ginger left for DC.
   b. Fred left for Chicago.
   c. Ginger left for DC.

Because this process can repeat without limit, the rules can form a potentially infinite number of new complex sentences from a finite vocabulary. Much the same is true of logical rules. For example, the logical rule of *And Introduction* stipulates that a conjoined sentence, such as (1a) follows deductively from its components, (1b) and (1c), taken together. Since this rule, too, can apply to its own output, it can produce an infinite number of new logical entailments (albeit dull ones, such as *Fred left for Chicago and (Fred left for Chicago and (... and (Fred left for Chicago and Ginger left for DC)...)))*. Linguistic and logic rules provide a straightforward way to describe and to implement these principles of combination. And in a psychological context, rules can help explain how people perform similar tasks like constructing an interpretation of a complex sentence from interpretations of its parts or drawing deductive inferences from given information. Analogous principles might even apply beyond language comprehension and deduction to all thinking. Rules might produce all complex mental representations by combining simpler ones.

By rules, we mean to encompass many procedures for determining the validity of inferences, including 'mental models' as described by Johnson-Laird and Byrne (1991). Although these theorists avoid the use of standard logical rules, such as And Introduction, they do not describe an approach that is outside the boundaries of the more general rule-based framework that we outlined above. Their proposal consists of specific procedures that combine individual mental representations to form new ones (Rips, 1994).

Fodor and Pylyshyn (1988) argue that the twin representational virtues of rule-based systems are *productivity* and *systematicity*. Rule-based systems are productive in that they can produce a theoretically unlimited number of new representations, as we have just seen. They are systematic in that their ability to produce one representation implies their ability to produce certain others. If a rule can combine representations A and B, and B' is of the same type as B, then the rule can combine A with B'. For example, the rule that combines (1b) and (1c) to produce (1a) could also combine (1b) with the sentence *Joan left for Spokane* to produce *Fred left for Chicago and Joan left for Spokane*. Human thought seems to have this character as well. Anyone who can imagine a person writing a sonnet also has the competence to imagine a person writing a ballad.

The properties of productivity and systematicity derive from the internal structure of rules—their abstract logical form and their use of variables. Productivity arises because rules can be applied in indefinitely long sequences, though they themselves are finite. For example, a rule like *Add 1 to integer N to produce the integer that is the successor of N* can be applied an infinite number of times to generate the entire class of integers. This is possible because of the presence of the variable N that allows the rule to apply to any integer. Systematicity arises because the abstract logical form of rules ensures that they apply to an entire class and not just to an individual object. Models of similarity generally compare representations without regard for logical form or variables. In this sense, similarity-based models seem to provide a natural contrast to rule-based ones.

4. The systems as computational devices

What kind of computational considerations can be brought to bear on the rule vs. similarity debate? Answering this question requires us to be more specific about the two kinds of systems. One fairly general approach to rules is to conceive of them as part of a *production system* (Newell, 1990). A production system consists of a large set of condition-action pairs (*production rules*) that specify an action to be performed if the condition holds. For instance, a production rule for producing the conjoined sentence in (1a) might be: IF S_1 and S_2 are each grammatical English sentences, THEN assert that S_1 and S_2 is a grammatical English sentence. You can use sets of production rules to implement most existing rule systems.

An inclusive approach to similarity-based systems is to identify them with any system whose processing of a representation is governed by the location of that representation relative to others in a continuous space. One large class of computational systems of this kind are called *dynamical systems*. These systems operate by associating representations with desired outputs, outputs that sometimes represent actions that the system can perform. It can be shown mathematically that production systems and dynamical systems have comparable degrees of computational power. Hence, on these assumptions, computational power is not sufficient to allow us to decide whether similarity or rules are preferable as a general 'language' of mental processing.

If power alone can't distinguish the approaches computationally, we must rely on criteria like efficiency, robustness, flexibility, and simplicity to evaluate their computational value. Here, systems of both kinds offer advantages. Debate over their relative merits is now common in the AI literature; some of it is reviewed in Chater and Hahn's paper. Note that in their paper, and in contrast with our position, Chater and Hahn argue that similarity should not be equated with an arbitrary associative system, in particular that connectionist systems are not similarity-based. The brunt of their effort is to specify the meaning of *rule-based* and *similarity-based* in an empirically consequential way.

Along with the virtue of compositionality, rule-based systems are often easier to analyze. We can sometimes prove that certain properties hold of rule-based systems because the rules come in discrete, explicit, and finite pieces. More generally, the ability to translate many theories directly into the kind of rules that conventional computer programs use makes many analyses easier and sometimes makes analyses possible. Moreover, the structure that rules share with natural discourse makes it easier to construct comprehensible explanations out of patterns of rule applications and to design interfaces between rule-based systems and humans.

In contrast, similarity-based models tend to be more robust to error and hardware failure because the models can more easily distribute computation across large portions of the system. They also tend to be flexible. Because such systems can generalize automatically on the basis of similarity, they can respond to stimuli that their designers didn't consider. When a computation requires retrieving information from a large data base, such systems are often efficient because they can retrieve instances in parallel that are similar to the memory probe.

Similarity-based models are closely related to conditional probability (Golden, 1988). The similarities among a set of objects, for example, maps into the probability that one of them has some property given that the others do. Prominent psychological theories have taken advantage of this relation, using similarity to predict the conditional probability of a response (e.g. Shepard, 1987), an inductive inference (Osherson et al., 1990; Sloman, 1993), or a categorization decision (e.g. Ashby, 1992).

In sum, computational considerations suggest that each approach has virtues and that these virtues are complementary. Roughly, rules provide precision, expressiveness, and generativity, and similarity provides flexibility and the means to deal with uncertainty.

5. Review of the data

We now briefly review some studies of human thinking with an eye toward answering two questions: Can we find evidence for or against rules and similarity? And, does this evidence throw further light on how to conceive of similarity? In a sense, this review wrote itself, for the distinction between similarity and rules turns up in all areas of cognitive science that deal with abstract thought.

5.1. Reasoning

The case for rules is clearest in the study of deductive inference—reasoning to certain conclusions. Several rule-based general theories of deduction have appeared that account for people's judgments of when a conclusion follows with certainty from a set of premises and when it does not (e.g. Braine et al., 1984; Rips, 1994). We know of no theories based on similarity that are successful over the same domain (predicate logic). The possibility remains, however, that people handle certain deductively valid arguments through procedures that do not themselves grind out valid conclusions (e.g. Sloman, 1998). If so, this opens the door for similarity-based theories.

By contrast, the field of inductive inference—reasoning to uncertain conclusions—is a battleground for the rules vs. similarity issue. The evidence is compelling that people sometimes use rules to make inductive inferences. Smith et al. (1992) make the case that people explicitly use certain probabilistic rules, although their discussion is limited to a small number of them. They found evidence that people apply the statistical law of large numbers when making inductive inferences. However, Kahneman and Tversky (1972) and Tversky and Kahneman (1973) demonstrated long ago the central role of heuristics in reasoning about probability—heuristics that at best approximate normative, rule-based procedures. Similarity-based machinery could easily implement two of these heuristics: the *representativeness* heuristic (which states that people make judgments of probability and frequency by determining the similarity of a description to the category being judged or to the outcome they would expect from the process being judged) and the *availability* heuristic (which states that people judge the likelihood of a class according to the ease with which instances of the class come to mind). The availability heuristic is similarity-based as it depends on a memory retrieval process that in turn depends on the similarity between an encoded event and retrieval cues.

Osherson et al. (1986) discuss the virtues and shortcomings of seven theories of inductive inference. Four of the theories derive from logic; another assumes the construction of causal schema; and another is based on a scale of 'conditional plausibility'. Osherson et al. (1990) conclude that each theory is likely to explain the source of some beliefs, but they also expose the shortcomings of each. A final theory is similarity-based. This theory differs from the others in applying to only a limited domain of arguments. It applies to arguments consisting entirely of category-predicate statements (e.g., *Turnips have vitamin T; therefore, parsnips have vitamin T*) that vary in the similarity among their categories or among their predicates. Further work (Osherson et al., 1990, 1994; Sloman, 1993) has developed this similarity-based approach in more detail and with a reasonable degree of empirical success. However, the framework's domain of application remains narrow.

The evidence so far suggests that both rules and similarity have places in a complete theory of inductive reasoning. Sloman (1996) has attempted to characterize their respective roles in the course of arguing that reasoning involves two complementary systems, a rule-based one and an associative one. That characterization remains underdetermined however. In this issue, Goldstone and Barsalou argue that both kinds of processing—indeed, all aspects of cognition—have a perceptual basis. They attempt to bridge the rule/similarity divide by constructing a continuum from perception to conception in which even the most abstract representations have some perceptual basis (and in which tasks differ in how much they depend on raw perceptual input).

5.2. *Categorization*

The standard lore in cognitive science is that categories are composed of similar instances. However, researchers have uncovered several dissociations between categorization and similarity. Barsalou (1985) demonstrated the existence of goal-derived categories (e.g. birthday presents) which group highly dissimilar items because they serve a common goal. Rips (1989) has shown that certain properties of natural kinds can differentially affect classification and similarity judgments. In particular, similarity judgments are more sensitive to perceptual properties than to other more central properties. Central properties of animals would include such things as their genetic structure and parentage. Keil (1989) has shown that the influence of these central properties grows over the course of development. Rips and Collins (1993) have used categories whose instances are distributed on a single dimension to show that similarity judgments depend on the distance of an instance from the distribution's center; categorization, however, depends on the relative frequency of instances. Finally, Rips (1989) has shown a dissociation between similarity and categorization produced by objects with a dimension value close to those of members of a category but nevertheless outside the category's boundary (e.g. an object that looks like a US quarter but has a 3-inch diameter). Subjects judge such objects similar to the category but nevertheless excluded from it. The quadrilateral at the right of Fig. 1 provides another example of this sort.

Some of these dissociations between categorization and similarity may depend on subjects adopting an analytical mode of processing rather than responding on an immediate, intuitive basis (Smith and Sloman, 1994). Nevertheless, the variety of dissociations between categorization and similarity have led a number of researchers to reject similarity as a basis for categorization in favor of the view that categorization depends on naïve domain theories (Carey, 1985; Keil, 1989). These researchers share the belief that instances are bound into a category by virtue of a common explanatory relation (Rips, 1989). Instances are classed together because their origin or function explains them in the same way. This view of categorization generally contrasts with prototype, exemplar, and connectionist models, all of which assume that similarity is the critical category-forming relation.

Taken together, we agree that the data cited demonstrate convincingly that categorization cannot be reduced in toto to a context-independent scale of similarity. Even so, we still find those who support the view that similarity plays a substantive role in categorizing. For example, Goldstone (1994a) argues that similarity is not so context-sensitive as to rob it of explanatory power. Abundant evidence shows that judgments of similarity can accurately predict classification performance for simple stimuli (e.g. Nosofsky, 1984).

The thinking of Quine (1977) about natural kinds led him to the conclusion that science often classes entities together because of a common explanatory link, and not because of their similarity to each other. The constituents of (say) the human immune system are in no sense similar to one another; they are members of a class only in that they participate together in a specialized biological function. Their commonality derives from the scientific account of the immune system. But such accounts—explanations—are not always available. In such cases, people may have to rely on their 'animal sense of similarity' by categorizing without an explanatory foundation (e.g. Smith et al., 1974). In general, people may have access to two distinct types of categorization processes—a rule-based one that is able to construct explanations, as well as a similarity-based one (Allen and Brooks, 1991; Smith and Sloman, 1994). Smith, Patalano, and Jonides in this issue report neuroimaging data showing that different parts of the brain are at work when people categorize on the basis of similarity to a stored exemplar than when they categorize according to a rule.

Keil, Smith, Simons, and Levin take issue with the Quinean hybrid model, according to which the explanatory process kicks in only after the stage has been set by similarity. They argue that, from the start, children struggle to explain the internal structure of the objects they encounter. Similarity-based processing, they argue, depends as much on explanation as explanation does on a stable similarity space. Hampton, in contrast, argues for the primacy of similarity in categorization. He shows strong correlations between people's judgment of the typicality of an item in a category, which he takes as a measure of similarity to a prototype, and the probability that people will classify the item as a member of the category. The correlations are not perfect, but Hampton is able to explain away most of the discrepancies by appealing to different demands of the typicality and categorization tasks.

5.3. Metaphor and analogy

One view of metaphor is that it is not substantially different from analogy. For example, a metaphor, such as (2), depends on the similarity between the metaphor's *topic*, Mozart, and its *vehicle*, pastry chef:

(2) Mozart is the pastry chef of composers.

Such an explicit comparison process is part of both the salience imbalance model of metaphor (Ortony, 1979) and the structure mapping approach to analogy (Gentner, 1983). On this view, understanding (2) requires comparing Mozart to pastry chefs in order to find a distinctive property of pastry chefs that can be ascribed to Mozart (perhaps the ability to create elaborate, beautiful, and enjoyable objects).

One provocative reaction to this view has been to deny that metaphor involves a similarity comparison. *Literal* statements that have the form *An X is a Y* often mean that *X*s are included among *Y*s (e.g. *An anteater is a mammal* means that anteaters are in the class of mammals). Glucksberg and Keysar (1993) argue that metaphors of this form should be understood as category inclusion statements too: The metaphor *An X is a Y* means that *X*s belongs to the category that *Y* typifies, not that *X* and *Y* are similar. For example, (2) means that Mozart belongs to the class of people who create elaborate, beautiful, and enjoyable objects. This debate about the interpretation of metaphor thus turns in part on the role of similarity in categorization. If categorization reduces to similarity, the difference between the two positions is negligible. But if Glucksberg and Keysar are right that metaphor comprehension is categorization and if metaphor comprehension depends on those aspects of categorization that are not reducible to similarity, then rules may govern metaphor in the same way they govern categorization.

According to both theories, understanding metaphors and analogies requires assigning properties of one entity to another, as our example suggests. So one framing of the basic issue in this literature is the extent to which such property-mapping emerges directly from alignment and comparison as opposed to rule-governed analysis and synthesis. In their paper, Gentner and Medina, make the case for alignment and comparison, not just in analogy, but as central processes in learning and in the abstraction and application of all kinds of rules.

5.4. Decision-making

Two main theories have dominated the study of decision-making. On one hand, there are models that mathematically combine subjective probability (e.g. your belief about the likelihood of rain) and subjective value (e.g. the strength of your desire to stay dry) to produce subjective expected utility (the overall desirability of taking your umbrella). (See Savage, 1954; cf. Fishburn, 1988). On the other hand, there are models that rely on heuristics to explain how people behave when confronted with choices (Kahneman et al., 1982). One of these heuristics, representativeness, claims that people make judgments of probability or frequency by determining the similarity of a description to a category or to the outcome of a process, as we mentioned earlier. Medin et al. (1995) have elaborated this observation by pointing out a number of parallels between choice and similarity. They suggest the possibility that choice may reflect the similarity of options to an ideal option. Rules may be staging a comeback in this area, however, in the guise of theories that use argumentation or explanation to guide choice (e.g. Shafir et al., 1993; Hogarth and Kunreuther, 1995).

5.5. Similarity judgments

Similarity can be regarded either as a form of judgment—what people say when asked to compare two entities—or as a theoretical comparison process that generates a similarity measure. Up to now, we have been considering similarity in the second sense, but we should also look at the way people judge similarity overtly. The need to distinguish similarity as a task from similarity as a theoretical construct arises because the study of the task once again raises the similarity versus rules issue. Sometimes automatic comparison processes seem to dominate similarity judgments. For example, Garner (1974; see also Goldstone, 1994b) has shown that when people must discriminate visual patterns according to their values on one dimension, variation on an irrelevant dimension can slow them down. Featural similarities on the second dimension are inhibitory even though they are irrelevant. In contrast, similarity judgments sometimes reflect the outcome of selective analysis. For example, falcons are judged more similar to chickens when the set of judged items includes wasps than when it includes sparrows (Tversky, 1977). The context in which judgments are made can selectively activate properties (for an extreme example of a 'cognitively penetrable' similarity task, see Bassock and Medin, 1997). Selective analysis may or may not implicate rules; nevertheless, different similarity tasks clearly require different explanatory models.

6. Conclusion

By characterizing similarity as we have, we believe that we have eliminated the possibility that all thought is similarity-based. Some rule-based mechanisms are necessary to explain (a) our competence to use language systematically and productively (Fodor and Pylyshyn, 1988); (b) the results of Smith et al. (1992); and (c) the sense of certainty associated with some inferences even in unfamiliar domains. To elaborate on (c), consider the argument *A, B, C, and D*, therefore *A*. We believe that all reasonable people consider this a conclusive argument. The certainty associated with it can be understood as a by-product of the application of a deductive inference rule like AND Elimination. It cannot be attributed to similarity-based computation because the argument *A, B, C, and D*, therefore *A, B, C, D, and E* is not conclusive, even though the premise is more similar to the conclusion than in the previous argument.

Of course, a dual view remains viable—that people are capable of explicit rule application, but they also have and use a special-purpose similarity-based inference system (Sloman, 1996). On this view, similarity-based processing obeys fundamentally different principles and uses different mechanisms than does rule-based processing.

How should we conceive of similarity? Which of the views outlined earlier should we accept (if any)? We believe that we can reject the Strong Similarity view, at least in the domain of abstract concepts. Similarity is too manipulable and too complex to be considered an irreducible relation. This may not be true in the perceptual domain, though. Analyses of color and of musical pitch have yielded similarity structures that may capture regularities across contexts (Shepard, 1980). No such reliable structure has been discovered at more abstract levels of analysis. Moreover, for similarity to have one of the virtues that we ascribe it—flexibility—it can't represent a set of fixed relations. Context-dependency must be intrinsic to its calculations.

Perhaps similarity can maintain some explanatory credentials, however, provided that it can be fitted with proper restraints (Goldstone, 1994a). In the Weak View (maybe even in the Feeble View), similarity remains a key building block in some forms of cognition. By giving it some special role, we can buy a lot of computational power while explaining why we often display a sensitivity to similarity, even when confronted simultaneously by a conflicting, more justifiable conclusion (Sloman, 1996). For unidimensional perceptual judgments, especially, similarity is hard to eliminate. Although it is possible to explain similarity away even in this context, attempts to do so seem to us forced and artificial.

Just what special role similarity has is yet to be decided. Rules are powerful entities, and the jury has yet to decide whether the data can support an autonomous notion of similarity. The purpose of this special issue is to help arrive at a more informed conclusion.

Acknowledgements

Steven Sloman was funded by NIMH grant MH51271 to Barbara Malt and Steven Sloman; Lance Rips by NSF grant SBR-9514491.

References

Allen, S.W., Brooks, L.R., 1991. Specializing the operation of an explicit rule. Journal of Experimental Psychology: General 120, 3–19.

Ashby, F.G., 1992. Multidimensional models of categorization. In: Ashby, F.G. (Ed.), Multidimensional Models of Perception and Cognition. Erlbaum, Hillsdale, NJ.

Barsalou, L.W., 1985. Ideals, central tendency, and frequency of instantiation as determinants of graded structure in categories. Journal of Experimental Psychology: Learning Memory, and Cognition 11, 629–654.

Bassock, M., Medin, D.L., 1997. Birds of a feather flock together: similarity judgments with semantically-rich stimuli. Journal of Memory and Language 36, 311–336.

Braine, M.D.S., Reiser, B.J., Rumain, B., 1984. Some empirical justification for a theory of natural propositional logic. In: Bower, G.H. (Ed.), The Psychology of Learning and Motivation: Advances in Research and Thinking, Vol. 18. Academic Press, New York, pp. 313–371.

Carey, S., 1985. Conceptual Change in Childhood. MIT Press, Cambridge, MA.

Fishburn, P.C., 1988. Nonlinear Preference and Utility Theory. Johns Hopkins Press, Baltimore, MD.

Fodor, J.A., Pylyshyn, Z.W., 1988. Connectionism and cognitive architecture: a critical analysis. Cognition 28, 3–71.

Garner, W.R., 1974. The Processing of Information and Structure. Erlbaum, Hillsdale, NJ.

Gentner, D., 1983. Structure-mapping: a theoretical framework for analogy. Cognitive Science 7, 155–170.

Glucksberg, S., Keysar, B., 1993. How metaphors work. In: Ortony, A. (Ed.), Metaphor and Thought, 2nd edition. Cambridge University Press, Cambridge.

Golden, R.M., 1988. A unified framework for connectionist systems. Biological Cybernetics 59, 109–120.

Goldstone, R.L., 1994a. The role of similarity in categorization: providing a groundwork. Cognition 52, 125–157.

Goldstone, R.L., 1994b. Influences of categorization on perceptual discrimination. Journal of Experiment Psychology: General 123, 178–200.

Goldstone, R.L., Medin, D.L., Gentner, D., 1991. Relational similarity and the nonindependence of features in similarity judgments. Cognitive Psychology 23, 222–262.

Goodman, N., 1955. Fact, Fiction, and Forecast. Harvard University Press, Cambridge.

Hogarth, R.M., Kunreuther, H., 1995. Decision making under ignorance: arguing with yourself. Journal of Risk and Uncertainty 10, 15–36.

Johnson-Laird, P.N., Byrne, R.M.J., 1991. Deduction. Erlbaum, Hillsdale NJ.

Kahneman, D., Tversky, A., 1972. Subjective probability: a judgment of representativeness. Cognitive Psychology 3, 430–454.

Kahneman, D., Slovic, P., Tversky, A., 1982. Judgment Under Uncertainty: Heuristics and Biases. Cambridge University Press, Cambridge.

Keil, F.C., 1989. Concepts, Kinds and Cognitive Development. MIT Press, Cambridge, MA.

Nosofsky, R.M., 1984. Choice, similarity, and the context theory of classification. . Journal of Experimental Psychology: Learning Memory, and Cognition 10, 104–114.

Medin, D.L., Goldstone, R.L., Markman, A.B., 1995. Comparison and choice: relations between similarity processes and decision processes. Psychonomics Bulletin and Review 2, 1–19.

Murphy, G.L., Medin, D.L., 1985. The role of theories in conceptual coherence. Psychological Review 92, 289–316.

Newell, A., 1990. Unified Theories of Cognition. Harvard University Press, Cambridge, MA.

Ortony, A., 1979. Beyond literal similarity. Psychological Review 86, 161–180.

Osherson, D., Smith, E.E., Shafir, E., 1986. Some origins of belief. Cognition 24, 197–224.

Osherson, D., Smith, E.E., Meyers, T.S., Shafir, E., Stob, M., 1994. Extrapolating human probability judgment. Theory and Decision 36, 103–129.

Osherson, D., Smith, E.E., Wilkie, O., Lopez, A., Shafir, E., 1990. Category-based induction. Psychological Review 97, 185–200.

Quine, W.V., 1977. Natural kinds. In: Schwartz, S.P. (Ed.), Naming, Necessity, and Natural Kinds. Cornell University Press, Ithaca, NY.

Rips, L.J., 1989. Similarity, typicality, and categorization. In: Vosniadou, S., Ortony, A. (Eds.) Similarity and Analogical Reasoning. Cambridge University Press, Cambridge.

Rips, L.J., 1994. The Psychology of Proof: Deductive Reasoning in Human Thinking. The MIT Press, Cambridge, MA.

Rips, L.J., Collins, A., 1993. Categories and resemblance. Journal of Experimental Psychology: General 122, 468–486.

Savage, L.J., 1954. The Foundations of Statistics. Wiley, New York.

Shafir, E., Simonson, I., Tversky, A., 1993. Reason-based choice. Cognition 49, 11–36.

Shepard, R.N., 1980. Multidimensional scaling, tree-fitting, and clustering. Science 210, 390–398.

Shepard, R.N., 1987. Towards a universal law of generalization for psychological science. Science 237, 1317–1323.

Sloman, S.A., 1993. Feature-based induction. Cognitive Psychology 25, 231–280.

Sloman, S.A., 1996. The empirical case for two systems of reasoning. Psychological Bulletin 119, 3–22.

Sloman, S.A., 1998. Categorical inference is not a tree: the myth of inheritance hierarchies. Cognitive Psychology, 35, 1–33.

Smith, E.E., Langston, C., Nisbett, R., 1992. The case for rules in reasoning. Cognitive Science 16, 1–40.

Smith, E.E., Shoben, E.J., Rips, L., 1974. Structure and process in semantic memory: a featural model for semantic decisions. Psychological Review 81, 214–241.

Smith, E.E., Sloman, S.A., 1994. Similarity– vs. rule–based categorization. Memory and Cognition 22, 377–386.

Tienson, J.L. Jr., 1988. Resemblance and general terms. Philosophical Studies 54, 87–108.

Tversky, A., 1977. Features of similarity. Psychological Review 84, 327–352.

Tversky, A., Kahneman, D., 1973. Availability: a heuristic for judging frequency and probability. Cognitive Psychology 5, 207–232.

Two dogmas of conceptual empiricism: implications for hybrid models of the structure of knowledge

Frank C. Keil*, W. Carter Smith, Daniel J. Simons, Daniel T. Levin

Department of Psychology, Uris Hall, Cornell University, Ithaca, NY 14853, USA

Abstract

Concepts seem to consist of both an associative component based on tabulations of feature typicality and similarity judgments and an explanatory component based on rules and causal principles. However, there is much controversy about how each component functions in concept acquisition and use. Here we consider two assumptions, or dogmas, that embody this controversy and underlie much of the current cognitive science research on concepts. Dogma 1: Novel information is first processed via similarity judgments and only later is influenced by explanatory components. Dogma 2: Children initially have only a similarity-based component for learning concepts; the explanatory component develops on the foundation of this earlier component. We present both empirical and theoretical arguments that these dogmas are unfounded, particularly with respect to real world concepts; we contend that the dogmas arise from a particular species of empiricism that inhibits progress in the study of conceptual structure; and finally, we advocate the retention of a hybrid model of the structure of knowledge despite our rejection of these dogmas. © 1998 Elsevier Science B.V.

Keywords: Dogmas; Conceptual empiricism; Hybrid models

1. Introduction

As this issue's opening article by Rips and Sloman makes clear, mature concepts have two central components: one that is largely associative and one that is explanatory. Proposals for such a hybrid stretch back at least to Locke and are very much with us today (Neisser, 1967; Sloman, 1996). The general acceptance of the hybrid model of thought and knowledge unifies the papers in this special issue of *Cognition*. Yet, controversy remains about how these components are involved in cognitive

* Corresponding author. Tel.: +1 607 2556365; fax: +1 607 2558433; e-mail: FCK1@Cornell.edu

development and in adult learning and use of concepts. These controversies are fueled by two distinct, but related assumptions (or Dogmas) that dominate most views of the origin and structure of concepts.

Dogma 1: Any new category is understood by first processing similarity and only later by considering causal or explanatory principles. The explanation-based component only arises given sufficient opportunity for cognitive reflection.

Dogma 2: Infants and young children initially represent categories using the association component of concepts. Only with development does the more abstract, explanatory component of concepts emerge.

Both of these dogmas presuppose that learning is perceptually driven, progressing from the simple processing of sensory features to forming complex representations and abstract thoughts; this presupposition eventually dooms them as reasonable models of knowledge acquisition. Indeed, we argue that the two dogmas fail both under principled considerations and under the bright light of experimental data. Yet, these dogmas are implicit in most models of concept development and of adult processing of categories. If these dogmas fail as explanations of category and concept acquisition and use, why, then, are they so prevalent and widespread? We show how empiricist biases influencing the choice of stimuli used to study concepts and the interpretations of data from these experiments have perpetuated and sometimes even reified these dogmas. First, however, we must briefly review the need for both the similarity and the explanatory components of concepts.

2. Do similarity and explanation account for separate aspects of concepts?

Many aspects of human thought seem to rely on relatively automatic processing, driven largely by the statistical properties of instances. Some aspects of our categorization, induction, and concept acquisition clearly are influenced by tabulations of feature frequencies (e.g. how frequently a feature occurs among members of one category versus others) and probabilistic comparisons to stored exemplars (see Smith and Medin, 1981 for a summary of earlier work). Indeed, the emergence and successes of the Roschean view of concepts in the 1970s suggested that probabilistic representations might sufficiently explain all of categorization, displacing earlier rule-based 'classical' models (Rosch and Mervis, 1975). These successes were particularly seductive because such models were able to account for much of categorization without delving into 'cause' and 'explanation'. Indeed, because the typicality of a feature often is directly related to its causal importance in determining category membership, models of categorization based on feature typicality alone seemed able to eliminate the explanatory component of concepts. For example, whiteness is both highly typical of and causally central to polar bears. Causally central features are those that are closely tied to other critical properties and are linked to the origins or essence of the object. 'White' is causally central to polar bears because the property is closely linked to survival in snow covered environments. Any other color would impair a polar bear's ability to hunt. Less central properties (e.g. a bear's tail shape) could more easily be variable without affecting the underlying nature or the basic behaviors of the bear. The causal mechanisms (evolutionary in this case) underlying the color of the polar bear explain why whiteness is a typical property. Given the substantial correlation between typicality and causal structure for real world categories, experimenters may miss a critical aspect of our concepts unless they empirically separate these components.

In many other cases, however, the properties most typically associated with members of a kind are not the most causally or explanatorily central. For example, virtually every washing machine ever encountered is white, yet we know that whiteness is irrelevant in determining that an object is a washing machine. Thus, although we do use typicality in categorization and induction, in many cases something other than mere similarity is needed, at least partly because some typicality information is not relevant. That 'something else' involves intuitions about why things are similar—about the causal forces underlying the similar properties themselves. Moreover, even variable properties can be causally central if the patterns of variation are linked to causal features of underlying category membership. For example, the variable colors of chameleons help determine category membership. Given that chameleons can change their colors, we rarely if ever encounter two chameleons that share identical coloring. Thus, the color variability for an individual chameleon leads to variability across chameleons as well. The variability itself is the feature that ties individuals to the larger category. Successful categorization requires us to ignore the typicality structure and rely on causal explanations for how color is involved in chameleon ecology. The same point can be made in cases where variability is even more lawfully and predictably related to causal interactions with the environment. For example, the color of iron varies considerably as a consequence of its surface being oxidized into rust. This variation is intimately linked to the interaction of iron's chemical nature and the environment. Even social categories such as 'teenager' can lead to variable, but nonetheless often depressingly predictable patterns of appearance. A concept of 'teenager' relies on causal accounts of how teens interact with their peers and adult society.

In some domains, the difference between similarity and rule-based categorization is even more striking. Categories such as odd numbers, prime numbers, and triangles are governed by formal, precise rules that transcend associative relations. Adults know and understand these logical constraints, but still easily and consistently judge some exemplars of these categories to be better than others (Armstrong et al., 1983). That is, even categories that are clearly defined by explicit rules can show typicality- or frequency-like effects. In other domains as well, we can clearly separate judgments based on typicality and on rules. For example, we can all appreciate that kinship terms such as 'uncle' have a dual representation. The typical uncle is a man about the same age as your parents who brings you gifts or sends cards on major holidays and often talks about things he and your mother or father did together as children. The rule-defined uncle is an individual of any age who shares a biological relationship to your mother or father. Whether or not he visits or brings gifts is irrelevant. Likewise, we know about the kinds of typical events that make one New Years' Eve similar to another, but we also know a rule defining that holiday.

Although the contrast between rules and typicality seems stark, we cannot fairly argue that these components are so discrete and independent that they function with little or no interaction. In fact, the cases described highlight the danger of generalizing from only one class of things. With nominal kinds such as triangle and uncle, the components may be fairly separable. However, for natural kinds, the interdependence of typicality and explanation is much more evident. If natural kinds are the most prevalent and typical type of category, such interdependence might well be the norm.

3. Natural kinds: the necessity of the hybrid

Knowledge of natural kinds clearly illustrates the need for a hybrid model of concepts. Surely the first human knowledge was largely of natural kinds in a world empty of artifacts. Thus, it is safe to assume that our first ways of meaningfully carving up the world and understanding its structure centered around our knowledge of natural kinds. Today, our knowledge about natural kinds is closely linked to the contemporary sciences, but how did these sciences ever get started? What cognitive processes account for the success of science in making predictions and increasing our understanding of the natural world? This question underlies much of the modern history and philosophy of science (Salmon, 1989). It should also be one of the foundational questions of cognitive science.

Science works because it links observations of associated variables with explanations of the causal mechanisms underlying those associations. Natural science is a union of the associative and the explanatory, of similarity and cause. For example, consider the class of metals occupying column 1B in the periodic table (i.e. copper, gold and silver) which tend to share many physical properties (reactivity, volatility, and malleability, etc.). We attribute these physical similarities to the nature of their electron shells: the causal mechanisms underlying the observable similarities depend on the behaviors of the electrons. Yet, even if the physical properties of these metals can be explained in terms of their electron shells, questions about the causal mechanisms responsible for the behavior of electrons remain. Diligently, we turn to particle physicists to find an explanation. They attribute the similarities to causal interactions of subatomic particles like quarks. We can proceed in this manner (e.g. what explains the behavior of quarks?) until eventually, this chain of linked mechanisms runs out and we must resort to less precise notions of what properties are causally relevant: 'at the end of every explanatory regress we must perforce shift from causal mechanisms to causal powers' (Harré, 1988, p. 142). Causal powers refer to our knowledge about the dispositions of entities to engage in some kinds of causal interactions but not others (see Harré and Madden, 1975; Harré, 1988). The distinction between causal mechanisms and causal powers mirrors the distinction between specific theories and framework theories (Wellman, 1990), where the frameworks constrain the kinds of information likely to be incorporated into a specific theory; that is, they highlight which properties are likely to be relevant to a particular causal explanation (see Brown, 1990; Gelman, 1990). With the accumulation of new observations, specific theories and explanations develop and sometimes are reinterpreted in different theoretical terms. These new observations often take the form of correlational evidence. Thus, further theory growth relies on an ever-growing similarity database. But this database is itself at least partially constrained by the assumption that similarities and correlations occur for a reason. We either seek to incorporate the observations into existing specific theories, or occasionally, if anomalous observations begin to accumulate, we attempt to significantly revise those theories (Kuhn, 1962).

For natural kinds then, there are at least three levels of conceptual understanding: precise knowledge of the causal mechanisms by which properties and kinds interact, notions of what kinds of properties are causally central in a domain (as well as what kinds of causal patterns and dispositions might be associated with a kind), and finally, a database of properties that tend to co-occur within a kind (i.e. the 'similarity' component). In terms of the hybrid structure of concepts, the explanatory component consists of both knowledge of precise mechanisms and framework notions of causal powers and patterns. This explanatory part draws on the 'similarity database.' New additions to that database, however, do not arise from a theory-neutral stance, but are in turn constrained by the explanatory component. That is, some similarities will be more readily noticed than others because they are more congruent with available systems of explanation. Each component, therefore, supports and helps guide the other. Indeed, without such mutual constraints each component would be dysfunctional.

Why do appeals to raw, theory-neutral similarity fail? Why cannot progressively higher-order tabulations of similarity fully account for our conceptions of natural kinds? The reason is simple: there are too many possible frequencies and correlations to be tabulated. Indeed the set of such possible tabulations is theoretically infinite. As has now been discussed in many places (Goodman, 1972; Keil, 1981; Murphy and Medin, 1985), depending on the features chosen for comparison, any two arbitrarily chosen objects can be maximally similar to each other. For example, a cloud and a white feather might be considered quite similar if color and ability to float in air are the comparison features, whereas they could not be more different if size and functional affordances are the comparison features. In the real world, every instance of every object we encounter has an indefinitely large number of features, any of which could be tabulated. Any attempt to store information about objects in terms of feature frequencies would fail without constraints on the inputs to such tabulations. Moreover, the whole notion of features as atomic primitives is suspect given that they can either proliferate or evaporate depending on the theoretical perspective adopted (see Wisniewski and Medin, 1994 for discussion). Thus, the idea of a theory-neutral set of primitive features is a fiction that, when acknowledged, makes the need for an explanatory component all the more obvious.

Empirical evidence bolsters this plausibility argument. In learning artificially constructed categories, in which the features are theory-neutral, adults are poor at detecting feature correlations even when doing so would enhance concept learning (Murphy and Wisniewski, 1989). Intuitive theories help people to assimilate statistical correlations (Wright and Murphy, 1984), and such intuitive notions of causation allow false beliefs to persist even when the statistical evidence contradicts the belief (e.g. Chapman and Chapman, 1967, 1969; Wright and Murphy, 1984). Thus, bottom-up statistical patterns do not always drive reasoning: we often use high level schema to impose interpretations on statistical patterns (see also Nisbett et al., 1983). Finally, in seeking to attribute the cause of an effect to some factor, adults prefer information about specific, underlying mechanisms over information about the covariation of surface events (Ahn et al., 1995).

In short, models of knowledge representation based solely on associative learning among properties are hopeless without some way of sharply limiting the set of properties to be associated. Empiricist approaches to knowledge representation cling to the assumption that such constraints will be imposed by the perceptual system. Accordingly, our sensory systems must provide a limited set of perceptual primitives so that exhaustive tabulations over those primitives are computationally possible. This assumption is nothing more than an article of faith and has never been even faintly satisfied. Even with a stock of a few hundred primitive features (e.g. colors, shapes, textures, sizes, and surface patterns), the number of potential associations to notice becomes massive. Add temporal and spatial factors to the tabulations (e.g. one feature is noticed at roughly the same time and place as another) and the computational task explodes once again.

Without constraints on the 'tabulation space' sufficiently more powerful than those imposed by the sensory system, associations alone cannot explain categorization of natural stimuli. In much of human cognition, those additional constraints come through rules, explanatory relations, and notions of mechanism. In other species, they may be less explicit and rule like, but still are radically different from pure association. If concepts were learned solely through association, those properties that co-occur more frequently should be more readily associated. Yet, classic work on phobias and taste aversion suggest that a single co-occurrence may indelibly link two properties or events. Many species form ecologically important links between properties of objects in the world in ways that run against the frequency of occurrence. Rats will associate nausea with the taste of a food ingested 8 hours earlier rather than with a physical trauma occurring minutes earlier (Garcia and Koelling, 1966; Rozin and Kalat, 1971). Also, monkeys more readily associate fear with snakes than with rabbits or flowers even when they have had equal exposure to both classes of entities (Cook and Mineka, 1989, 1990). These preferred linkages cannot be explained easily by different saliency of features; instead, the animal is predisposed to be especially sensitive to those associations that make sense for that organism's ecological niche.

Humans show similar constraints in their understanding and categorization of natural kinds; higher-order criteria determine the particular frequencies and correlations we choose to notice and remember. When learning about a new kind of animal, we expect certain property relations to be causally and explanatorily useful. These expectations can override similarity-based information. Although the nature of these constraints is still unclear (they could take a range of forms from causal intuition to precise rules), our concepts of natural kinds are a blend of frequency information and constraints on the particular relations we choose to consider. In fact, we could not have concepts of natural kinds without both components, any more than science could proceed without both theoretical expectations to guide our inquiry and feature tabulations to gather as yet uninterpretable information. Hybrid concepts are necessary to adequately represent any natural kind.

The hybrid model of concepts occupies the middle ground in the ccntinuum offered by Rips and Sloman and acknowledges that both similarity and rules are needed without reducing one to the other. Adopting a hybrid model neither entails a particular representational format for each component nor specifies the nature of the interaction between the components. We still need to know more about how the two components interact and how each is represented. Over many different versions of the hybrid model of concepts, the two dogmas outlined above are the primary assumptions that have shaped current theory and research. Our main purpose here is to place these dogmas in a broader context and to discuss why they must fail for any model of natural kind concepts.

4. Dogma 1—New categories are initially similarity-based: only with time do we come to apply rules and explanations

Although, at first glance, it seems plausible that adults acquire new knowledge via an association to theory shift, research on causal attribution and the development of domain specific expertise in adults directly contradicts this characterization. This research shows that causal theories often exert a powerful influence on the acquisition process itself and furthermore that associationistic principles are not eventually replaced by explanatory knowledge but remain important even in experts' classification schemes.

Traditional models of causal attribution propose that people use information about the covariation of factors and effects to determine what caused an event (e.g. Kelley, 1967; Cheng and Novick, 1990, 1992). But an examination of the information search strategies people use to develop explanations for events challenges this view (Ahn et al., 1995). In seeking to learn why an event occurred, people solicit information about hypothesized causal mechanisms much more often than they seek information about co-occurring events (Ahn et al., 1995). For example, when trying to discover why John had a car accident on Route 9 last night, people tend to ask questions that either propose specific underlying mechanisms (e.g. 'Was John drunk?' 'Did John's brakes fail?') or that seek more information about the elements described (e.g. 'Was there something wrong with John's car?' 'Was there something peculiar about last night?'). Generally, they do not ask questions about the frequency with which John has car accidents, the frequency of car accidents last night, or the frequency of accidents on that particular road. So, in learning about a novel event, people do not often seek information about covarying factors, nor do they seem to use such information when given it directly. However, as Ahn et al. (1995) point out, these findings do not diminish the importance of covariation information: such information may be used to generate hypotheses or to confirm the presence of a particular underlying mechanism.

Covariation models of causal attribution, with their emphasis on common and

distinctive 'factors' are analogous to similarity-based accounts of concept formation, in which categories are learned by attending to common versus distinctive
features. A still-thriving tradition of research on adult concept learning is based
on the premise that raw computations of similarity relations adequately describe
an early state of concept learning. Much of this research uses simple, semantically
meaningless stimuli that vary continuously on two dimensions to test predictions of
universal exemplar models of category structure. For example, the Generalized
Context Model (GCM; Nosofsky, 1984, 1986) predicts classification and recognition behavior by assessing the similarity between a test stimulus and stored representations of other, previously acquired exemplars (i.e. the two categories of
artificial stimuli used in a given experiment). This similarity measure is a weighted
function of the features across which a test stimulus is compared to stored exemplars. Stimuli that are very similar to a large number of stored exemplars from either
category will provoke a recognition response, whereas stimuli that are more similar
to exemplars from one category than those of another will be classified accordingly.
This ability to predict performance across a number of tasks using simple generalizable principles is one of the most important aspects of the GCM model and other
similarity based models.

Nosofsky (1992) provides the groundwork for a plausible interface between these
generalizable similarity computations and a more rule-based component of concepts
by suggesting that exemplar models be understood in terms of representation-pro-
cess pairs (Anderson, 1976) whereby representations are given separate status from
the processes that work on them. Accordingly, similarity-based exemplar spaces
represent a stable ground upon which various processes (e.g. summed similarity)
operate to produce predictable patterns of behavior. This kind of model implies that
associative principles are fundamental in organizing concepts, but that theory laden
processes can supplement these basic representations to produce a complete explanation of more complex concepts (such as real world categories). The most concrete
mechanism purported to govern the interaction of the associative and explanatory
components is selective attention. Both the GCM and the earlier Context Theory
(Medin and Schaffer, 1978) suggest that selective attention changes the weighting
given to each stimulus feature in different task contexts. Thus, selective attention
takes into account the relevance of particular features to particular classification
goals. Therefore, a resulting hybrid model of concepts might borrow this distinction
between representations and processes by positing theory and explanation as processes akin to selective attention that operate a posteori on stable associative networks by determining which features will be most heavily weighted in a given
comparison. Advocates of this kind of model appeal to a combination of basic
perceptual filters and task-specific principles to constrain the properties represented
and thus render the similarity comparison process more plausible than a brute force
associative engine (Goldstone, 1994; Medin et al., 1993).

Such models directly instantiate Dogma 1 whereby learning begins as an accumulation of a series of exemplars encoded according to domain-general associative
principles and is gradually enriched by attentive processes that select critical features more carefully, which, in turn, drives the emergence of more sophisticated,

perhaps causal, principles relating those features. This progression seems to account for the learning of categories of artificial stimuli devoid of real-world meaning. The use of such stimuli effectively eliminates the possibility that existing explanatory knowledge can contribute to the organization of novel categories. Thus, this instantiation of Dogma 1 seems to follow by necessity: it is difficult to imagine how a rule-based 'process' can function until a sufficient number of exemplars have been coded associatively into a sufficient 'representation'.

However, when items in a novel category do evoke real world knowledge, the importance of causal theories and explanations to even the earliest stages of the acquisition of new concepts becomes evident. Unlike the arbitrary categories described above, natural kinds and even humanmade implements have features that tend to be causally interwoven. When features are causally interrelated, explanatory knowledge speeds both category learning and the identification of features (Murphy and Allopena, 1994). In Murphy and Allopena's study, participants learn to classify novel animals with either interrelated or non-interrelated features. For example, one animal might have 'pointed ears' and 'spots' and another animal might 'eat meat,' and have 'sharp teeth.' Having pointed ears does not causally entail the presence of spots or any other surface marking. However, 'eating meat' likely entails the presence of 'sharp teeth'. Species that eat meat have generally evolved sharp teeth. Participants who learn categories with causally interrelated features are faster and more accurate at identifying isolated features than subjects who learn non-interrelated features. Moreover, causally interrelated, but infrequently mentioned features are identified just as quickly and are rated as being just as typical as frequently mentioned features. In contrast, participants who learn non-interrelated features rate infrequently mentioned features as atypical and identified such features more slowly than frequently mentioned features (Murphy and Allopena, 1994). This effect is not likely to be merely a consequence of earlier stored correlations about the features of animals. Even if one taught a new, plausible causal mechanism, it should produce the same effects in a replication of the Murphy and Allopena study.

When the features available for learning novel instances of natural categories are interrelated, people use knowledge of these interrelations to guide learning a new category without having to attend to raw feature frequencies. But when the features are not interrelated, people must resort to strategies using only the raw statistical frequencies of features. Thus, knowledge about a domain can aid in learning about new categories in a domain.

Knowledge from one domain can also be used during the initial learning of another domain, as shown by research on the acquisition of expertise. Not only do novices immediately use domain-specific causal theories, they also recruit theories from other domains when analyzing new information. Learners seem compelled to immediately organize new information using causal theories. Yet similarity is still central to concept learning; it highlights associations needing further explanation. Thus, explanation and association both play important roles throughout the course of learning.

In one of the best studied areas of expertise, medicine, there is ample evidence that novices use causal knowledge right from the start. The presence of such theories is perhaps most evident in the reasoning errors made by both novices and experts. Beginning medical students assimilate and misconceptualize new medical knowledge because they rely on causal theories learned in school and everyday life. For example, students may recruit knowledge about kitchen plumbing when trying to learn properties of the circulatory system (Feltovich et al., 1989). As a result, they fail to understand the contribution of the elasticity of arteries in amplifying the power of the heart to pump blood because kitchen pipes are rigid. Even experts in medicine sometimes mistakenly assume that an enlarged heart implies overstretching of its muscle filaments because they incorrectly recruit knowledge of skeletal muscles which can become stretched enough to lose efficiency (Feltovich et al., 1989).

In addition to recruiting knowledge from other domains novices rely heavily upon causal theories within the new domain. They may even recruit causal theories more frequently than experts. For example, Boshuizen and Schmidt (1992) asked students and experts to diagnose case summaries, and found that students engaged more frequently in explicit biomedical reasoning. When asked, experts could produce more biomedical information, but only relatively infrequently did they spontaneously refer to this information in their protocols. The acquisition of medical expertise begins with biomedical knowledge (i.e. rules and theories), and only later is enriched by associations with the examples gained from practical experience (Boshuizen and Schmidt, 1992). Even in cases where the medical school curriculum emphasizes an exemplar-based approach, specific examples are almost always connected with pre-existing, causal, biomedical knowledge (Norman and Schmidt, 1992).

Experts may even use associations more rapidly than novices. Novices appear to use a seemingly unwieldy process of backward chaining in which reasoning progresses from initial hypotheses to the observation of disease features and back to a subsequent revision of the diagnosis if the features do not match the hypothesis (Patel and Groen, 1991). Experts, on the other hand, appear to use forward chaining in which reasoning jumps directly from features to hypotheses or disease schemas (Patel and Groen, 1991). This procession from features to hypotheses is typical of an associative process, yet it is observed more frequently in later stages of the learning process, not in the initial stages.

Although the medical knowledge literature supports neither a shift from exemplars to causal theories nor a shift from perceptual to conceptual processing, other contrasts between experts and novices have been taken to support Dogma 1. The best known example comes from the classification of physics problems. Chi et al. (1981) found that experts classify problems according to deep structural principles (e.g. the kinds of physical laws applicable to solving the problem) but that novices classify based on surface features (e.g. the kinds of objects involved in the physical mechanism under examination). Expert and novice math problem solvers (as defined by Scholastic Aptitude Test scores) also seem to differ in their use of association (Novick, 1988). Expert students showed positive transfer from an example word problem to a new one which shared a structural component—the particular mathematical solution procedure. Novices, on the other hand, attempted to transfer based on a match between the surface features of the old and new problems and therefore often selected the wrong solution procedure.

In both examples, however, the things identified as 'surface' features are more complex than primitive perceptual attributes: 'surface features' include non-concrete terms and structural relations between objects. For the physics problems, surface structure was defined as '(a) the objects referred to in the problem (e.g. a spring, an inclined plane); (b) the literal physics terms mentioned in the problem (e.g. friction, center of mass); or (c) the physical configuration described in the problem (i.e. relations among physical objects such as a block on an inclined plane)' (Chi et al., 1981, p. 125). In Novick's (1988) mathematical problem solving task, two problems were said to share surface similarity if they involved the same kind of activity (e.g. gardening). The characterization of such abstract, relational features as mere surface features seems to lead inherently to an underestimation of the depth of processing in which novices engage. Although it might be the case that novices encode problems more shallowly than experts, it is equally plausible that novices are relying on a different (possibly more domain-general) set of causal principles to code the problems. If this were true, then describing novice's reasoning as 'shallow' and more instance-bound would be a mischaracterization.

For example, college students who learn to solve a physics problem involving a constant change in the speed of some object will often spontaneously transfer the appropriate equation from this base problem to a target problem concerning a constant change in the rate of population growth. These same participants are less likely to use this equation to solve a problem concerning a constant change in the rate of increase in attendance at an annual fair (Bassock, 1996). Because participants represent speed and population growth as continuously changing quantities, whereas they represent increases in attendance at an annual fair as a discretely changing quantity, transfer between the former problems is less difficult than transfer from the physics problem to the attendance problem (Bassock, 1996). Thus, novices may engage in sophisticated causal reasoning and mental-model building even if they do not happen to exploit the particular mathematical principles or structural correspondences considered important by the experimenter. Furthermore, the activities described in a problem often *do* signal a particular formal procedure: expert problem solvers readily use such content, or 'surface,' cues to select appropriate solution schemas (Blessing and Ross, 1996).

In any problem solving situation, even novices exclude certain features from consideration. For example, in assessing the force required to push a block up an inclined plane, what novice would seriously consider the color of the block, the gender of the pusher, or whether the plane ends in the back of a Ryder or a Hertz rental truck? Rather, the typical novice would employ a whole series of implicit and explicit theories about the properties of the plane's surface, the tilt of the plane, and the weight of the object. A strict empiricist might argue that the process of importing this information is one of sophisticated association. Perhaps the learner has directly experienced the process of pushing something along a surface, walking up a plane, and carrying heavy and light objects. Therefore, each problem element might be associated with a relevant experience. Such a model would, of course, have to be modified to include more abstract associations than simple perceptual features. It would require representations of prior problem solving experiences with particular ways of selecting features. Such an approach is, of course, not new to learning theory in either its behaviorist (e.g. the concept of a discriminative stimulus) or neural net instantiation (e.g. adaptive resonance theory; see Carpenter and Grossberg, 1987).

However, by allowing more abstract associations, this model cannot explain behavior solely through the interaction of a domain-general learning system with the structure of the environment. One of learning theory's major goals is to explain behavior without positing complex representations or domain-specific rules. The need for constraints on feature selection forces learning theory to adopt just this type of complex, domain-specific apparatus. Whether feature selections are driven by domain-specific theories or discriminative stimuli, both require modifications to supposedly objective associations in order to allow the domain-general apparatus to accommodate domain-specific regularities. Such modifications imply that existing knowledge, whether it be association weights, connections, propositions, or images, cannot be ignored when modeling even the simplest interactions with a stable environment. To claim that a carefully structured neural network that has been fed precisely selected information can model behavior only using domain general learning rules is to purposely black-box all of the domain-specific processes that would be necessary to get the net to explain anything about real world behavior.

In summary, the development of expertise in adults does not support Dogma 1. Not only do novices immediately recruit domain specific causal theories or theories from other domains when acquiring new concepts, but experts continue to rely on a blend of similarity-based computations and explanatory reasoning. Association and similarity remain important throughout the course of learning, neither predominating nor becoming relegated to the periphery. Clearly, similarity, perceptual or otherwise, can play an important role in isolating potentially important correlations when theory runs out or an initial hypothesis is contradicted. But similarity will rarely be the sole basis for conceptualizing: in real world contexts, expertise develops from a symbiosis of preconceived theory and experience with new material.

In addition to the expertise differences explicitly adopted by Dogma 1, a second, less frequently mentioned assumption was prominent in many earlier discussions of concepts and is still tacitly presupposed in contemporary discussions. The assumption rests on the following line of reasoning: (a) The similarity-based component of concepts is simpler than the explanation-based aspect (this assumption is clearly linked to the belief that novices are driven by similarity); (b) Simpler aspects of cognition are performed more rapidly than complex aspects; (c) Simple, quickly formed aspects of cognition often serve as preprocessing for more complex aspects; (d) therefore, in real-time use of concepts (e.g. categorization and induction), the similarity-based component is processed first, and only later does the explanation-based component come into play.

The idea that initial 'rough and ready' or 'quick and dirty' processing relies more heavily on similarity was proposed explicitly in the 1970s (Smith et al., 1974) and has been left largely unchallenged by contemporary work. Yet, this assumption may not describe real-world cognition. Even in the briefest glance at a scene, viewers could have theory-based expectations about which features count. For example, a brief glimpse of a whale may lead to the perception of a fish or of a mammal depending on which features the viewer considers given a prior theory that emphasizes some features over others. Of course ignorance may lead to mistakes (e.g. observers may misclassify bats as birds and dolphins as fish), but mistakes reflect the use of different theory-based expectations not a complete reliance on similarity. Our perceptions are often influenced by what was causally and explanatorily relevant in the past. Only with stimuli so arbitrary and decontextualized that no prior information could be relevant will the 'similarity first' rule of processing apply.

Although the conclusion that initial processing of new entities is driven solely by perceptual primitives and the laws of association may be correct under such decontextualized circumstances, we cannot generalize this conclusion to cases of conceptual apprehension in the real world. In some intriguing studies, researchers have found that people with psychological disorders show Stroop-interference effects for words related to their own individual diagnosis (for review, see Williams et al., 1996). These studies suggest that a priori thoughts or emotions can create schemas that affect early stages of perceptual processing. Research on natural scene processing provides further evidence suggesting that the initial steps in encoding objects and scenes involve mutual constraint satisfaction in which scene context facilitates object recognition (Biederman et al., 1982; Rayner and Pollatsek, 1992). Other research on rapid identification of pictures shows it is possible to detect an object that does not belong to a target category even when each image is visible for only 114 ms (Intraub, 1981). To detect an exemplar that is not a member of a specified category requires participants to activate category knowledge at a higher level than perceptual similarity; perceptual similarity is less useful in this case because the participant does not know what features define the target. Therefore, on-line expectations about upcoming events can direct early visual processing in searching for something as abstract as the non-occurrence of a given category of object. In both of these cases, early object recognition processes are sensitive to the surrounding scene context and current task demands, which implicate the use of more abstract knowledge than perceptual primitives. We are not resurrecting aspects of the 'new look' in perception (e.g. Bruner and Goodman, 1947; Bruner and Postman, 1947), a movement that foundered in a methodological morass, but we are suggesting that abstract conceptual information is involved in the interpretation and use of information from the earliest stages of processing.

5. Dogma 2—Children initially rely on associations and only later begin to use theories to constrain their concepts

The notion has long persisted that children have different patterns of thought and different concepts than adults. Such apparent differences suggest the need for a transition between undeveloped and mature thinking. The transition most frequently proposed to account for these differences is one in which similarity precedes and acts as the cradle for rules and explanation. In this view, knowledge emerges through ever more complex associations over perceptual primitives. The child is seen as initially nothing more than a frequency and correlation detector, and the massive collections of associations eventually yield impressions of causality, rules, and explanation. In other words, young children are initially instance bound, but gradually develop principled ways of understanding. Many theorists have argued for a shift from concrete, instance-based knowledge to abstract, rule-based concepts. For example, Vygotsky (1962) argued that the development from similarity to rules parallels the acquisition of language; language serves as a tool for stating and using rules. Others argued for a shift from concrete representations to abstract ones (Werner and Kaplan, 1963) or from accidental features to essential ones (Inhelder and Piaget, 1969).

Despite the prevalence of the concrete to abstract shift in models of development, no one has ever been able to describe how senses of explanation, mechanism, and cause gradually arise out of statistical operations over primitives. Models based on the second dogma offer no plausible account of how the second part of the hybrid might emerge from the first. Threshold models in which associations of sufficient strength become causal cannot account for our ability to reject causal explanations for some cases of perfect, but indirect or arbitrary correlations. Thus, the shadow of a flagpole at any given time of day may be perfectly correlated with its height, but no one assumes that the shadow of the flagpole causes it to have a particular height. In the 1950s in the US, hair length was almost perfectly correlated with gender, but no one thought that gender caused hair to be of different lengths or that hair length somehow caused an individual to be a certain gender. In contrast to such threshold models, which do not capture our ability to posit mediating variables or to reject nonsensical explanations, recent papers have argued that theory often precedes, or operates in concert with considerations of similarity (e.g. Simons and Keil, 1995).

The second dogma also encounters the problem discussed earlier in the context of adult concepts of natural kinds. If children merely tabulate feature frequencies, how do they know which frequencies and correlations to encode? Even if the features considered are constrained to a relatively small set of perceptual primitives, the number of possible relations to tabulate seems overwhelming. Thus, in principle, children could not acquire a rule-based concept of a natural kind from similarity relations alone. Not surprisingly, then, research with human infants increasingly suggests a sensitivity to features and relations that are anything but the sorts of perceptual primitives embraced by those adopting Dogma 2. Young infants appear to perceive causal relations over mere contiguities (Leslie, 1995), to evaluate the rationality of an agent's actions in relation to its inferred goals (Gergely et al., 1995), to intermodally integrate information at birth (Gibson and Walker, 1984), to imitate high order relational patterns (Meltzoff, 1988), and to discriminate biological from non-biological motion (e.g. Fox and McDaniel, 1982). All of these abilities seem to require representations of interactions among features or entities. Apparently, infant concepts are not so impoverished that they are trapped by similarity of perceptual features.

Several recent findings from work with preschool-aged children also raise serious questions about the developmental progression described by Dogma 2 (Simons and Keil, 1995; Wellman and Gelman, 1992). For example, children's inductions about novel, unobservable properties seem to be based preferentially on information about category membership as opposed to information about perceptual similarity (Gelman and Markman, 1986, 1987). In such tasks, preschool children are shown an animal or artifact which is given a label. They are then told about an unobservable property or part of that object and are asked which of several other objects have that part. The test objects vary in their perceptual similarity to the original object and in whether they have the same label as the original. Thus, the task directly pits category membership against perceptual similarity. Dogma 2 would suggest that preschoolers form categories using perceptual similarity alone, and that only later do children begin to use more abstract rules to form categories. If so, then inductions of unseen properties should be based on the similarity of the original and queried object. However, even 2-year-old children override perceptual similarity and attribute unobservable parts to members of the same category (Gelman and Coley, 1990; Gelman and Markman, 1986). These children also seem to know which properties should be inferred on the basis of category membership; they know that category membership is more central than perceptual similarity. Although these findings do not directly speak to the developmental origins of preschooler's concepts, they do suggest that children's categories are based on more than perceptual similarity. The findings suggest that 'even before children can make use of subtle perceptual cues to determine category membership, they readily use category labels as the basis of their inferences' (Gelman and Coley, 1990, p. 803).

Other evidence suggests that preschoolers develop knowledge of unobservable internal parts in the opposite order to that suggested by Dogma 2. Children initially have abstract expectations which guide their search for more concrete information (Simons and Keil, 1995). In these studies, children were shown a target animal or machine along with a set of potential 'insides': the insides of an animal, of a machine, a pile of blocks, and a pile of rocks. On each trial, children were asked to pick the insides that belonged with the target animal or machine. Even preschool children expected the insides of animals and machines to differ, but they did not have specific expectations for the physical appearance of the insides. Children consistently chose different insides for animals and machines. However, their mistakes across several studies were particularly revealing. In one study, when they picked the wrong insides for animals, they picked the rocks rather than the machine insides. In a second study, when they chose the wrong insides for machines, they tended to choose the blocks rather than the animal insides. Although children lack concrete knowledge of the insides of animals and machines, they have abstract expectations about the differences between these categories and use the expectations to guide their inductions about unfamiliar properties. By 8 years, children have acquired enough concrete knowledge that they rarely choose the wrong insides (Simons and Keil, 1995). Abstract expectations about the differences between animals and machines guide children's search for more concrete details; concepts of animals and machines become more like those of adults by refining broad initial expectations with specific concrete details. Although studies of children's knowledge of insides do not directly assess the relationship between perceptual similarity and rule based components of concepts, they do suggest that young children are guided by rule-like expectations for the differences between superordinate level categories. Pre-schoolers know that only natural kind insides belong in animals and only artificial insides belong in machines. They can use this abstract distinction to draw inferences without having to rely exclusively on perceptual groupings.

Some have argued that demonstrations like these are based on an excessively impoverished notion of perceptual similarity. As a result, early categorization is falsely portrayed as non-perceptual, and thus by necessity conceptual, when a richer view of perceptual similarity makes clear the primacy of perception in development (e.g. Jones and Smith, 1993). We need not enter that debate here (but for related commentary see Barsalou, 1993; Gelman and Medin, 1993; Mandler, 1993; Mervis et al., 1993; and Smith and Jones, 1993), but we should note that these more elaborated forms of 'perceptual similarity' have little in common with the notion put forth in Dogma 2. Instead, these richer versions of perceptual similarity include highly relational and abstract structural properties and are heavily influenced by context and relevant prior experience. There may be good reasons for attempting to define a more principled perceptual/conceptual boundary, but they are beyond the scope of this article.

If infants are sensitive to more complex forms of information from the start, they must be biased to notice certain feature patterns over others. What, then, is the nature of these biases and how do they transcend the laws of a raw similarity system? One developmental model posits very crude initial sensitivity to relational patterns that pick out some limited domain of information such as the human face. These crude sensory biases isolate face-relevant information and then learning occurs via domain-general mechanisms (Johnson et al., 1991). Thus, infants might first pick out and attend to human faces by relying on the crude triangular configuration of the eyes and mouth (see Johnson, 1992). Such information may be sent to one region of the cortex which, other than being the endpoint for face related configural informa-tion, has no a priori specialization for face processing. This modern variant of empiricism accounts for distinct causal explanations by adopting minimal prior biases (possibly embodied in the neural architecture of the perceptual system) which help to separate distinct domains into separate representational systems.

An alternative approach argues for initial sensitivity to many complex patterns at both perceptual and cognitive levels. These might range from the particular temporal patterning of social interactions to having expectations about the mechanics of physical objects (Spelke et al., 1992). At a minimum, this approach requires early sensitivity to informational patterns which uniquely specify important kinds in the world. Positing sensitivity to complex patterns or invariants in the environment does not require that infants have theories, conscious or otherwise, or even sets of beliefs, but it does require a learning system that is tuned to particular kinds of causal patterning and that uses such tuning to build and structure knowledge in a domain. Despite these arguments and evidence against Dogma 2, it continues to resist extinc-tion. One reason for its persistence arises from the tendency of some to mistake other developmental patterns for versions of Dogma 2.

6. Mistakenly interpreting developmental trends as evidence for Dogma 2

In recent years, more sophisticated versions of Dogma 2 have arisen that are not so easily rendered implausible. Rather than simply positing a shift from similarity to rules, recent models argue for more subtle transitions. For example, the acquisition of word meanings and their corresponding concepts seems to follow a 'characteristic-to-defining shift' (Keil and Batterman, 1984; Keil, 1989). Other similar developmental trends include a shift from processing surface to deep features (Chi, 1992) and a gradual transition from noting properties, to detecting relations between properties, and finally to detecting relations between relations (Gentner and Toupin, 1988). In all of these cases, the first kind of knowledge seems more like similarity and the second more like rules and/or explanations. Real developmental changes have inspired all of these claims (as well as all earlier ones), but a closer look at the nature of children's knowledge suggests that the changes have little to do with the pattern described by Dogma 2.

Consider, for example, the shift from characteristic to defining features. Young children regularly identify instances as members of a category on the basis of shared typical or characteristic features even when 'defining' ones are absent. For example, young children claim that a gift-giving, male, unrelated adult is an uncle, but an adolescent who is their father's brother is not. These children seem to be tabulating the features most frequently associated with uncles and neglecting any use of the kinship rule. Older children accurately reject such cases, but accept ones that have almost no characteristic features when a defining feature is present (Keil, 1989).

A closer look at the characteristic to defining shift, however, reveals that it is not truly a shift from similarity to rules, or from association to definitions. Even the youngest children never rely solely on tabulations of the most perceptually salient features associated with instances and adults rarely rely exclusively on rules or explanations. The features children tabulate in demonstrations of a characteristic to defining shift are always constrained; they limit their consideration even of characteristic features to those likely to be relevant. For example, even if every 'uncle' a child encounters is seen wearing glasses, it is unlikely that the child would weigh this feature as heavily as certain social, behavioral, and personality traits that are characteristic of uncles. Typicality is always harnessed to the particular explanatory framework currently active; which typical features are taken to be 'characteristic' depends critically on the child's cognitive 'point of view'.

More broadly, younger children can differ from older ones in two ways that give the illusion of reinforcing Dogma 2: (1) they know less about the world; and (2) they may have different biases about what information they regard as explanatorily relevant. In the first case, children might well be ignorant of specific causal mechanisms or rules underlying a phenomena and therefore may be forced to rely on notions of causal frameworks much sooner than adults. Furthermore, given the necessary vagueness of those frameworks, they may in turn have to rely more heavily on similarity to structure the information they encounter. However, they do not and could not ever use similarity exclusively. At most, there is a shift in the ratio of their use of similarity-based vs. explanation-based knowledge. But by neglecting the less precise aspects of explanatory knowledge (such as notions of causal potency), researchers might mistakenly attribute to children a full association to explanation shift. In the second case, when trying to assimilate new information, a child may implicitly adopt an inappropriate theory (e.g. psychological versus biological; see Carey, 1985) that makes it appear as if she is ignoring critical features and simply tabulating features indiscriminately when, in fact, she is using a theory, albeit one inappropriate to the domain.

7. Causal potency of properties: an initial study

If explanatory knowledge constrains initial tabulations of similarity, how is such knowledge represented? The early explanatory component of concept representation might consist of a discrimination between causally central and causally peripheral properties even when specific mechanisms are unknown. Such knowledge must distinguish between causal centrality and typicality of properties (even though they are often closely related). Knowledge of this distinction is easy to demonstrate in adults. For example, adults view the property 'curvedness' as equally typical of bananas and boomerangs, but do not regard it as equally central to determining category membership (Medin and Shoben, 1988). Although a straight 'banana' could still be a banana, a straight 'boomerang' would be a stick. Research on the causal centrality of properties typically asks participants to consider a hypothetical situation in which a typical property (curvedness) is not present, and then to judge whether this counterfactual vitiates the inclusion of an instance in a category. We have used such counterfactual questions to examine the properties that adults believe are causally central to categories such as animals, artifacts and non-living natural kinds. Importantly, judgments of centrality are distinct from judgments of typicality; the most typical properties are not always thought to be causally central (Keil and Smith, 1996).

Although several researchers have considered the distinction between typicality and centrality with adults, the development of notions of causal centrality has remained largely unexplored. Children under 6 years of age usually do not greet sets of counterfactual questions with much pleasure. Often, they simply refuse to entertain the counterfactual (but see Harris et al., 1996). However, by describing a novel category and posing less structurally complex questions, we have been able to explore intuitions about causal centrality in children as young as 5 years.

In the following study, we read stories about a novel kind of animal ('glicks') and a novel kind of machine ('nilards') to 5-, 7-, and 9-year-olds. Each story described six property types: size, weight, color, surface markings, number of important inside parts, and appearance of functional outside parts. Subsequently, we asked children if other instances of the described category had to share the same property as those described in the story, or whether something could still belong to the category if it differed on a particular property type (e.g. if a something had a different color than the glicks described, could it still be a glick?). Because both the machine and animal stories described the same property types, we were able to assess to degree to which children believed that a particular property type was relevant to a decision about category membership for different ontological kinds[1].

8. Method

8.1. Participants

Sixty-eight children participated: 22 5-year-olds, 24 7-year-olds, and 22 9-year-olds (mean ages, 5 years 6 months, 7 years 6 months, 9 years 6 months). Children were tested individually outside their preschool classroom. Each session lasted roughly 10 min.

8.2. Materials and procedure

The stimuli consisted of two animal stories and two machine stories. Each child heard one animal and one machine story, with half of the children of each age hearing a 'glick' and 'nilard' pair and the other half hearing a 'bleek' and 'jullet' pair. The artificial labels, 'glick' and 'bleek,' each referred to a novel kind of animal; 'nilard' and 'jullet' each referred to a novel kind of machine. The order of presentation of the stories was counterbalanced across subjects. Each story contained a set of property types that could in fact apply to either an animal or machine, and only an introductory statement told the children the category (animal or machine). Because each child heard an animal story and a machine story, the stories were not word for word duplicates in terms of the properties described: although both stories indicated the color of the 'glick' or 'nilard', in one story this color was black while in the other story this color was, for example, yellow. This design was necessary to avoid situations in which a child might confuse the two stories; however both stories contained the same six property types. (See Tables 1 and 2 for examples).

After hearing a story, children responded to a series of questions about the properties mentioned in the story. Specifically, they were asked whether the object they heard about would be the same kind of thing if a target property were changed. For example, they might be asked 'Do you think that all Glicks have to have black stripes on their backs, or could something still be a Glick even if it didn't have black stripes on its back?' We explored six different property types presented in a pseudo-random order for each child: surface markings (e.g. stripes), the number of internal parts, the shape of external parts, color, size, and weight.

To make sure children understood the task, two control questions were asked: 'Could something still be a Glick even if it didn't have dirt on its tail?' and 'Could something still be a Glick if it was made out of butter?' All but one child answered these control questions correctly ('yes' for the first question and 'no' for the second); this child's data were not included in the analyses.

[1]To avoid confusion, we distinguish between property types and particular properties. That is, color is a property type, while 'red' is a particular property or instantiation of that property type.

Table 1
Animal story and questions read to 5-, 7-, and 9-year-olds

There is a kind of animal called a Glick. Have you ever heard of a Glick?
I certainly had not, but the other day, I was walking through the woods, and
I saw one. Do you want to hear what the Glick looked like? Well, it was
brown, had black stripes on its back, was about this big [gesture] and
weighed about 10 pounds. It also had 26 really important parts on the inside
of it. The Glick I saw really liked to eat berries, and had four parts on the
outside of it that it used to pick apart the berries. It also was sitting in a tree
with 16 branches and had a little bit of dirt on its tail.

Do you think Glicks really have to have dirt on their tails, or could some-   [Dirt]
thing still be a Glick even if it didn't have dirt on its tail?

Do you think Glicks have to be the same size as the one I saw, or could   [Size]
something still be a Glick even if it was a different size?

Do you think that Glicks have to be brown, or could something still be a   [Color]
Glick even if it was a different color?

Do you think that all Glicks have to have black stripes on their backs, or   [Surface markings]
could something still be a Glick even if it didn't have black stripes on its
back?

Do you think that all Glicks have to weigh the same as the Glick I saw, or   [Weight]
could something still be a Glick even if it weighed something different?

Do you think that all Glicks have the same number of important inside   [# Of inside parts]
parts, or could something still be a Glick even if it had a different number of
important inside parts?

Do you think that all Glicks have the same kind of parts on the outside of it   [Shape of outside parts]
or could something still be a Glick and have different looking parts on the
outside?

Could something be made of butter and still be a Glick?   [Butter]

8.3. Results

A belief that the hypothetical object with the changed property was still a member
of the labeled category was coded as '0', and a belief that changing the property
precluded category membership was coded as '1'. These scores correspond to how
relevant a child thought a particular attribute was to determining an object's category membership. And, when averaged across children, they provide the proportion
of children of each age group who believed that property to be central.

The mean responses for each age group are represented graphically in 'spider
web' plots (see Figs. 1–3). Each axis radiating from the center represents one
property, and distance from the origin indicates the degree to which children judged
the property to be central (i.e. that it had to be shared by all members of the labeled
category). For example (see Fig. 1), whereas about 75% of the children (averaging
across age) thought that all animals called 'glicks' had to have outside parts that
looked the same, only 20% of the children thought that all machines called 'nilards'
had to share similar looking outside parts.

A 3 (Age: 5, 7, or 9 years) by 2 (Kind: animal or machine) by 6 (Property: stripes,
color, size, weight, # of internal parts, shape of external parts) mixed-design
ANOVA with Kind and Property as repeated measures compared children's

Table 2
Machine story and questions read to 5-, 7-, and 9-year-olds

There is this kind of machine called a Nilard. Have you ever heard of a Nilard? I certainly had not, but the other day, I was walking through the hardware store, and I saw one. Do you want to hear what the Nilard looked like? Well, it was yellow, and had green stripes on it, was about this big [gesture] and weighed about 50 pounds. It also had 30 really important parts on the inside of it. The Nilard I saw is used to dig holes in the ground, and had 5 parts on the outside of it that would dig those holes. It was sitting on a shelf and had some dust on it.	
Do you think Nilards really have to be dusty, or could something still be a Nilard even if it wasn't dusty?	[Dirt]
Do you think Nilards have to be the same size as the one I saw, or could something still be a Nilard even if it was a different size?	[Size]
Do you think that Nilards have to be yellow, or could something still be a Nilard even if it was a different color?	[Color]
Do you think that all Nilards have to have green stripes on their backs, or could something still be a Nilard even if it didn't have green stripes on its back?	[Surface markings]
Do you think that all Nilards have the weigh the same as the Nilard I saw, or could something still be a Nilard even if it weighed something different?	[Weight]
Do you think that all Nilards have the same number of important inside parts, or could something still be a Nilard even if it had a different number of important inside parts?	[# Of inside parts]
Do you think that all Nilards have the same kind of parts on the outside of it or could something still be a Nilard and have different looking parts on the outside?	[Shape of outside parts]
Can something be made of butter and still be a Nilard?	[Butter]

responses to the property changes for each story[2]. The analysis revealed significant main effects only of Property ($F_{(5,58)} = 21.94$, $P < 0.0001$) and Kind ($F_{(1,62)} = 22.69$, $P < 0.0002$) and a significant Property × Kind interaction ($F_{(5,58)} = 21.87$, $P < 0.0001$)[3]. No other main effects or interactions reached significance, although the main effect of Age approached significance ($F_{(2,62)} = 2.481$, $P = 0.092$). Post-hoc analyses confirmed that each age group showed this same pattern of results. For each age group a 2 (Kind) by 6 (Property) repeated measures ANOVA revealed significant main effects of, and a significant interaction between, kind and property: For 5-year-olds, Kind $F_{(1,21)} = 3.80$, $P = 0.065$, Property $F_{(5,17)} = 4.83$, $P = 0.006$, Property by Kind $F_{(5,17)} = 6.39$, $P = 0.002$; for 7-year-olds, Kind $F_{(1,21)} = 7.09$, $P = 0.015$, Property $F_{(5,17)} = 6.97$, $P = 0.001$, Property by Kind $F_{(5,17)} = 7.91$, $P < 0.0006$; for 9-year-olds, Kind $F_{(1,20)} = 13.81$, $P = 0.001$, Property $F_{(5,16)} = 16.37$, $P < 0.0001$,

[2]Three participants (two 7-year-olds and one 9-year-old) were excluded from these overall analyses because their responses to one of the property questions were ambiguous and were coded as missing values. These subjects were included in analyses of the individual properties for which they gave unambiguous responses.

[3]We do not report MSEs here because they are meaningless for repeated factors having more than two levels. In mixed designs such as ours, the standard univariate tests of significance, with their accompanying neatly partitioned sums of squares, are invalid due to violations of the assumption of compound symmetry (see Winer, 1971). We thank Richard Darlington for pointing this out.

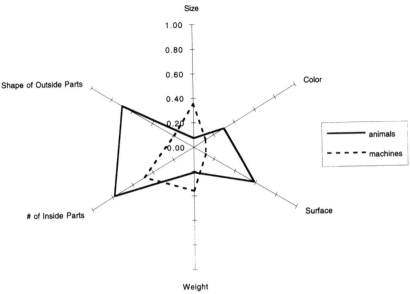

Fig. 1. Mean proportion of children (averaging across ages) who judged that all members of a novel category of animals or machines must share a given property. Each axis of the radial graph represents one of the properties about which children were asked. Distance from the center corresponds to the proportion of children (out of 68 total) who indicated that all members of a particular category had to share the same property (e.g. having black stripes) as the exemplar described in the story. Thus, high values on an axis indicate the relative centrality of the designated property to category membership. The dashed plot line shows the response profile for the novel machine category and the solid plot line shows the response profile for the novel animal category.

Property by Kind $F_{(5,16)} = 8.23$, $P < 0.0006$. In addition, we conducted follow-up analyses to examine the effect of category for each property individually. For each property, we subtracted responses to the machine story from responses to the animal story to get a single difference score for each participant. Six separate one-way ANOVAs compared the three age groups (5, 7, and 9 years) for each of the six properties. No significant main effects were found for any property (color, $F_{(2,65)} = 2.31$, $P > 0.10$; surface markings, $F_{(2,65)} = 1.66$; weight, $F_{(2,65)} < 1$; inside parts, $F_{(2,65)} < 1$; outside parts, $F_{(2,65)} = 1.67$; size, $F_{(2,65)} < 1$). Thus, children of all ages tested were sensitive to differences among the properties they were asked to consider and to the differential relevance of particular attributes to animals vs. machines.

In order to directly assess the significance of the differences in the profiles for animals and machines, we averaged across the age groups and conducted McNemar tests for each property[4]. Here, the McNemar test considers cases in which children responded that changing that property casts doubt on category membership for one kind but not on the other (e.g. all 'glicks', a novel animal, have to have stripes, but all 'nilards,' a novel machine, do not). Children significantly differentiated animals and

[4]The McNemar test compares responses on two related, dichotomous variables based on a χ^2-distribution. The standard χ^2-test is inappropriate when a single participant would be counted in multiple cells.

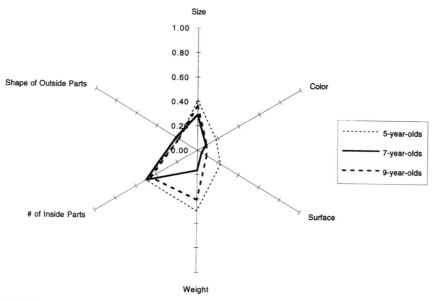

Fig. 2. Proportion of children at each age tested (5-, 7-, and 9-years-old) who judged that all members of a novel category of machines must share a given property. Small dashed line shows response profile of 5-year-olds; solid line shows response profile of 7-year-olds; and large dashed line shows response profile of 9-year-olds. To interpret this radial graph, see detailed description of similar graph in Fig. 1.

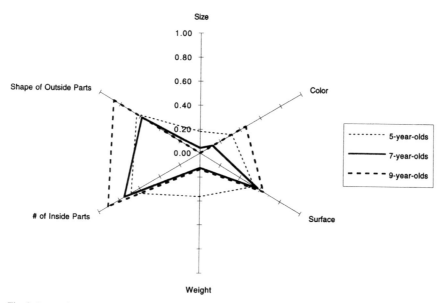

Fig. 3. Proportion of children at each age tested (5-, 7-, and 9-years-old) who judged that all members of a novel category of animals must share a given property. Small dashed line shows response profile of 5-year-olds; solid line shows response profile of 7-year-olds; and large dashed line shows response profile of 9-year-olds. To interpret this radial graph, see detailed description of similar graph in Fig. 1.

Table 3
Number of children ($n = 68$ total) who judged that a property change was, or was not, relevant to membership in an Animal vs. a Machine novel category

Changed property	Irrelevant to both animal and machine categories	Relevant to both animal and machine categories	Relevant to *animal* but not to machine categories	Relevant to *machine* but not to animal categories	McNemar χ^{2b}
Kind of outside parts[a]	19	10	34	2	30.44***
# Of inside parts	10	32	20	6	7.54**
Color	41	2	18	7	4.84*
Surface markings	26	7	34	1	31.11***
Size	44	3	2	19	13.76**
Weight	39	8	5	16	5.76*

[a] Three participants gave ambiguous responses and are not counted for this property.
[b] Whenever the expected frequency of a McNemar cell is below 5, the McNemar χ^2 tends to be inflated; in these cases, we relied on the exact binomial formula to obtain a P-value. χ^2 degrees of freedom=1.
***$P < 0.0001$; **$P < 0.005$; *$P < 0.05$.

machines for all six properties. Changing the shape of outside parts had a greater effect on animals than machines (i.e. changing the shape of outside parts disrupted category membership more for animals than for machines). Similarly, changing the number of inside parts, the surface markings, and the color had a greater effect on animals than machines. Changing the size and the weight mattered more for machines than for animals. See Table 3 for the frequencies of the four possible response patterns.

9. Discussion

This study revealed that children as young as 5 years recognize the differential importance of specific property types for animals and machines. The majority of children indicated that all members of a novel animal category must share the same color, surface markings, number of inside parts and appearance of outside parts[5]. The same children thought that members of a novel machine category could vary along these attributes yet still belong to the category. In contrast, children indicated that members of an animal category could vary more in size and weight than could members of a machine category.

Interestingly, the pattern of responses shows no systematic developmental changes (as confirmed by the post hoc analyses; see Figs. 2 and 3). This consistency

[5] As long as the outside parts of a particular machine perform the same function as other members of its class, the actual appearance of those parts might vary; but the same is not likely to be true for members of an animal class: if the outside parts look different despite serving the same function for the animal, we would probably think that the animal belonged to a different class. For example, both squirrels and nuthatches dig holes to cache food, but they do not have similarly shaped parts for digging those holes. In contrast, different lamps may have highly dissimilar parts for turning them on and off, yet we would hardly consider this difference significant enough to warrant classifying lamps on the basis of the appearance of their on/off switches.

indicates that children of different ages had the same notions about which types of properties were most central to each category. Across a substantial developmental period notions of centrality for these sets of properties remain remarkably stable. Given the similarity of response profiles across ages 5, 7, and 9, there is no basis to presume that children even younger than those tested here would have radically different knowledge about the fundamental differences in the causal relevance of particular properties to particular kinds of things.

We have suggested that children were responding on the basis of *causal* notions. Children might not, however, have clear notions of the causal reasons for the differential importance of, say, color, to animals versus machines. Instead, such notions might develop from an accumulation of observations about property variation rates within different kinds. If so, the children in this study may have based their responses not so much on an understanding of the causal importance of property types to particular ontological kinds but rather on this accumulation of frequency-based information[6]. The children's protocols suggest otherwise. Although children varied in their verbal precocity, those children who did justify their responses often did so in causal terms. For example, a large proportion of 5-year-olds spontaneously appealed to notions of 'growth' to explain why all 'glicks,' a kind of animal, did not have to be the same size. We did not conduct a systematic protocol analysis (partly because younger children are notoriously bad at articulating explanations), but we suggest that if children were asked to choose between a covariation explanation and a causal explanation (similar to Ahn et al., 1995) for these results, they would overwhelmingly prefer the causal account.

These data may not, then, rule out interpretations that appeal to frequency tabulations, but they do pose a challenge to such accounts. If younger children are insensitive to causal potency and must rely solely on correlational evidence, then when do they start using causal notions—do causal notions click into place once a certain threshold of correlational evidence has accumulated? But then, where do such causal notions come from? Certainly children are not explicitly taught why, for example, surface markings are relevant to what an animal is but not to what a machine is. Furthermore, correlational accounts, in which information accrues from concrete instances in the absence of later-developing abstract notions, would predict that local explanations would develop first only to be replaced later by abstract notions of how the mechanisms of growth, inheritance, and human intention apply broadly to animals or artifacts in general. That is, children should first generalize locally before generalizing observations about properties to all animals as a broad class. But in our study, the animal is a novel one, and the description gives no information that would allow local generalizations—indeed we forced children to consider 'glicks' as a specific type of animal, a very broad level of classification (i.e. as opposed to a specific type of mammal, or pet, or insect). Finally, such accounts would seem to have particular difficulty accounting for children's belief that all animals of the same kind should have the same number of inside parts, given that children very likely have not ever seen, much less counted, the inside parts of various animals.

[6]We thank an anonymous reviewer for pointing this out.

These results also accord with a related task in which two groups of 8-year-olds were familiarized with a single set of features, half of which characterized one category, half of which characterized a contrasting category (Barrett et al., 1993). One group of children was told that the features described two types of animals, while the other group was told that those same features described two types of tools. Subsequently, children's classification of test items (with novel combinations of the familiar features) differed, depending on whether or not the features had been introduced as belonging to two kinds of animals or two kinds of tools. Thus, these older children's knowledge was structured and guided by intuitive notions of the differential importance of certain features to animals vs. tools.

As suggested by the infant research reviewed earlier, these basic notions of causal centrality may emerge early, possibly as early as sensitivity to the typicality of properties. We are not suggesting that infants innately 'know' patterns of causal centrality for different kinds (although even that possibility has not been ruled out). Instead, we are suggesting that the ability to perceive and learn causal patterns may be just as fundamental as the ability to learn typicality and frequency distributions; typicality and causal centrality may go hand in hand in development.

10. Differential knowledge of local causal mechanisms

Knowledge about things such as living kinds and machines does develop. A framework of causal understanding of the differential centrality of properties for different kinds is only that—a framework. Within this framework, a great deal of cognitive growth and conceptual change occurs. Although the results of our study revealed no developmental differences, dramatic developmental changes can occur even for the properties we examined. If we queried details about the causal mechanisms underlying a given property, undoubtedly, we would see developmental changes. However, our questions required only a preliminary understanding of general causal patterns. We did not ask children, for instance, about the inner workings of a gasoline engine, the adaptive value of claws vs. hooves, or how being white helps a polar bear. This distinction between detailed knowledge of local causal mechanisms and less precise frameworks is an important one, as we emphasized earlier. Failure to acknowledge this distinction has sometimes led to mistaken endorsements of Dogma 2 and may foster false controversies regarding developmental change when some research focuses on local mechanism knowledge and other research emphasizes general explanatory frameworks (see Simons and Keil, 1995 for discussion).

We have recently begun to examine more carefully which aspects of causal knowledge emerge early in development to form a relatively fixed explanatory framework and which show change with increasing age. A full account of this distinction will require an extensive set of studies, but the general point can be illustrated through thought experiments. The study reported in this paper demonstrated that, during a developmental period marked by many changes in detailed knowledge of living kinds and artifacts, a general framework of causal knowledge is likely to exist early on, side by side with a sensitivity to typicality information. This somewhat counterintuitive prediction required an initial empirical demonstration. One other, more intuitive pattern will almost certainly be found, although the details of the developmental course can only be revealed through future studies:

   For sufficiently complex mechanisms, even most adults will not have a precise causal understanding (e.g. Au, in press). Thus, we might expect there to be relatively stable causal intuitions across lay people and little developmental change in these intuitions, but more dramatic, though highly specific, expert-novice differences. That is, only the most sophisticated experts would have such knowledge, and even for them it would likely be incomplete. An extreme example would be properties that no one outside of the leading laboratories has ever encountered. But even when almost everyone has heard of a property, only a few experts may understand how it is involved in specific mechanisms. For example, color is a salient property for both machines and animals, but only expert chemists might be able to explain the chemical composition of paint pigments or the biological under-pinnings of skin and fur pigments. Furthermore, such experts are likely to be the only ones who could explain how the organic and inorganic compounds in animals and machines produce colors differently. Similarly, only certain ecologists would be able to explain in detail how a particular pattern of coloration distinct to a species has adaptive value. For each of the properties used in our study, we could pose similar sorts of questions about mechanisms that only a tiny fraction of adults would know. Moreover, it would be almost trivial to demonstrate that some aspects of knowledge about any particular mechanism take a lifetime of devoted study to acquire.

   Aside from such cases of extreme expertise, lay knowledge of both causal mechanisms and typicality often will develop during childhood. Without further careful studies, we cannot easily predict the developmental time course for parti-cular properties, but few would doubt that many such cases exist. For example, children of different ages would likely give quite different answers to questions about the local mechanisms at work in such domains as biology, chemistry, and physics: 'Is the process that makes things rust like the process that makes people get grey hair, or is it more like the process that makes batteries run down?' In our preliminary studies we have found that answers to such detailed questions about color, size, and weight may change with age. For example, 5-year-olds do not distinguish between an animal and a machine when asked which is more likely to change its weight during the course of a day, but older children and adults think animals are more likely to show weight fluctuations.

11. Dogma 2: summary

   Children do learn as they get older, but the sorts of things they are capable of learning may not undergo qualitative changes such as a shift from similarity to causal frameworks or rules. Young children surely know fewer detailed mechanisms in domains ranging from the germ theory of disease to the actions of levers and fulcrums. They will also know less about typicality distributions of disease types and machine types. They may also acquire some new frameworks of causal understanding. However, our study suggests that such causal frameworks can be stable across large periods of development. Even when children default to typicality to distinguish classes of entities, they do not necessarily undergo a shift from strictly similarity-based reasoning to explanation-based reasoning. The illusion of this shift results from our neglect of their more abstract forms of non-associative knowledge.

12. The unnecessary commitments of empiricism

We have not yet explained why the two dogmas have influenced so much research in cognitive science. One powerful reason may be a tendency within cognitive science to adopt the several unnecessary commitments of the empiricist approach to the acquisition of knowledge. The strongest version of empiricism adopts the view that all knowledge and constraints on learning are acquired through the senses. This extreme view is untenable. Even the British empiricists (e.g. Locke) understood the need for constraints on knowledge acquisition; the sensory organs are clearly tuned to different kinds of information. Rather, they argued that there are no specialized knowledge acquisition devices tuned to different kinds of information. Instead a single general learning capacity accounts for all knowledge acquisition (e.g. Hume's account of learning about causation). Most nativists objected not to the absence of innate beliefs or knowledge but to the lack of domain-specific knowledge acquisition systems. They believed that different systems were biased to acquire different kinds of knowledge, that knowledge is constrained both by the sensory organs and by cognitive biases as well.

If these were the only differences between nativists and empiricists (and in fact they seem to be the only reliable, principled differences), then neither group should be particularly disposed towards the two dogmas. However, many empiricists tend to make additional assumptions that do not logically follow from their fundamental position but which lead to the dogmas. Specifically, they assume that the domain-general learning mechanism relies on association across a stock of perceptual primitives provided by the sensory apparatus. Accordingly, they believe that new associations must build on earlier associations such that higher-order relations can only be represented after all of their constituents are firmly in place. Following Hume, researchers often assume that causal relations can only be appreciated after they are built from pre-existing correlational constituents.

There is, however, no obvious reason why a domain-general learning device must rely on associations among sensory primitives. In fact, the strong form of this empiricist model is clearly false. Infants perceive intermodally at birth and seem to perceive causal relations as early as they have been tested (e.g. Leslie, 1982, 1984; Leslie and Keeble, 1987). In addition, newborns can imitate the facial expressions and body movements of their parent, revealing a sensitivity to particular kinds of complex, relational information from the start. This message, of course, was the key theme of the Gibsonian view of perceptual development. The Gibsons argued that we are all capable, at any age, of picking out complex relational patterns in the environment, especially those that form invariants that could be used to guide action (Gibson, 1966, 1979; Gibson, 1991). Their position was not clearly nativist or empiricist because it did not commit to a domain-general or domain-specific system for detecting invariants. We see no reason why a similar approach cannot be extended to the apprehension of relations that are more cognitive in nature (an extension that was not proposed by the Gibsons). Perhaps a domain-general learning system could be sensitive to and immediately encode such relations as cause, containment, and temporal precedence. If so, we could quickly learn abstract relational patterns that have immediate behavioral consequences. Such a learning system would fit with empiricist principles to the extent that it applied equally well to all sorts of information. There appear to be some innovative and clever attempts to further such a position. Mandler's early image schemas could possibly be interpreted in this way (see Mandler, this issue). For example, containment may be a fundamental image schema accessible to young infants (Baillargeon et al., 1995).

The nativist perspective argues that different aspects of the mind are innately tuned or optimized for picking up different kinds of high-level relational information. Thus, one aspect may be optimized for understanding physical, mechanical causation and another for social causation. The difference between empiricist and nativist accounts is closely linked to the number of distinct learning systems. If there are only two different learning systems that are optimized for two very large domains (e.g. social relations and mechanical forces), the differences between empiricist and nativist accounts are less dramatic. Alternatively, if there are thousands of distinct systems with highly local biases and prejudices, the differences between nativists and empiricists are large but potentially uninteresting as each highly local bias appears trivial and hardly the basis for a system of knowledge or explanatory insight. The middle ground between these extremes, with about a dozen different learning systems, may best capture the heterogeneous causal structure of the world without sacrificing coherency.

Our purpose here is not to determine whether particular kinds of knowledge acquisition problems are best solved by empiricist or nativist approaches, nor is it to argue that only one of these approaches fits with hybrid views of concepts. We do suggest, however, that a certain brand of empiricism seems to lead naturally to the two dogmas. Unfortunately, that brand seems to dominate many current models of how we acquire and use concepts.

Acknowledgements

F.K. was supported by NIH grant R01-HD23922 and D.S. was supported by a Jacob K. Javits fellowship. Many thanks to Bethany Richman for helping to design the study and for collecting all of the data. Thanks also to the children, parents, and teachers at the Ithaca area daycares and schools who made this research possible. We thank three anonymous reviewers for comments that helped to strengthen and clarify our arguments in several areas.

References

Ahn, W., Kalish, C.W., Medin, D.L., Gelman, S.A., 1995. The role of covariation versus mechanism information in causal attribution. Cognition 54, 299–352.

Anderson, J.R., 1976. Language, Memory, and Thought, Earlbaum, Hillsdale, NJ.

Armstrong, S., Gleitman, L., Gleitman, H., 1983. What some concepts might not be. Cognition 13, 263–308.

Au, T., Romo, L., in press. Mechanical causality in children's "folkbiology". In: Medin, D.L., Atran, S. (Eds.), Folkbiology. MIT Press, Cambridge, MA.

Baillargeon, R., Kotovsky, L., and Needham, A., 1995. The acquisition of physical knowledge in infancy. In: Sperber, D., Premack, D., Premack, S.J., Causal Cognition: A multidisciplinary debate, Clarendon Press, Oxford.

Barrett, S.E., Abdi, H., Murphy, G.L., Gallagher, J.M., 1993. Theory-based correlations and their role in children's concepts. Child Development 64, 1595–1616.

Barsalou, L.W., 1993. Challenging assumptions about concepts. Cognitive Development 8, 169–180.

Bassock, M., 1996. Using content to interpret structure: effects on analogical transfer. Current Directions in Psychological Science 5, 54–58.

Biederman, I., Mezzanotte, R.J., Rabinowitz, J.C., 1982. Scene perception: detecting and judging objects undergoing relational violations. Cognitive Psychology 14, 143–177.

Blessing, S.B., Ross, B.H., 1996. Content effects in problem categorization and problem solving. Journal of Experimental Psychology: Learning, Memory, and Cognition 22, 792–810.

Boshuizen, H.P.A., Schmidt, H.G., 1992. On the role of biomedical knowledge in clinical reasoning by experts, intermediates and novices. Cognitive Science 16, 153–184.

Brown, A.L., 1990. Domain-specific principles affect learning and transfer in children. Cognitive Science 14, 107–133.

Bruner, J.S., Goodman, C.C., 1947. Value and need as organizing factors in perception. Journal of Abnormal Social Psychology 42, 33–44.

Bruner, J.S., Postman, L., 1947. Emotional selectivity in perception and reaction. Journal of Personality 16, 69–77.

Carey, S., 1985. Conceptual change in childhood, MIT Press, Cambridge, MA.

Carpenter, G.A., Grossberg, S., 1987. A massively parallel architecture for a self-organizing neural pattern recognition machine. Computer Vision, Graphics, and Image Processing 37, 54–115.

Chapman, L.J., Chapman, J.P., 1967. Genesis of popular but erroneous diagnostic observations. Journal of Abnormal Psychology 72, 193–204.

Chapman, L.J., Chapman, J.P., 1969. Illusory correlation as an obstacle to the use of valid psychodiagnostic signs. Journal of Abnormal Psychology 74, 272–280.

Cheng, P.W., Novick, L.R., 1990. A probabilistic contrast model of causal induction. Journal of Personality and Social Psychology 58, 545–567.

Cheng, P.W., Novick, L.R., 1992. Covariation in natural causal induction. Psychological Review 99, 365–382.

Chi, M.T.H., 1992. Conceptual change within and across ontological categories: Examples from learning and discovery in science. In: Giere, R. (Ed.), Cognitive models of science: Minnesota studies in the philosophy of science, University of Minnesota Press, Minneapolis, MN.

Chi, M.T.H., Feltovich, P.J., Glaser, R., 1981. Categorization and representation of physics problems by experts and novices. Cognitive Science 5, 121–152.

Cook, M., Mineka, S., 1989. Observational conditioning of fear to fear-relevant versus fear-irrelevant stimuli in rhesus monkeys. Journal of Abnormal Psychology 98, 448–459.

Cook, M., Mineka, S., 1990. Selective associations in the observational conditioning of fear in rhesus monkeys. Journal of Experimental Psychology: Animal Behavior Processes 16, 372–389.

Feltovich, P.J., Spiro, R.J., Coulson, R.L., 1989. The nature of conceptual understanding in biomedicine: the deep structure of complex ideas and the development of misconceptions. In: Evans, D.A., Patel, V.L. (Ed.), Cognitive Science in Medicine: Biomedical Modeling, MIT press, Cambridge MA, pp. 113–172.

Fox, R., McDaniel, C., 1982. The perception of biological motion by human infants. Science 218, 486–487.

Garcia, J., Koelling, R.A., 1966. The relation of cue to consequence in avoidance learning. Psychonomic Science 4, 123–124.

Gelman, R., 1990. First principles organize attention to and learning about relevant data: number and the animate-inanimate distinction as examples. Cognitive Science 14, 79–106.

Gelman, S.A., Coley, J.D., 1990. The importance of knowing a dodo is a bird: categories and inferences in 2-year-old children. Developmental Psychology 26, 796–804.

Gelman, S.A., Markman, E.M., 1986. Categories and induction in young children. Cognition 23, 183–209.

Gelman, S.A., Markman, E.M., 1987. Young children's inductions from natural kinds: the role of categories and appearances. Child Development 58, 1532–1541.

Gelman, S.A., Medin, D.L., 1993. What's so essential about essentialism? A different perspective on the interaction of perception, language, and conceptual knowledge. Cognitive Development 8, 157–168.

Gentner, D., Toupin, C., 1988. Systematicity and surface similarity in the development of analogy. Cognitive Science 10, 277–300.

Gergely, G., Nádasdy, Z., Csibra, G., Bíró, S., 1995. Taking the intentional stance at 12 months of age. Cognition 56, 165–193.

Gibson, E.J., 1991. An odyssey in learning and perception, MIT Press, Cambridge, MA.

Gibson, E.J., Walker, A.S., 1984. Development of knowledge of visual and tactual affordances of substance. Child Development 55, 453–460.

Gibson, J.J., 1966. The senses considered as perceptual systems, Houghton-Mifflin, Boston.

Gibson, J.J., 1979. The ecological approach to visual perception, Houghton-Mifflin, Boston.

Goldstone, R.L., 1994. The role of similarity in categorization: providing a groundwork. Cognition 52, 125–157.

Goodman, N., 1972. Problems and Projects, Bobbs-Merrill, New York.

Harré, R., 1988. Modes of explanation. In: Hilton, D.J. (Ed.), Contemporary science and natural explanation: commonsense conceptions of causality, Harvester Press, Brighton, Sussex.

Harré, R., Madden, E.H., 1975. Causal powers: a theory of natural necessity. Totowa, NJ: Rowman and Littlefield.

Harris, P.L., German, T., Mills, P., 1996. Children's use of counterfactual thinking in causal reasoning. Cognition 61, 233–259.

Inhelder, B., Piaget, J., 1969. The early growth of logic in the child, classification and seriation. New York: W.W. Norton.

Intraub, H, 1980. Rapid conceptual identification of sequentially presented pictures. Journal of Experimental Psychology: Human Perception and Performance 7, 604–610.

Johnson, M.H., 1992. Imprinting and the development of face recognition: From chick to man. Current Directions in Psychological Science 1, 52–55.

Johnson, M.H., Dziurawiec, S., Ellis, H., Morton, J., 1991. Newborns' preferential tracking of face-like stimuli and its subsequent decline. Cognition 40, 1–19.

Jones, S.S., Smith, L.B., 1993. The place of perception in children's concepts. Cognitive Development 8, 113–139.

Keil, F.C., 1981. Constraints on knowledge and cognitive development. Psychological Review 88, 197–227.

Keil, F.C., 1989. Concepts, kinds, and cognitive development, MIT Press, Cambridge, MA.

Keil, F.C., Batterman, N., 1984. A characteristic-to-defining shift in the development of word meaning. Journal of Verbal Learning and Verbal Behavior 23, 221–236.

Keil, F.C., Smith, W.C., 1996. Is there a different 'basic' level for causal relations? Paper presented at the 37th annual meeting of the Psychonomic Society (November), Chicago, IL.

Kelley, H.H., 1967. Attribution theory in social psychology. Nebraska Symposium on Motivation 15, 192–238.

Kuhn, T.S., 1962. The structure of scientific revolutions, University of Chicago Press, Chicago.

Leslie, A.M., 1982. The perception of causality in infants. Perception 11, 173–186.

Leslie, A.M., 1984. Spatiotemporal continuity and the perception of causality in infants. Perception 13, 287–305.

Leslie, A.M., 1995. A theory of agency. In: Sperber, D., Premack, D., Premack, A.J. (Eds.), Causal Cognition: A multidisciplinary debate, Oxford: Clarendon Press, pp. 121– 141.

Leslie, A.M., Keeble, S., 1987. Do 6-month-olds perceive causality? Cognition 25, 265–288.

Mandler, J.M., 1993. On concepts. Cognitive Development 8, 141–148.

Medin, D.L., Shoben, E.J., 1988. Context and structure in conceptual combination. Cognitive Psychology 20, 158–190.

Medin, D.L., Schaffer, M.M., 1978. Context theory in classification learning. Psychological Review 85, 207–238.

Medin, D.L., Goldstone, R.L., Gentner, D., 1993. Respects for similarity. Psychological Review 100, 254–278.

Meltzoff, A.N., 1988. Infant imitation after a 1-week delay: long-term memory for novel acts and multiple stimuli. Developmental Psychology 24, 470–476.

Mervis, C.B., Johnson, K.E., Scott, P., 1993. Perceptual knowledge, conceptual knowledge, and expertise: comment on Jones and Smith. Cognitive Development 8, 149–156.

Murphy, G.L., Allopena, P.D., 1994. The locus of knowledge effects in concept learning. Journal of Experimental Psychology: Learning, Memory, and Cognition 20 (4), 904–919.

Murphy, G.L., Medin, D., 1985. The role of theories in conceptual coherence. Psychological Review 92, 289–316.

Murphy, G.L., Wisniewski, E.J., 1989. Feature correlations in conceptual representations. In: Tiberghien, G. (Ed.). Advances in cognitive science: Vol. 2. Theory and applications, Ellis Horwood, Chichester, UK, pp. 23–45.

Neisser, U., 1967. Cognitive Psychology. Englewood Cliffs, NJ: Prentice-Hall.

Nisbett, R.E., Krantz, D.H., Jepson, C., Kunda, Z., 1983. The use of statistical heuristics in everyday inductive reasoning. Psychological Review 90, 339–363.

Norman, G.R., Schmidt, H.G., 1992. The psychological basis of problem based learning. Academic Medicine 67, 557–565.

Nosofsky, R.M., 1984. Choice, similarity, and the context theory of classification . Journal of Experimental Psychology: Learning, Memory and Cognition 10, 104–114.

Nosofsky, R.M., 1986. Attention, similarity, and the identification-categorization relationship. Journal of Experimental Psychology: General 115, 39–57.

Nosofsky, R.M., 1992. Similarity scaling and cognitive process models. Annual Review of Psychology 43, 25–53.

Novick, L.R., 1988. Analogical transfer, problem similarity, and expertise. Journal of Experimental Psychology: Learning, Memory and Cognition 14, 510–520.

Patel, V.L., and Groen, G.J., 1991. The general and specific nature of medical expertise: a critical look. In: Ericsson, K.A., Smith, J. (Ed.), Toward a general theory of expertise, Cambridge University Press, New York, pp. 93–125.

Rayner, K., Pollatsek, A., 1992. Eye movements and scene perception. Canadian Journal of Psychology 46, 342–376.

Rosch, E., Mervis, C.B., 1975. Family resemblances: studies in the internal structure of categories. Cognitive Psychology 7, 573–605.

Rozin, P., Kalat, J.W., 1971. Specific hungers and poison avoidance as adaptive specializations of learning. Psychological Review 78, 459–486.

Salmon, W.C., 1989. Four decades of scientific explanation, University of Minnesota Press, Minneapolis, MN.

Simons, D.J., Keil, F.C., 1995. An abstract to concrete shift in the development of biological thought: the insides story. Cognition 56, 129–163.

Sloman, S., 1996. The empirical case for two systems of reasoning. Psychological Bulletin 119, 3–22.

Smith, E.E., Medin, D.L., 1981. Categories and concepts, Harvard University Press, Cambridge, MA.

Smith, E.E., Shoben, E.J., Rips, L.J., 1974. Structure and process in semantic memory: a featural model for semantic decisions. Psychological Review 81, 214–241.

Smith, L.B., Jones, S.S., 1993. Cognition without concepts. Cognitive Development 8, 181–188.

Spelke, E.S., Breinlinger, K., Macomber, J., Jacobson, K., 1992. Origins of knowledge. Psychological Review 99, 605–632.

Vygotsky, L.S., 1962. Thought and language (E. Hanfmann and G. Vakar, Trans.), MIT Press, Cambridge, MA.

Wellman, H.M., 1990. The child's theory of mind, MIT Press, Cambridge, MA.

Wellman, H.M., Gelman, S.A., 1992. Cognitive development: Foundational theories of core domains. Annual Review of Psychology 43, 337–375.

Werner, H., Kaplan, B., 1963. Symbol formation: An organismic-developmental approach to language and the expression of thought, Wiley, New York.

Williams, J.M.G., Mathews, A., MacLeod, C., 1996. The emotional Stroop task and psychopathology. Psychological Bulletin 120, 3–24.

Winer, B.J., 1971. Statistical principles in experimental design, 2nd ed., McGraw Hill, New York.

Wisniewski, E., Medin, D.L., 1994. On the interaction of theory and data in concept learning. Cognitive Science 18, 221–281.

Wright, J.C., Murphy, G.L., 1984. The utility of theories in intuitive statistics: the robustness of theory-based judgments. Journal of Experimental Psychology: General 113, 301–322.

3

Similarity-based categorization and fuzziness of natural categories

James A. Hampton*

Department of Psychology, City University, Northampton Square, London EC1V OHB, UK

Abstract

The adequacy of similarity to prototype as an account of categorization in natural concepts was assessed by analyzing the monotonicity of the relation between typicality of an item in a category and the probability of a positive categorization response using data from McCloskey and Glucksberg (1978). The analysis revealed a strong underlying similarity-based threshold curve, with systematic deviations. Further data collection showed that deviations from the curve could be attributed to the effects of unfamiliarity and non-categorial associations on typicality judgments, as well as differences between the perceptual appearance of an item (which tended to boost typicality) and its underlying nature (which tended to boost categorization). The results are discussed in terms of the different presuppositions and task constraints involved in rating typicality as opposed to performing a categorization. © 1998 Elsevier Science B.V.

Keywords: Categorization; Fuzzy; Concepts; Similarity

1. Introduction

A critical issue in current theorizing about the psychological representation of natural concepts concerns the degree to which *similarity* can provide an account of our conceptual categorization of the world. Whereas similarity-based models, such as prototype and exemplar-based models (Rosch, 1975; Nosofsky, 1988) propose that conceptual categories are formed as clusters held together by the similarity of their instances, others have argued that categorization is based on a more rule-like or

* Fax: +44 171 4778581.

theory-like semantic representation (Osherson and Smith, 1982; Murphy and Medin, 1985; Rips, 1989).

According to Rosch (1975), objects in the world can be clustered together on a number of correlated attributes. For example, creatures are clearly differentiated from inanimate objects and plants in terms of their spontaneous behavior, their internal organs and a great many other respects. Within the class of creatures, there are also correlations between attributes. Possession of one attribute (for example a creature that has feathers) tends to correlate within the general class of creatures with the possession of other attributes (such as having wings and flying). According to Rosch, this cluster of inter-correlated attributes leads to the formation of prototype concepts, such as BIRD and FISH within the class of creatures—where the prototype represents the idealized category member possessing all of the attributes in the cluster. Membership in the prototype concept category of FISH or BIRD is determined by judging how similar any instance is to this prototype, where similarity itself is defined in terms of the weight and number of the prototype attributes that the instance possesses[1].

Giving the prototype model a more formal treatment and extending its representational power, Hampton, (1993, 1995b) proposed that the central notion in the model involves an *intensional* representation (as a set of attributes) characterizing the average or idealized category member (that is to say, the prototype is an abstraction, and not simply the most typical category member). The attributes could themselves be structured in a frame or schema format. The representation of a particular prototype concept then involves three essential aspects: the intensional representation, a metric for determining similarity of an instance or a subclass to that representation, and a threshold criterion which can be placed on the resulting similarity measure in order to generate a binary Yes/No decision about the categorization. (Classifying instances as opposed to subclasses on the basis of similarity requires a different treatment—see Hampton, 1995b). Some may object that by increasing the representational power of prototype models to include structured representations and non-perceptual information one loses the distinctive nature of the theory. On the face of it 'similarity to a prototype' appears to imply perceptual resemblance. However, a moment's consideration shows that a model that is limited to representing purely perceptual information with no deeper structural, functional or abstract attributes is simply a 'straw man' as a model for representing most concepts. One has simply to point to things which commonly appear to be what they are not (such as whales or silk flowers) to dismiss such a model. Nor is it the case that those researching prototype theory have adopted such a restriction. Rosch and Mervis (1975), in their series of experiments on family resemblances, based similarity to prototype on attribute overlap, where the attributes were subject-generated verbal predicates which ranged over a wide variety of features (see also Hampton, 1979). Hampton (1976) had subjects cluster attributes generated by others as true of categories on the basis of the type of information involved, and found in addition to

---

[1]It should be understood that the concepts of Fish and Bird described in this way are the mental representations of these categories possessed by the average person, and are not the same as the corresponding biologically defined concepts.

physical/perceptual characteristics there were clusters corresponding to function, location, superordinate categorization and behaviour. Prototype theory has also been applied among other things to abstract concepts (Hampton, 1981), personality traits (Cantor and Mischel, 1977, 1979), psychological situations (Cantor et al., 1982), psychiatric diagnoses (Cantor et al., 1980), and a range of linguistic effects in syntax (Lakoff, 1987), none of which can sensibly be considered as perceptually based concepts. By allowing more powerful representational formats, the revised theory also avoids the weaknesses associated with simple 'feature list' models (Barsalou and Hale, 1993), without losing the essential premise that categorization is based on similarity to a prototype.

Hampton (1995a) also pointed out that if the correlation among attributes is very high so that (presumably for reasons to do with the nature of the world) there are no borderline cases, then it may be possible to give a category 'definition' in terms of individually necessary and jointly sufficient attributes. Discovery of natural concepts with conjunctive definitions (such as the category of Birds as 'feathered bipeds' for example) does not, therefore, invalidate the prototype account[2].

Along with the development of the prototype theory, Rosch (1975) also introduced a new variable—the notion of 'typicality'. Typicality of an instance or subclass refers to how representative it is of the category or concept. Typicality predicts performance across a range of cognitive tasks (see Hampton, 1993 for a review). Of central importance to prototype theory is the idea that this variable of typicality reflects the same underlying similarity to the category prototype as is used in making categorization decisions. Similarity here is not an empty notion (Goodman, 1970) but means 'similarity in respect of those attributes which form the intensional representation of the prototype concept'. This point is particularly important, since similarity can be a notoriously unconstrained variable, depending on the perspective adopted and the respects in terms of which things are judged to be similar. Typicality, then, is a constrained form of similarity, in which the respects (and their relative importance) are determined by the conceptual representation itself.

It is clear that classifying on the basis of similarity must involve 'rules'—there must be a rule for determining a similarity value for any pair of concepts (or instance-concept pair), and there must be a rule for deriving degree of category membership (either as a binary outcome via a threshold criterion, or as a fuzzy judgment on a response scale) on the basis of this similarity. In each case, different possible rules exist as variants of the prototype model. However, a stricter notion of 'rule-based' categorization has been developed as a direct contrast to the similarity-based approach.

The major alternative to the prototype theory's similarity clustering account of natural concepts was summarized in a seminal paper by Rips (1989). Reviewing arguments from Goodman (1970), Osherson and Smith (1982), Armstrong et al. (1983), Murphy and Medin (1985), and others, Rips made the case that membership

---

[2]Well defined concepts such as rectangle or prime number would, of course, be outside the scope of the theory, since the necessity of their defining properties is a matter of analytic stipulation or deductive inference, rather than an empirical generality based on observation.

in natural categories was not primarily dependent on similarity. The argument is that the way in which category membership is determined is different from the way in which typicality is derived. For example, Murphy and Medin suggested that, whereas typicality in a category may depend largely on similarity to a prototype, the membership of some instance or subclass in the category depends on whether or not that instance or subclass fits the underlying causal/explanatory structure of the category, and it is this underlying 'theory' which lends coherence to the whole conceptual domain. Just as a doctor will classify a case by considering which known medical condition best accounts for the symptoms presented by the patient, so we classify an item in the category that best *explains* the set of attributes that it possesses. The existence of a causal theory of how observable attributes arise from an object's deeper underlying nature allows us to over-ride a simple similarity account with a more rule-like or logical classification. One could even say that we see things as being similar *because of* their category membership, rather than categorizing them because of their similarity.

One example of where typicality and category membership apparently have very different determinations is the case of concepts that have well known explicit definitions, such as kinship terms in English (Landau, 1982). Whether someone is a grandmother depends *only* on whether or not she is female and is the mother of a parent (or some logically equivalent definitional rule). Whether someone is a *typical* grandmother however depends on whether the stereotypical grandmother characteristics—white hair, rocking chair, bakes cookies—apply. In this case, similarity to the prototype (or more properly the stereotype) does not provide any more than probabilistic information about true membership of the category[3].

Few theorists would wish to argue that kinship terms like uncle or grandmother, or other explicitly defined terms, such as prime number or triangle are represented by prototype concepts. Such concepts are perhaps paradigm cases of rule-based classification, in the narrow sense of categorization based on a logical conjunction of a small set of criterial features. However, to concede this limitation on prototype theory is not to abandon the notion that the bulk of our common sense everyday concepts, for which explicit definitions are much harder to frame, might not still have prototype representations. Doctors and scientists do indeed have well developed theories that allow for a more satisfactory classification of their particular domain of expertise according to deeper explanatory principles. The question remains to what extent this model of concepts as elements of theories is appropriate for the everyday reasoning of the non-specialist. Could it be that the model overestimates the sophistication of most people's conceptual representations?

Evidence on this score concerning common biological and artifact kinds is mixed. Studies on adult's concepts of natural kind and artifact terms (Malt, 1990, 1994; Malt and Johnson, 1992; Hampton, 1995a; see also Kalish, 1995; Braisby et al., 1996) suggest that rule-based models of category membership often provide a poor

---

[3]Lakoff (1987) points out that motherhood itself may be a prototype concept. Mothers normally satisfy multiple criteria—donors of genetic material, conception, pregnancy, birth, nursing and rearing. Where these multiple criteria can be separated, then it is possible to argue that motherhood becomes a matter of degree, depending on how many of the criteria are satisfied, and how important they are to the concept.

account of the way in which people actually categorize classes of biological and artifact objects. For example Malt's research has shown that people do not classify liquids as 'water' solely on the basis of their chemical constituency, but also take into account the origins and human functions of the liquid. Malt also found that categorization in artifact categories was not simply based on the intended function of the object, but also reflected less explanatorially relevant attributes such as appearance.

Hampton (1995a) found that people's categorization in common everyday categories was affected by aspects of the concept ('characteristic features') that would normatively be expected to be irrelevant. For example, when told that a fruit had been grown from an orange tree, but that because of special growing conditions it had the appearance and taste of a lemon, only a third of subjects judged it to be really an orange. Or consider the following description:

'The offspring of two zebras, this creature was given a special experimental nutritional diet during development. It now looks and behaves just like a horse, with a uniform brown color'.

When asked if this was really a zebra, again only a third of the subjects agreed, the rest of the subjects ignoring the genotype in favor of the phenotype, contrary to the assumptions of psychological essentialism (Medin and Ortony, 1989; Rips, 1989). The 'rule' for species membership that requires that two creatures will always have an offspring of the same type, was overruled for most subjects by the lack of similarity of the instance to the class[4].

Kalish (1995) asked participants to judge whether category membership in a class was a matter of fact (as in the case of whether the number 349231 is prime) or a matter of opinion (as in the case of whether Florida is a good place to take a vacation)[5]. One could expect that if people feel that categories are based on rules, then they would judge their membership to be a matter of fact, even if in individual cases the rule was unknown or the application of the rule was hard to determine. In his study, Kalish did not find clear evidence that either biological or artifact categories were considered to be rule-based.

In the developmental literature, Keil (1989) found that children's understanding of concepts may shift from a surface similarity-based concept to a deeper 'theory-based' concept. Several other studies in the developmental literature have also drawn out the fact that children do not rely on purely *perceptual* similarity to define their concepts (Carey, 1985; Gelman, 1988). However, if similarity is defined as above—in terms of the attributes that are relevant to the concept—then there is no reason to suppose that children's or adult's prototypes should be represented by

---

[4]Keil (1989) found that even relatively young children can appreciate the rule that parenting determines the species of the offspring. The data from Hampton (1995a) suggest that, although people understand this general rule, they may not be fully confident in applying it, when faced with contradictory evidence. Subjects in the experiment may have believed it to be possible that a special diet could in fact change the physical nature of a creature or plant in such a way as to change its categorisation. Alternatively, they may not have been using their concept of 'species' in determining whether it is appropriate to label an organism as a zebra or an orange.

[5]These are my examples.

purely *perceptual* information. The shift from perceptual to 'hidden' aspects of objects is evidence of growing levels of knowledge on the part of the child, and an increase in the attention and importance accorded to deeper functional and relational kinds of attribute in concept representations. The data do not, however, show that categorization is not still similarity-based. It is not enough to show a developmental trend in the understanding of a concept in order to argue that the format of the representation (as opposed to its content) has actually changed. This point has important implications for many criticisms of the prototype model. It has often been assumed that 'similarity' refers only to similarity in visual appearance. If such were the case, similarity-based categorization would of course fail to capture any but the most trivial of concepts—those based on obvious visual features. Prototype theory does not make this assumption however. From the first, Rosch argued that a multiplicity of types of feature may be involved in categorization, including common function, origin, common ways of interacting with an object, and so forth. As I argued in Hampton (1995a), the central tenet of a similarity-based categorization model is that, for most concepts, people use a wide range of information for judging category membership, and this information is combined to form an overall assessment of closeness to the category prototype in a way that allows for contextual and individual variation in categorization. 'Deeper' aspects of the nature of an object (such as the innards, or the parentage of a biological kind) are clearly valid sources of information which can be used in categorization, and will be accorded weight in the computation of similarity depending on the individual's understanding of the conceptual domain, and the contextual purposes of the categorization.

If similarity is to be given more than a 'straw-man' status in categorization, then how might one otherwise differentiate similarity and rule-based categorization? One critical piece of evidence concerns the relation between *typicality* and category membership. If categorization depends on similarity, then there should be a monotonic relation between measures of similarity to the prototype (which ratings of typicality are assumed to provide), and measures of category membership. It should not be possible to find cases where object A is more typical of a concept than object B, but yet object B is more likely to be in the concept category than object A. Accordingly, Rips (1989) aimed to demonstrate cases where this monotonicity is violated, from which it could be argued that categorization could not be based on similarity—or at least not on the same kind of similarity as is reflected in judgments of typicality to prototype.

1.1. Rips' studies

In one study Rips asked subjects to consider a range of objects that were each half way between two conceptual categories—one a 'fixed' category, and the other a 'variable' category. To use an illustrative example, coins tend to have a fixed diameter (more or less), whereas pizzas can vary in size considerably. Rips therefore asked participants to think of a circular object that had a diameter half way between the largest example of an American quarter they could think of and the smallest example of a pizza they could think of. One group of participants were then asked to decide whether the object was a pizza as opposed to a quarter (presumably they chose whichever option they considered more probable, given that no other information was available). Others judged for which category the object was more typical, and a third group judged to which category the object was more similar. While the object was more often judged to be a pizza (overall, 63% chose the variable category), it was more likely to be judged as similar to the quarter (69% chose the fixed category), and was about equally likely to be judged as typical of either category (54% chose the fixed category). Hence, there was a non-monotonicity of the kind required to disprove the prototype account. The object in question was more similar to category A than to category B, but was more likely to belong in B than in A.

Notwithstanding some problems with the generalizability of this result (Smith and Sloman, 1994, found that unless subjects were 'thinking aloud' as they did the categorization task, the dissociation did not occur), even as it stands it provides poor evidence against similarity-based categorization. First, the argument is only valid if one assumes equal generalization gradients for each concept. But there is no reason to restrict prototype concepts in this way. According to the model, categorization depends on placing a threshold on the similarity measure (Hampton, 1993, 1995b, 1997). Differences in the placement of the threshold could explain differences in the allowed range of variability of concepts. Rips' fixed categories could have high thresholds, whereas his variable categories could have low thresholds— for example the similarity to prototype needed for something to count as a quarter could be much greater than the similarity to prototype needed for something to count as a pizza[6]. Furthermore, where to place the similarity threshold of concepts relative to their internal variability is something that can be learned from experience with exemplars (Fried and Holyoak, 1984), so there is no need for a rule-based 'theory' to explain the difference between fixed and variable conceptual classes. (Lamberts, 1995, offers a similar account using a mathematical model of similarity). Hampton (1995b) argued that what, in fact, differentiates the prototype representation of a class from the representation of an individual is just this inclusion of the range of variability allowed on different semantic dimensions. An *individual* apple has just one color and just one size, whereas the *class* of apples has a *distribution* of values for color and size.

In a second ingenious study, Rips (1989) presented participants with a story in which a creature metamorphosed from a bird-like form into an insect-like form. When the transformation was caused by hazardous chemicals, then the object was judged overall to be more similar to (and typical of) an insect, but more likely to be a bird. By contrast, if the transformation was portrayed as a normal part of the life cycle of the creature, then the immature form (before transformation) was judged more similar to (and typical of) a bird, but more likely to be an insect.

Different generalization gradients could not explain these results since merely changing the *source* of the transformation (accidental versus maturational) changes the category to which the object is considered most likely to belong. Rips' demon-

---

[6]This is to ignore, for the present, the additional important role of historical origin in determining whether a coin is a true coin as opposed to a fake. Only a few of Rips' examples were of this type.

stration is a prima facie example of non-monotonicity between similarity and categorization. This second study can also be criticized in several ways[7]—for example, each subject responded to the scenarios for one condition only, yet all three responses were collected at the same time from each subject, leading to the possibility of demand characteristics (would a subject feel happy to always give the same response to all three questions?) The accidental transformation condition did not allow participants to express the anti-essentialist belief that the creature changed category as a result of the accident, since they were only asked for a single classification of the creature—'the one that changed'. There was also poor agreement amongst the subjects in the classification of the creatures, and while categorization was expressed as a 'likelihood' (suggesting relevant information was missing), typicality and similarity were judged directly (implying that all relevant information was given). Pending a replication of the study, it does, however, appear that counterfactual examples of this kind may break the normal relation between typicality/similarity and categorization (see Hampton, 1996a, for further evidence based on a study by Kalish, 1995).

A third set of studies by Rips and Collins (1993) employed categories with bimodal distributions to demonstrate non-monotonicity. If a population of people was composed of (for example) 5th graders and their fathers, then the height of individuals in the set would have two modal values, one for a typical child and one for a typical father. In this situation participants were willing to rate similarity and typicality by distance from the mean, but to rate likelihood of being in the population on the basis of actual frequency of the value. Thus, someone with the mean height would be more typical of the class but judged less likely to belong in it than someone else whose height was one of the two modal values. Similar results were obtained with a range of different distributions other than bimodal mixtures of this kind.

These last studies also provide clear prima facie examples of non-monotonicity between similarity and classification. They achieved this by providing very explicit distributional information (participants were shown graphs of the distributions of values across the population of instances) which invoked extensional reasoning processes in judging likelihood of category membership. People are, thus, apparently able to use extensional reasoning to make judgments of likelihood of category membership, although they still prefer to use distance from the average value when judging similarity or typicality[8]. Others have stressed the important differences between extensional and similarity-based reasoning. Tversky and Kahneman (1983) showed that people often engage in similarity-based reasoning ('representativeness' was the term they used) when they should be thinking extensionally—in particular, when estimating the likelihood of membership in a conjunction of two categories compared with likelihood of membership in just one. When frequencies are emphasized in the presentation of these problems, however, people are apparently able to reason extensionally, and their responses are more in line with the

[7]My ability to criticise Rips' study is largely owing to his providing me with copies of his experimental booklets—a generous gesture which I gratefully acknowledge.

[8]Note that exemplar models use extensional representation of category members, and would predict the categorization performance here, but not the similarity judgments.

axioms of subjective probability theory (Kahneman and Tversky, 1996, but see Gigerenzer, 1994, 1996 for an alternative interpretation). Similar effects could have occurred in the Rips and Collins studies. The 'intuitive' reasoning that judges typicality or similarity as distance from the average exemplar could be replaced with a frequency-based assessment of subjective likelihood when doing the categorization task. Note that in all three of Rips' demonstrations—the fixed/variable categories, the metamorphosis study, and the bimodal distribution experiments – participants are not actually categorizing an instance about which everything is known. They are always asked to assess, *on the basis of the available evidence*, the *likelihood* that the object is in one category or another. The evidence offered is usually very limited. This way of framing the categorization task is very different from the standard categorization question—'is an X an instance of category Y?', where the task is not framed in a way that presumes that the participant is making a judgment with an associated probability of being true or false (cf. Kalish, 1995).

The problem with many of these demonstrations is that the reasoning processes elicited from the participants may be quite specific to the unusual kinds of materials presented. For example, there are a few familiar cases of biological metamorphoses (caterpillars to butterflies, tadpoles to frogs), but most of our conceptual categories are remarkably stable and most objects fall clearly into one class or another. The issue of whether categorization of the familiar everyday world is based on some form of similarity is not, therefore, always well addressed by these studies. The remainder of this paper, therefore, turns to the question of whether non-monotonicity can be observed in data of a more traditional kind—namely the situation where participants decide whether a particular subclass falls in a more general category.

None of the studies so far described have adopted the most direct way to test the monotonicity between similarity and category membership. This would be to obtain measures of category membership and typicality from independent groups of participants and to test the monotonicity of the results directly. Such an experiment would be simple to set up, and in fact McCloskey and Glucksberg (1978) published data for just this design. In the Appendix to their paper they listed 492 items in 18 categories, together with (a) their mean rated typicality, (b) the probability that they were categorized positively, and (c) the degree of within subject disagreement. (These 492 items were selected from an original total of 540 items by excluding those which were considered by any one of ten participants as referring to *overlapping* rather than nested categories). Using these three sources of information, the aim of the following analysis is to see to what extent the prototype model can provide an adequate account of the data. The strategy will be first to determine how well typicality predicts the likelihood that someone will categorize an item in a category. This initial model will then be taken as a base-line from which to identify cases where non-monotonicity is occurring—that is to say items which are either more likely or less likely to be categorized in a category than would be predicted from their typicality. A study will then be described in which ratings were collected to test possible accounts of these deviations from a straightforward similarity-based model of categorization.

2. Analysis

The 492 items in 18 categories together with their published normative measures were entered for analysis into SPSS for Windows with variables of mean rated typicality, and probability of a Yes categorization[9] (a fuller account of the statistical analysis, including an analysis of the within-subject inconsistency data is to be found in Hampton, 1996b). One category (*Carpenter's Tool*) was omitted since there were only ten items left in the norms after the rejection of overlapping concepts, presumably because most carpenter's tools are also used in other skilled trades. There remained 17 categories with 482 items, with between 24 and 30 items per category. If there is a monotonic relation between categorization probability and mean rated typicality, then a plot of one variable against the other should show a monotonically rising curve, asymptoting at a probability of one at the top of the typicality scale, and at a probability of zero at the bottom of the typicality scale. More specifically the curve should follow a threshold function. A scatterplot with categorization probability as the vertical axis and mean typicality as the horizontal axis (see Fig. 1) revealed the expected threshold curve, but with a considerable spread of items above and below the curve. The overall linear correlation between the variables was 0.89. Of course a reasonable level of correlation was to be expected under any model. A more detailed analysis was therefore carried out.

2.1. Inter-category differences in threshold

Scatterplots were produced for each category individually, and representative examples of the range of results are shown in Appendix A. The graphs show that some categories (e.g. Bird, Sport) show a neat monotonically rising threshold function relating categorization probability to typicality, whereas others (e.g. Disease, Fish) do not. For Fish, for example, items with typicalities in the range from 5 to 6 showed categorization probabilities ranging from 0.2 to 0.9.

It was also very noticeable that different categories had different 50% categorization threshold points on the typicality scale. This difference was probably owing to scaling factors resulting from the different proportions of members and non-members in each category list. In fact across categories, threshold point correlated at 0.55 with mean number of positive categorizations. These differences in threshold point could also have been exacerbated by the use of a blocked presentation of items in each category for the typicality ratings, but a randomized presentation of item-category pairs for the membership decisions. Range effects were therefore more

---

[9]The analysis involves data summed over subjects, and so necessarily confounds individual subject differences with within-subject variance. It would, of course, be hard to do the analysis in any other way, given that the assessment of probability requires repeated sampling of a binary judgment. McCloskey and Glucksberg did, however, show that within-subject inconsistency in categorization across an interval of a few weeks was highly correlated with overall fuzziness as reflected in categorization probability for the group as a whole. There is, therefore, a reasonable basis for assuming that analyzing the structure of categories based on group data will give a representative account of individual's conceptual representations and thought processes.

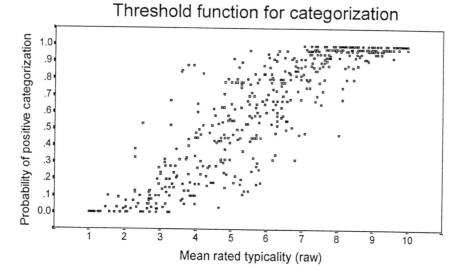

Fig. 1. Scatterplot of the raw data relating probability of a positive categorization (*P*) to mean item typicality.

likely to have occurred in the typicality judgments than in the categorization responses.

In order to remove between-category range effects from the typicality scales, a correction constant was subtracted from the typicality scores for each category so that mean typicality for each category was a linear function of mean normalized categorization probability. Effectively this removes between category effects using a single parameter to estimate the correction factor based on the average proportion of items in each category list that were considered category members. (Statistical details may be found in Hampton, 1996b). The new typicality variable incorporating the subtracted constant is referred to as *corrected typicality*. Combining the data from all categories once more, the corrected typicality scales correlated with categorization probability *P* at 0.905, and with normalized categorization probability *zp* at 0.927 (*zp* is a transformation of *P* which would show a straight line function with typicality if the threshold curve followed the cumulative normal distribution function). A regression model was calculated to predict *zp* from corrected typicality. The regression equation was

$$zp' = -2.91 + 0.57 \times (CorrectedTypicality) \tag{1}$$

Using this equation, predicted values of *zp* were found, and retransformed back into predicted probabilities of categorization using the inverse of the previous normalization function. The observed and predicted *P* also correlated at 0.927. Thus, using a single parameter to estimate the range effect on typicality and assuming a normally distributed criterion placement, some 86% of the variance in categorization probability could be predicted on the basis of mean rated typicality alone. An alternative analysis was run which calculated individual correction factors for each category separately and achieved a correlation of 0.947.

Part of the successful fit of the regression model is owing to the inclusion in the lists of words of items which were clearly not members of their categories—for example, Car as an Animal or Bee as a Bird. It was important to keep these items in the statistical analysis, in order to anchor the threshold function at the bottom end, and to enable calculation of the range effect, but at the same time the ability to predict low typicality and low categorization probability for such items is not too surprising. To examine the effect of these items on the fit of the model, a subset of data were selected by eliminating any items with categorization probability less than 0.05 (allowing for occasional lapses in concentration on the part of the participants). The correlation of observed and predicted categorization probability fell to 0.903, based on 444 of the original 482 words. The model is clearly still a reasonable fit to the data. Finally, a similar argument could be made concerning items that are very *clearly* category members, which may be exerting strong leverage on the regression equation. Accordingly the 324 items which had categorization probabilities between 0.05 and 0.95 were selected. These items constitute the borderline region of fuzzy categorization where the test of monotonicity is most critical. The correlation for these items between predicted and observed categorization probability was still high at 0.850[10]. Across the individual categories, taking just the borderline region of items, typicality correlated with normalized categorization probability with values between 0.68 (for Fish and Animal) and 0.98 (for Bird) with an estimated mean of 0.87. The range of correlations across categories was not consistent with the hypothesis that they were from a homogenous population ($\chi^2(16) = 33.4$, $P < 0.01$). There were, therefore, significant inter-category differences in how well typicality correlated with zp, but these differences did not reflect any obvious semantic distinction.

The purpose of the analysis was first to identify how well typicality alone could predict normalized categorization probability. The second purpose was to use the typicality model as a base-line in order to identify cases where typicality is *not* a good predictor of categorization, such as those seen in the Disease and Fish categories in Appendix A. It is these cases that break the expected pattern of a monotonic increase in categorization probability with typicality which are of particular interest from the point of view of similarity-based accounts of categorization. To identify such cases as accurately as possible, typicality was corrected individually for each category, so that each category had a 50% threshold point corresponding to 5 on the typicality scale. A scatterplot of the observed and predicted values of P based on this corrected typicality was plotted (see Fig. 2) and the residuals examined.

The distribution of residuals showed significant positive kurtosis, suggesting that there were outlier cases which were not simply reflecting normally distributed random error in the measurements. Cases with absolute standardized residuals greater than 2 were examined. There were 36 such outliers (7.5% of the cases). These

---

[10]In a later analysis the 324 borderline items were 'refined' by removing a further 20 which had more than 85% 'clear' categorization responses in the following experiment. Correlation with categorization increased from 0.85 to 0.88.

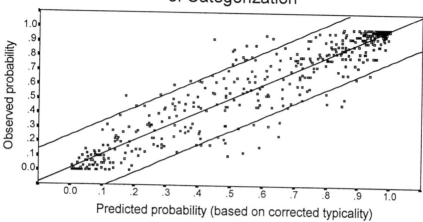

Fig. 2. Scatterplot of observed probability of a positive categorization *P* against predicted values based on corrected typicality scores, together with 95% C.I.s.

outliers are shown in Table 1. They constitute evidence against a single similarity dimension underlying both typicality and categorization judgments. They, therefore, deserved further exploration.

2.2. Accounting for residual variance

Various hypotheses suggested themselves to explain why items should have been

Table 1
Cases with *P* greater than or less than expected from their typicality

Category	*P* greater than expected	*P* less than expected
Animals	Sea anemone, hydra, euglena, sponge, yeast	Cocoon, egg
Clothing	–	Cuff links, bracelet
Disease	Schizophrenia, depression neurosis	Heart attack, fever
Fish	Lamprey	Whale, porpoise, seal
Fruit	Tomato, olive	Orange juice
Furniture	–	Sewing machine, stove, refrigerator
Kitchen utensil	–	Stove
Natural earth formation	Sinkhole	Forest
Precious stone	–	Industrial diamond
Science	Linguistics	Nursing, geometry
Ship	Sampan	Sailboat
Vegetable	Sauerkraut	–
Weather phenomenon	Waterspout	Autumn

categorized with a probability higher or lower than that predicted from their typicality. First, there may have been factors other than similarity affecting the typicality
ratings.

Familiarity is known to play a role in how people rate typicality (Barsalou, 1985;
Hampton and Gardiner, 1983; Malt and Smith, 1982; McCloskey, 1980). When
items are unfamiliar they are normally given lower typicality ratings. However,
unfamiliar items are not necessarily rejected from categories (in fact category membership may be all that is known of some unfamiliar animals or diseases). Unfamiliar
items would be expected therefore to be judged as less typical than would be
warranted by their category membership. This effect is possibly seen in Table 1
for items such as Sea anemone, Hydra, Euglena, Lamprey, Sinkhole, and Sampan,
all of which have observed P greater than predicted—that is they all have depressed
values of typicality.

Superficial similarity could also be playing a role in *boosting* typicality ratings.
For example, in the Fish category, all three aquatic mammals were found to have
categorization P lower than expected from their typicality ratings. Tadpole was also
in this position (although not extreme enough to be shown in Table 1). The account
offered here would be that greater weight is accorded to perceptual similarity in
typicality judgments than in categorization judgments. This hypothesis would lend
support to the notion of a differentiation between the information used in typicality
judgements and that employed in categorization, as predicted by the 'binary' view of
concept structure (Osherson and Smith, 1982) and as proposed by Rips (1989),
although it could also be understood as a shift in the weight given to different aspects
of a concept in judging similarity for the purpose of categorization, as opposed to
similarity for the purpose of making a typicality judgment.

The converse of this effect is that items with a poor superficial similarity but a
better match to 'technical' definitions should have greater P than predicted on the
basis of typicality – Tomato and Olive as Fruits, and Sponge and Yeast as Animals
might well fall into this category.

Membership in contrasting categories could also play a role in reducing categorization probability below its predicted level. There is a bias—noted particularly in
the developmental literature—for people to assume that categories are mutually
exclusive (Clark, 1973; Pinker, 1984; Slobin, 1973). In a similarity-based categorization scheme, categorization can proceed either in a contrastive way (where each
item is classed with the category to which it *best* belongs) or in a non-contrastive
way (where each item is classed with any category to which it is sufficiently similar,
and may thus be included in a number of overlapping categories). One possible
cause of items deviating from the threshold function would be that in categorization
judgments people are more inclined to think contrastively than when making typicality judgments. For example, in the Furniture category, the three items Sewing
Machine, Stove, and Refrigerator may have been thought by many participants to be
better classified in a contrasting category such as Appliances, and so were rejected as
Furniture in line with the Mutual Exclusivity heuristic. When considering typicality
however, participants may have been driven more by similarity to the category itself,
and less by consideration of alternative contrasting categories. There is a presuppo-

sition in judging typicality that the item in question is actually a category member, and so closeness to other category prototypes may have less influence on the typicality judgments than on categorization itself[11]. (This point is taken up further in Section 5). This account might explain the low P value for Bracelet and Cuff-links as Clothing (in that they may be better classed as Jewellery or Accessories), and for a number of Ships which might be better categorized as Boats (Sailboat, Rowboat and Lifeboat).

Finally, *non-categorial associations* could act to boost typicality without affecting categorization. When a word refers to something that is not logically of the right kind (for example a *part* or *product* of a fruit, like Orange juice, a *symptom* of a disease like Fever, a *time* of characteristic weather like Autumn) then typicality ratings may tend to reflect this association, without any corresponding effect on categorization probability. That is, typicality ratings could be influenced by semantic associatedness involving other types of semantic relation. Recent work by Bassok and Medin (1997) suggests that similarity itself can also be influenced by thematic (co-occurrence) as opposed to categorial (taxonomic) associations. Included in this heading would also come Cocoon and Egg in the Animal category—items strongly associated with the lives of animals but probably not considered to be animals in themselves.

3. Experiment

In order to test these post-hoc hypotheses, the 17 lists of category items from the norms were presented to 20 participants with instructions to rate each word according to a number of different criteria.

3.1. Method

3.1.1. Participants
Participants were 20 student volunteers at the University of Chicago who were paid $6 for their help.

3.2. Procedure

There were three main sections to the task:

3.2.1. Familiarity
Participants checked one column if the word was unfamiliar, and a second column if the thing that the word referred to was unfamiliar. If they checked either column, they moved directly on to the next word.

3.2.2. Categorization
Participants categorized each word in the category at the head of the list, choosing

[11]Alternatively, McCloskey and Glucksberg's use of a blocked presentation for typicality ratings may have drawn less attention to alternative categories than did the random presentation of different category-item pairs used for the categorization group.

just one of the following responses A to D, by checking the appropriate column (quotes indicate literal quotation from the instructions given):

1. *Member (OK)*—'if the word is clearly a member of the category, e.g. horse as a mammal';
2. *Only technically speaking a member*—'if the word refers to a thing which is '*only* technically speaking' in the category. In other words it is *not like* other typical category members, yet in a technical sense it does belong in the category. An example might be human being as a mammal';
3. *Technically speaking not a member*—'if the word refers to a thing which may loosely speaking be called by the category name but is 'technically speaking' *not* a member of the category. It may be similar to or easily confused with other category members, but in a technical sense it does not belong. An example might be a kangaroo[12] as a mammal, if marsupials are not mammals.'
4. *Non member*—'if the word is clearly not a member of the category, e.g. a snake as a mammal'.

3.2.3. Other things

The final two columns required two further judgments. The first was headed *Part or Associated Property* and had the following rubric: 'For some words you may feel that the categorization was problematic because the word referred to something that was not the right sort of thing—for example it might be a *part* or a *property* of an object that was in the category (like fur as a mammal), or it might refer to some other closely associated notion (like milk or pork as a mammal). If you feel this is the case, then check this column'. The second was headed *Other categories* and had the following rubric: 'For some of the words which you judged to be members you may also feel that while the word in question can be considered as a category member, it is actually a *better* example of another category (not necessarily one of those in this booklet) with which it is more closely associated. For example a hammer could be considered a Weapon, but it would be more natural to classify it as a Tool. If this is the case then check this column. (Don't worry about this one if you did not class the word as a member)'.

Participants were asked to read through the list of words on each page first, and then to work down the page completing all questions for each word, unless the word or object was unfamiliar in which case they did not need to answer any further questions about it. The task took approximately 45 min to complete.

4. Results

The aim of collecting new data was to test the post-hoc hypotheses of why certain

[12]Examples used for instructions had to employ words and categories not used in the norms—hence the choice of mammal as a category. The example of kangaroos was perhaps unfortunate, as the author later discovered that marsupials *are*, in biological classification, a subclass of mammals, thus rendering the example counterfactual for those participants with a detailed knowledge of biological classification. No participants referred to this problem however.

items were poorly fit by the simple similarity-based model predicting categorization probability from mean typicality. To show the distribution of the different responses across categories, Table 2 shows (a) the overall number of items receiving at least one 'unfamiliar' response either to the word or the object, (b) the mean percentage of valid responses per item for each of the four categorization judgments, and (c) the mean number of items with at least 10% responses to the Associated part or property, and Contrast category questions. It can be seen that in most categories there were items attracting responses in answer to the different questions. On average there were 3 or 4 unfamiliar items per category, with most falling in the three categories of Birds, Precious Stones and Ships. On average, around 10% of categorization responses were of the 'technical member' kind, and another 10% of the 'technically not a member' kind. There was considerable variability across categories here, with for example only about 3% technical members for Birds and Insects, and as many as 25% technical members for Vehicles. For the last two responses, the part/property response occurred for an average of 4.5 items, and the contrast category for an average of 3.6 items per category.

A regression model predicting categorization probability was developed in the following way. First, categorization probability was normalized as before, so that (according to the model) the relation with typicality may be expected to be approximately linear. Normalized categorization probability zp was treated as the dependent variable. Corrected mean typicality was entered into the regression first as in the

Table 2
Number of items receiving at least one response to either of unfamiliarity questions, the mean percentage of responses per item for each of the four categorization judgments, and the mean number of items with at least 10% responses to the associated part or property, and contrast category questions

Category	Categorization (%)						
	Unfamil-iarity	OK	Tech mem	Tech not	Not	Part/ property	Contrast category
Animal	3	47	13	10	30	3	6
Bird	7	71	3	5	21	2	0
Clothing	0	22	12	16	51	11	2
Disease	2	38	10	14	38	8	4
Fish	3	23	9	19	50	0	9
Fruit	2	44	8	6	42	2	3
Furniture	0	25	11	11	54	9	2
Insect	4	59	2	9	31	3	0
Kitchen utensil	0	43	10	10	36	13	4
Natural earth formation	4	74	12	3	12	3	0
Precious stone	11	50	6	13	31	1	1
Science	1	61	15	7	17	8	5
Ship	8	51	7	14	27	5	1
Sport	5	63	16	8	13	0	11
Vegetable	3	58	6	8	28	3	4
Vehicle	1	41	25	5	29	4	6
Weather phenomenon	3	51	7	8	34	2	3
Mean	3.4	48	10	10	32	4.5	3.6

model described previously. On subsequent steps, each of the following variables were then entered individually in a forwards stepwise fashion (entering the next best predictor at each step) to assess whether they explained residual variance, not accounted for by typicality alone. The variables were: unfamiliarity of the word/object (UNFAMILIAR), scored as the number of participants checking either of the two unfamiliarity responses; only technically a member (ONLY TECHNICAL); technically not a member (TECHNOT); associated part or property (PART/PROP); and membership of contrast categories (CONTRAST). Each of these last four variables was coded as the proportion of all participants who were familiar with the word and object who then checked the appropriate column. In order to concentrate on the prediction of categorization probability within the region of interest, the analysis was run using only the 324 items with categorization probability between 0.05 and 0.95.

The results of the regression analysis are shown in Table 3. After typicality, four variables entered significantly, using a significance criterion of 0.05. The table shows the statistics for this equation. Multiple R was 0.900, corresponding to 81% of the variance.

Of the various hypothetical accounts of residual variance in categorization probability, all but the Contrast category hypothesis were born out in the data. (The Contrast variable still made no significant contribution if forced into the equation immediately after Typicality and before the other variables). Items with categorization probability P higher than expected from typicality tended to be more unfamiliar, or to be only technically speaking category members. Those with lower P than expected from typicality tended to be associated parts or properties, or to be technically speaking *not* members of the category.

Four of the five new variables were shown to predict significant residual variance in categorization probability. The question remains finally of whether *all* remaining reliable variance has now been captured, or whether there is still some variance remaining to be explained. In order to answer this question, a test is needed of the reliability of the residual variance for the final model. One test of this reliability is to compare the residual categorization probability with another measure of categorization probability. If the residuals are truly based on random noise then they should not

Table 3
Regression statistics for predicting z-transformed categorization probability zp

Variable	B	β	t	P
Typicality	0.459	0.866	35.1	0.001
Unfamiliar	0.064	0.110	4.4	0.001
Only technical	0.756	0.090	3.5	0.001
Tech not	−0.469	−0.053	−2.1	0.04
Part/property	−0.646	−0.064	−2.47	0.02
Contrast	–	–	–	Not significant
(Constant)	−2.30			

B, regression coefficient; β, standardized regression coefficient; not significant, not significant at the 0.05 level.

correlate with any other variables. An independent measure of categorization probability was available in the data from the categorization phase of the experiment. By calculating the proportion of participants giving a categorization response who responded with either a clear yes or an 'only technically speaking yes', an estimate of categorization probability was obtained. This variable was entered into the regression equation after all other variables were entered, and explained significant additional variance. The Multiple R rose from 0.953 to 0.961 in the full analysis, and variance explained (adjusted R^2) rose from 90.7 to 92.3%. In the restricted data set of 324 borderline items, R rose from 0.900 to 0.915, and adjusted R^2 from 80.8 to 83.4%. The answer to the question, therefore, appears to be that not all reliable variance has been explained by typicality plus the four new variables.

4.1. Between category differences

Another question of particular interest is whether deviations from the similarity-based categorization threshold function were attributable to different factors depending on the type of semantic category. The regression model used the same coefficients to fit all categories. Remaining systematic variance may then reflect differences among categories. Biological categories, for example, are differentiated by the existence of a technical classification scheme based on biological theory, which could influence participants' categorization through encouraging essentialist beliefs. It may, therefore, be expected that the influence of the ONLY TECHNICAL and TECHNICAL NOT variables may be stronger in biological categories. To investigate this possibility, the 17 categories were collapsed into five groups. The first two were clear groupings: four biological kinds (fish, insects, birds and animals) and five categories of artifacts (clothing, furniture, kitchen utensils, ships and vehicles). The remaining groups were more approximate clusters of: natural kinds (natural earth formation, precious stone, weather phenomenon); food (fruit, vegetable); and other categories (sport, science, disease). Within each group, regression analyses were run predicting residual categorization probability (after regression on typicality) from the five variables collected in the experiment. Table 4 shows the pattern of significant variables.

Table 4
Significant predictors in regression equations predicting residual categorization probability for each of five groups of categories

Group	Positive predictors		Negative predictors		
	Unfam	Only tech	Tech not	Part/property	Contrast
Biological	√	√	√		
Artifact					√
Natural kind	√		√		
Food		√		√	
Other				√	

Unfam, unfamiliarity; only tech, only technically a member; tech not, technically not a member; part/property, an associated part or property; contrast; better member of a contrasting category.

For biological kinds, UNFAMILIAR, ONLY TECHNICAL and TECHNICAL NOT were all significant. 'Technical only' members were more likely to be categorized, and technically not members were less likely to be categorized than would be expected on the basis of typicality. This result confirms the idea that there is an influence of biological knowledge on people's classification of birds, fish, insects and animals. People were more inclined towards technical definitions when classifying than when rating typicality. The story is not quite so simple however. When the proportion of people giving an ONLY TECHNICAL and a TECHNICAL NOT response was correlated across items, it emerged that there was a significant *positive* correlation between the two variables for biological kinds ($r(119) = 0.25, P < 0.01$). This correlation was largely owing to the category of Fish where the correlation was 0.59 (df = 28, $P < 0.001$). The significance of this unexpected positive correlation is that many items were being labelled *both* as 'only technically' members *and* also (by other participants) as 'technically not' members. Items in the Fish category with this pattern of responses were tadpole, shark, lamprey, stingray and seahorse. These two response classes were therefore being used to signal a borderline case, rather than to indicate that there was a commonly agreed theoretical basis for classifying the item which differed from its similarity-based categorization. Alternatively, it might also have indicated that participants felt that there was a different (more technical) basis for categorization, but that they lacked sufficient knowledge about either the category or the individual items to be able to apply it consistently.

For artifacts neither of the technical variables was significant, in spite of relatively high rates of use of the two responses (see Table 2). However for artifacts, the CONTRAST CATEGORY variable was significant. Thus, for artifacts but not for biological kinds an item might be less likely to be classified in the category if it was judged to be a better member of some contrasting set. This result makes good sense given that biological kinds rarely show overlap (other than cases of class inclusion) while it is quite common for an object to fall in more than one artifact category. An object may be at the same time a weapon and a vehicle, or an electrical appliance and an item of furniture.

5. Discussion

In the course of this analysis, I have hypothesised a mathematical relationship between typicality and categorization probability—namely a monotonically increasing threshold function based on the cumulative normal distribution. I have fit this function to the data, and sought to account for those data points that did not fit the predicted relationship. While this procedure is clearly post hoc, and so runs the risk of 'explaining' effects which may reflect random noise in the data, the method is appropriate to use as a way of identifying outliers and, hence, generating interesting hypotheses about the conditions in which the relation between typicality and P deviates from the monotonic threshold function. The procedure is particularly interesting methodologically since it very clearly reveals the cases that deviate from an expected similarity-based categorization function.

The underlying trend of a monotonic function is compelling in many of the categories, and the outliers are in a majority of cases just those which would be expected to be outliers on the basis of reasonable assumptions, supported in the literature. One area where there was clear evidence that categorization involves more than typicality was in biological kinds, where items with poor superficial similarity and better match of core qualities were more likely to be included in the category than expected, while those which had good superficial similarity but poor match of deeper aspects were less likely to be categorized positively. However, even in these biological categories categorization was far from clear-cut. Much has been made in the literature (e.g. Smith et al., 1974) about the well-definedness of BIRDS for example. Smith et al. used the clear distinction between birds and non-birds to argue for a distinction between defining features, and merely characteristic features. However, when the data are plotted relating typicality to P for birds (see Fig. 3), it is seen that there is a clear distinction not only in P but also on the horizontal axis of Typicality. The function is quite consistent with the smoothly rising threshold function seen for other categories, indicating that there is no reason to suppose that Birds are any different from other similarity-based categories.

In contrast to the biological categories, the artifact categories showed no evidence for deep/surface information differentiating categorization and typicality. Where typicality did not provide a good prediction of categorization, one reason was identified as the effect of possible contrast categories. Many objects can fall in more than one category (for example a knife may be a tool, a weapon and a kitchen utensil). The data analysis presented here suggests that when making categorization judgments people are more inclined to take note of contrasting categories than when judging typicality (but see [11]). They may be willing to say that a hammer is quite a typical weapon (it has all the properties necessary to function as such), but prefer to say it is *not* in the category, since it is more fittingly categorized as a tool.

In conclusion, similarity-based categorization has been shown to provide a good base-line model for understanding the structure of natural categories. Some systematic deviations from a monotonic relation between typicality and categorization probability were observed, and the best account of these deviations appeared to be in terms of (a) unfamiliarity, (b) a greater weight accorded to superficial similarity in rating typicality than in categorization, particularly in biological kinds (c) a greater account taken of contrasting categories in categorization than in typicality rating, particularly in artifact kinds, and (d) an effect of non-similarity-based associations on typicality ratings but not on categorization. Given that typicality ratings are known to be impure reflections of similarity to a category prototype (Barsalou, 1985) the influence of familiarity and other associative effects need not be taken to undermine the similarity-based categorization account of the structure of these categories. Likewise, the increased emphasis on contrasting categories in the categorization task can easily be accommodated within a similarity-based account. Given two prototype representations, categorization can be made in a contrastive manner (by classifying any item with the category to which it has the greatest similarity—relative to the similarity-membership function for each category), or in a non-contrastive manner (by classifying relative to each category independently and allowing the categories to overlap). Indeed most exemplar models (Medin and Schaffer, 1978; Nosofsky, 1988) incorporate a contrastive categorization rule, classifying items in the class to which they bear the greatest average similarity.

The non-monotonicity which gives best support to the rule-based view offered by Rips (1989) is the effect contrasting superficial similarity with more definitional or diagnostic features. For example, whales, seals and dolphins were considered more typical of Fish than was warranted by their low level of categorization. Conversely, tomatoes and olives were judged less typical of Fruit than was warranted by their high probability of categorization. There are a number of ways to interpret this result. One could take this as evidence for rule-based classification, showing an effect of deeper knowledge based on biological theory. Alternatively, one could propose that there is a shift in the weights used to compute similarity in the two tasks. Rips (1989) has argued that this theoretical move greatly weakens the prototype model, since giving up the notion of fixed weights, independently determined, allows the modeller to fit any categorization data. If one takes whatever criteria are in the categorization rule, and sets them up as highly weighted attributes in a prototype, then effectively the rule- and similarity-based models converge. Actually, this is not quite true since the similarity-based model requires that categories be linearly separable in terms of the available features, whereas rules presumably have no structural constraints on what can form a category, instead deriving their constraints from the nature of higher level theories within which the categories are embedded (Murphy and Medin, 1985). In fact, a demonstration that natural concept categories are commonly *not* linearly separable would be excellent evidence against the similarity view. Although it has been shown that certain non-linearly separable categories are as easy (or difficult) to learn as linearly separable ones (Medin and Schwanenflugel, 1981), I am aware of no direct evidence of this kind.

The categorization data shown in the graphs in Appendix A and summarized as the vertical axis in Figs. 1 and 2 show little evidence of rule-based classification. McCloskey and Glucksberg were correct in concluding from their study that membership in these categories is not all-or-none but shows clear signs of gradedness, and it is quite unclear how rule-based models can account for that gradedness. At the least an account is required of the source of the observed disagreement and inconsistency in classification. (McCloskey and Glucksberg demonstrated that people are not particularly consistent in their classifications across a period of a few weeks, so the fuzziness in categorization cannot be just a matter of individual differences in people's beliefs about the correct classification rule).

5.1. Theories and prototypes

A reasonable reaction to the view of concept representations presented here is to ask how the more powerful version of prototype theory advocated by Hampton (1995b) differs from rule-based 'theory' theories of concepts of the kind discussed by Murphy and Medin (1985) or Rips (1989). Both are capable of representing relational and abstract kinds of information about concepts, and it is not immediately clear whether differential predictions can be derived. One important difference is in the emphasis for prototype theory on the abstract representation of the most common attributes of the class. The theory argues that the reason that conceptual borderline disputes are so common and so puzzling is that category borderlines themselves are *not* firmly represented in memory. Changes in perspective and classification context may then affect how different attributes are weighted and how broadly or narrowly the category should be defined. Rule-based theories by contrast appear to argue for the involvement of *inferential reasoning* as a part of categorization. Items are categorized with the concept that best generates their observed attributes through reasoning processes applied to the concept representation. Both theories remain grossly under specified in terms of processing accounts of exactly how these representations are learned, retrieved into working memory, or operated upon. It is perhaps time to consider a compromise model that will both have the representational power to represent theory-laden concepts such as natural kinds, but also provide an account of the process of categorization that fits with empirical data on the fuzziness of category boundaries and accounts for the influence of typicality on a wide range of cognitive tasks.

5.2. A pragmatic account on non-monotonicity

One approach which may prove fruitful is to consider the vagueness of the categorization task itself in terms of the lack of a clear discourse context offered to the categorizer (Braisby and Franks, 1996, unpublished manuscript). A recent study by Hampton and Dubois (1996) tested this notion, but found little or no evidence that clarifying the context reduces the fuzziness of categorization. Participants classified borderline cases either under conditions where an elaborate scenario was provided, or in a condition with no scenario. Levels of disagreement and inconsistency were unaffected by the manipulation. Alternatively, it may be that by developing research into the kinds of feature that influence typicality as opposed to categorization, similarity can be constrained sufficiently to provide a predictively adequate account of categorization.

If the notion that both typicality and categorization employ a common conceptual representation of the category is to be preserved, then the way in which attributes are selected and weighted as relevant to the decision must differ between the two judgments. The question is then how this selective weighting might be predicted. Note that this proposal is also consistent with many of the points made by Rips in his critique of similarity. Perhaps the two positions can be integrated if a proper understanding can be reached of how a common conceptual representation is processed differently in arriving at typicality or categorization judgments. The analysis of factors differentially affecting the two judgments presented earlier goes some small way towards this goal.

To pursue the question of discourse context a little further, consider how participants may construe the meaning of the instructions given in a typicality task. When asked to say 'how typical is this of the category?' or 'how good an example is this of the category?', a case can be made that there is a presupposition to the question — namely that the example actually does belong in the category. We do not normally ask 'how typical is Sydney as an American City?' or 'how good an example of US

Presidents is Joseph Stalin?' The problem here began with Rosch and Mervis (1975) who included non-members of categories in their typicality rating lists. The application of typicality ratings to non-members has continued in the literature (e.g. from McCloskey and Glucksberg, 1978, through to Kalish, 1995), although it can be argued that one is distorting the meaning of typicality by asking the question this way (Hampton and Gardiner, 1983, provided subjects with a 'does not belong' response on the typicality rating scale, while Hampton, 1988, adopted a two stage decision in which typicality was asked as a supplementary question once subjects had given a positive categorization). At the least it may be argued that there is an ambiguity to the judgment, as between rating the relative typicality of members within a category, and rating the typicality of just anything in a category.

If typicality were to apply just to category members (as seems the most natural interpretation of the task), then it would involve attribute weights that would differ from those appropriate to categorization per se. This is because the weight of an attribute will depend on its diagnosticity for the task in hand (Tversky, 1977). Suppose that the weight of an attribute were determined statistically by computing the correlation of each attribute with the sum of the remaining attributes across a range of items, as in an item-total correlation for assessing reliability of items in psychometric tests. The calculated weight will vary as a function of the range of items considered. If only potential category members are included (that is the range from typical category members down to borderline members), then the feature weights will correspond to those that determine typicality. If, on the other hand, the full range of items is considered, including related non-members and totally unrelated items, the relative weight of features will be optimised for determining categorization.

What effect will these two sets of weights have on ratings? The typicality weights will highlight attributes that best differentiate most typical from least typical category members. What do typical cars, horses, or sports have that atypical ones do not? The answer is the 'incidental' trappings of the most common and familiar examples. Typical cars have four wheels, atypical may have 3 or 6. Typical horses are brown or black, atypical may be piebald or white. Typical sports have teams, competition and a ball, atypical ones may involve individuals pitting themselves against the elements. What will *not* get high weights are those attributes which are more 'defining', in that they are true of most category members, and untrue of many non-members. Being able to carry people around determines membership in the car category, but is relatively unimportant in determining typicality. Having a horse for a mother is important for being a horse, but is not important for being a typical one.

The argument then is that the two sets of attribute weights needed to preserve a basis in similarity for both typicality and categorization, in the face of evidence of non-monotonicity, can be derived from the Diagnosticity Principle of Tversky (1977). Weights are determined by the diagnosticity of the attributes for the task in question. Typicality carries with it the assumption of a range restricted to category members, while category membership clearly requires the full range of related and unrelated non-members also to be taken into account. As a result, when typicality judgments are applied to non-members, the attributes which differentiate items *within* the category are applied to items outside the category. Consider how one might answer the question 'How typical is Sydney as a US city?'. If the question is to be answered sensibly, one may interpret it as asking 'How similar is Sydney to typical US cities?'. This question will then automatically produce a judgment based on what differentiates typical from atypical US cities, and which ignores that which differentiates US cities from others—namely their location within the USA.

This argument is (for the moment) entirely speculative, and needs to be supported by empirical evidence if it is to help in shedding light on the processes involved in typicality and categorization judgments. Little is as yet known about the stability of either type of judgment in the face of changing discourse contexts.

In conclusion, it has been argued that a critical difference between similarity- and rule-based accounts of categorization lies in their expectations that categorization probability and typicality will always vary in step with each other. Rips (1989) offered evidence of a number of unusual cases in which a dissociation between the two measures can be observed. The approach adopted here has been to look not at artificially created test cases, but at a data set in which borderline cases in 17 different natural categories were assessed on both measures. Further experimentation then examined cases of non-monotonicity and found that they could be attributed to several interesting factors. Among these were some relating to typicality judgments—such as unfamiliarity and non-categorial semantic associations—and others relating to categorization such as the effect of overlapping or contrasting categories. There was also evidence for a difference in emphasis between typicality and categorization, with the former giving more weight to surface similarity, and the latter more weight to 'technical' similarity. Whether this effect is to be accounted for by a sophisticated similarity model, or by an equally sophisticated rule-based model, is perhaps of less immediate interest than the pursuit of the question of just how and why these effects do occur. A speculative account based on pragmatics of the two tasks was offered as an example of one way in which this interesting question may be pursued.

Acknowledgements

The author acknowledges support for this research from the British Academy, the French Ministry for Higher Education and Science, and the Nuffield Foundation (UK). The hospitality of the Fulbright Commission and the University of Chicago is also gratefully acknowledged. Wenchi Yeh provided invaluable help and advice with the experiment, and the author thanks Lawrence Barsalou, Daniele Dubois, Zachary Estes, Dedre Gentner, Barbara Luka, Gregory Murphy, Lance Rips, Steven Sloman and Karen Solomon, for help and comments on the work and on an earlier draft.

References

Armstrong, S.L., Gleitman, L.R., Gleitman, H., 1983. What some concepts might not be. Cognition 13, 263–308.

Barsalou, L.W., 1985. Ideals, central tendency, and frequency of instantiation as determinants of graded structure in categories. Journal of Experimental Psychology: Learning Memory, and Cognition 11, 629–654.

Barsalou, L.W., Hale, C.R., 1993. Components of conceptual representation: from feature lists to recursive frames. In: van Mechelen, I., Hampton, J.A., Michalski, R.S., Theuns, P. (Eds.), Categories and concepts: theoretical views and inductive data analysis, Academic Press, London, pp. 97–144).

Bassok, M., Medin, D.L., 1997. Birds of a feather flock together: similarity judgments with semantically rich stimuli. Journal of Memory and Language 36, 311–336.

Braisby, N., Franks, B., Hampton, J.A., 1996. Psychological essentialism and concept use. Cognition 59, 247–274.

Cantor, N., Mischel, W., 1977. Traits as prototypes: effects on recognition memory. Journal of Personality and Social Psychology 35, 38–48.

Cantor, N., Mischel, W., 1979. Prototypes in person perception. In: Berkowitz, L. (Ed.), Advances in Experimental Social Psychology, 12, Academic Press, New York, pp. 3–52.

Cantor, N., Mischel, W., Schwartz, J.C., 1982. A prototype analysis of psychological situations. Cognitive Psychology 14, 45–77.

Cantor, N., Smith, E.E., French, R., Mezzich, J., 1980. Psychiatric diagnosis as prototype categorization. Journal of Abnormal Psychology 89, 181–193.

Carey, S., 1985. Conceptual change in childhood, MIT Press, Cambridge, MA.

Clark, E.V., 1973. Meanings and concepts. In: Flavell, J.H., Markman, E.M. (Eds.), Handbook of child psychology: Vol. 3. Cognitive development, Wiley, New York, pp. 787–840.

Fried, L.S., Holyoak, K.J., 1984. Induction of category distributions: a framework for classification learning. Journal of Experimental Psychology: Learning, Memory, and Cognition 10, 234–257.

Gelman, S.A., 1988. The development of induction within natural kind and artifact categories. Cognitive Psychology 20, 65–95.

Gigerenzer, G., 1994. Why the distinction between single-event probabilities and frequencies is important for Psychology (and vice versa). In: Wright, G., Ayton, P. (Eds.) Subjective Probability, Wiley, New York.

Gigerenzer, G., 1996. On narrow norms and vague heuristics - reply. Psychological Review 103, 592–596.

Goodman, N., 1970. Seven strictures on similarity. In: Foster, L., Swanson, J.W. (Eds.), Experience and theory, Amherst: University of Massachusetts Press, pp. 19–29.

Hampton, J.A., 1976. An Experimental Study of Concepts in Language. Doctoral thesis, University of London.

Hampton, J.A., 1979. Polymorphous concepts in semantic memory. Journal of Verbal Learning and Verbal Behavior 18, 441–461.

Hampton, J.A., 1981. An investigation of the nature of abstract concepts. Memory and Cognition 9, 149–156.

Hampton, J.A., 1988. Overextension of conjunctive concepts: evidence for a unitary model of concept typicality and class inclusion. Journal of Experimental Psychology: Learning, Memory and Cognition 14, 12–32.

Hampton, J.A., 1993. Prototype models of concept representation. In: van Mechelen, I., Hampton, J.A., Michalski, R.S., Theuns, P. (Eds.), Categories and concepts: Theoretical views and inductive data analysis, Academic Press, London, pp. 67–95.

Hampton, J.A., 1995. Testing prototype theory of concepts. Journal of Memory and Language 34, 686–708.

Hampton, J.A., 1995. Similarity-based categorization: the development of prototype theory. Psychological Belgica 35, 103–125.

Hampton, J.A., 1996. Non-monotonicity between categorization and typicality in transformed items: an analysis of data from Kalish (1995).

Hampton, J.A., 1996. The relation between categorization and typicality: an analysis of McCloskey and Glucksberg's (1978) data.

Hampton, J.A., 1997. Psychological representation of concepts. In: Conway, M.A. (Ed.) Cognitive Models of Memory, Psychology Press, Hove, pp. 81–110.

Hampton, J.A., Dubois, D., 1996. Effects of perspective on categorization in natural concept classes. Paper presented to the Annual Convention of the Psychonomic Society, Chicago IL, November.

Hampton, J.A., Gardiner, M.M., 1983. Measures of internal category structure: a correlational analysis of normative data. British Journal of Psychology 74, 491–516.

Kahneman, D., Tversky, A., 1996. On the reality of cognitive illusions. Psychological Review 103, 582–591.

Kalish, C.W., 1995. Essentialism and graded membership in animal and artifact categories. Memory and Cognition 23, 335–353.

Keil, F.C., 1989. Concepts, Kinds, and Cognitive Development, MIT Press, Cambridge, MA.

Lakoff, G., 1987. Women, Fire and Dangerous Things, University of Chicago Press, Chicago.

Lamberts, K., 1995. Categorization under time pressure. Journal of Experimental Psychology: General 124, 161–180.

Landau, B., 1982. Will the real grandmother please stand up? The psychological reality of dual meaning representation. Journal of Psycholinguistic Research 11, 47–62.

Malt, B.C., 1990. Features and beliefs in the mental representation of categories. Journal of Memory and Language 29, 289–315.

Malt, B.C., 1994. Water is not H_2O. Cognitive Psychology 27, 41–70.

Malt, B.C., Johnson, E.C., 1992. Do artifact concepts have cores?. Journal of Memory and Language 31, 195–217.

Malt, B.C., Smith, E.E., 1982. The role of familiarity in determining typicality. Memory and Cognition 10, 69–75.

McCloskey, M., 1980. The stimulus familiarity problem in semantic memory research. Journal of Verbal Learning and Verbal Behavior 19, 485–502.

McCloskey, M., Glucksberg, S., 1978. Natural categories: Well-defined or fuzzy sets?. Memory and Cognition 6, 462–472.

Medin, D.L., Ortony, A., 1989. Psychological Essentialism. In: Vosniadou, S., Ortony, A. (Eds.), Similarity and Analogical Reasoning, Cambridge University Press, Cambridge, pp. 179–195.

Medin, D.L., Schaffer, M.M., 1978. Context theory of classification learning. Psychological Review 85, 207–238.

Medin, D.L., Schwanenflugel, P.J., 1981. Linear separability in classification learning. Journal of Experimental Psychology Human Learning and Memory 7, 355–368.

Murphy, G.L., Medin, D.L., 1985. The role of theories in conceptual coherence. Psychological Review 92, 289–316.

Nosofsky, R.M., 1988. Exemplar-based accounts of relations between classification, recognition, and typicality. Journal of Experimental Psychology: Learning. Memory and Cognition 14, 700–708.

Osherson, D.N., Smith, E.E., 1982. Gradedness and conceptual conjunction. Cognition 12, 299–318.

Pinker, S., 1984. Language learnability and language development, Harvard University Press, Cambridge, MA.

Rips, L.J., 1989. Similarity, typicality and categorization. In: Vosniadou, S., Ortony, A. (Eds.), Similarity and Analogical Reasoning, Cambridge University Press, Cambridge, pp. 21–59.

Rips, L.J., Collins, A., 1993. Categories and resemblance. Journal of Experimental Psychology: General 122, 468–486.

Rosch, E., 1975. Cognitive representations of semantic categories. Journal of Experimental Psychology: General 104, 192–232.

Rosch, E., Mervis, C.B., 1975. Family resemblances: studies in the internal structure of categories. Cognitive Psychology 7, 573–605.

Slobin, D.I., 1973. Cognitive prerequisites for the development of grammar. In: Ferguson, C.A., Slobin, D.A. (Eds.), Studies of child language development, Springer, New York, pp. 45–54.

Smith, E.E., Shoben, E.J., Rips, L.J., 1974. Structure and process in semantic memory: a featural model for semantic decisions. Psychological Review 81, 214–241.

Smith, E.E., Sloman, S., 1994. Similarity- versus rule-based categorization. Memory and Cognition 22, 377–386.
Tversky, A., 1977. Features of similarity. Psychological Review 84, 327–352.
Tversky, A., Kahneman, D., 1983. Extensional versus intuitive reasoning: the conjunction fallacy in probability judgment. Psychological Review 90, 293–315.

Appendix A

Figs. 3, 4, 5, 6.

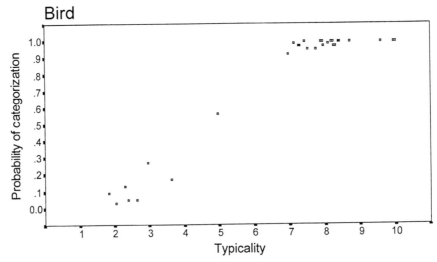

Fig. 3. Scatterplot of probability of a positive categorization *P* vs. mean item typicality for the category Bird.

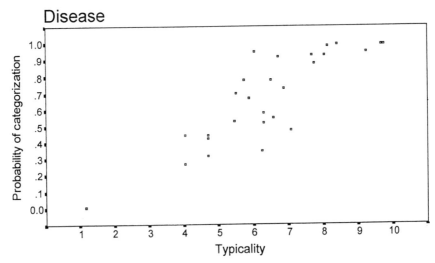

Fig. 4. Scatterplot of probability of a positive categorization *P* vs. mean item typicality for the category Disease.

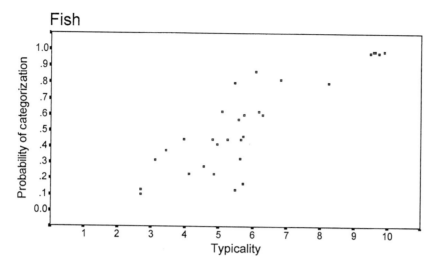

Fig. 5. Scatterplot of probability of a positive categorization *P* vs. mean item typicality for the category Fish.

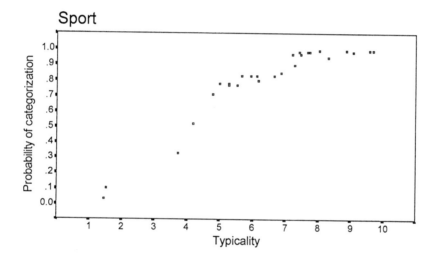

Fig. 6. Scatterplot of probability of a positive categorization *P* vs. mean item typicality for the category Sport.

4

Alternative strategies of categorization

Edward E. Smith*, Andrea L. Patalano, John Jonides

Department of Psychology, University of Michigan, 525 East University, Ann Arbor, MI 48109, USA

Abstract

Psychological studies of categorization often assume that all concepts are of the same general kind, and are operated on by the same kind of categorization process. In this paper, we argue against this unitary view, and for the existence of qualitatively different categorization processes. In particular, we focus on the distinction between categorizing an item by: (a) applying a category-defining rule to the item vs. (b) determining the similarity of that item to remembered exemplars of a category. We begin by characterizing rule application and similarity computations as strategies of categorization. Next, we review experimental studies that have used artificial categories and shown that differences in instructions or time pressure can lead to either rule-based categorization or similarity-based categorization. Then we consider studies that have used natural concepts and again demonstrated that categorization can be done by either rule application or similarity calculations. Lastly, we take up evidence from cognitive neuroscience relevant to the rule vs. similarity issue. There is some indirect evidence from brain-damaged patients for neurological differences between categorization based on rules vs. that based on similarity (with the former involving frontal regions, and the latter relying more on posterior areas). For more direct evidence, we present the results of a recent neuroimaging experiment, which indicates that different neural circuits are involved when people categorize items on the basis of a rule as compared with when they categorize the same items on the basis of similarity. © 1998 Elsevier Science B.V.

Keywords: Categorization; Similarity; Rule application; Neuroimaging

1. Introduction

Since the beginning of the experimental study of categorization in psychology (Hull, 1920), there has been a tendency to assume that all acts of categorization are accomplished by the same means. In the seminal studies of Bruner et al. (1956),

* Corresponding author. Tel.: +1 313 7640186; e-mail: eesmith@umich.edu

people were assumed to rely primarily on rules when categorizing novel items; in the current models of Estes (1994) and e.g. Nosofsky (1992), people are assumed to categorize new objects solely on the basis of their similarity to remembered exemplars of known categories; and in the discussions by Keil (1989) and Rips (1989), categorization inevitably comes down to applying a 'theory' of the category. The alternative to such unitary views, of course, is that there are multiple strategies of categorization. This issue of unitary vs. multiple strategies is of foundational importance. If there are multiple strategies or procedures but we act as though there is only one, then results from different situations will no doubt conflict, with few or no generalizations emerging and no true accumulation of research findings[1].

Though much of the research motivated by the various unitary views is of great importance, it is not difficult to devise counterexamples to the idea of a unitary view. One can generate pairs of extreme situations, such that just about everyone would agree that categorization is based on one strategy in one case and on a different procedure in the other case. Thus, if a person has to categorize two-digit numbers as odd or even, presumably all researchers would agree that the categorizer does it by applying the rule of 'Divisible by 2 or not' (Armstrong et al., 1983); but if that same person has to categorize novel people with respect to whether they are as friendly as the neighbors on their block, presumably most would agree that the categorizer now relies on memories of his or her neighbors (Kahneman and Miller, 1986). Note, however, an important aspect of this counterexample—the different putative categorization procedures are applied to different kinds of categories, where one category is part of a rule-based formal system and the other one is completely *ad hoc*. If we ask instead whether there are multiple categorization procedures that are routinely applied to the same categories, then the issue of unitary versus multiple strategies is very much alive. It is this more stringent question that is the subject of the present paper.

Another aspect of the issue of one or many procedures is whether the multiple procedures are qualitatively different from one another. Some have argued for multiple categorization strategies that are qualitatively similar. For example, Nosofsky et al. (1994) have proposed a rule-plus-exception model, in which the representations used by the two procedures—rules and stored exemplars—differ quantitatively rather than qualitatively (e.g. the representation of a simple rule specifies a single attribute value, whereas the representation of a remembered exemplar might specify two or three attribute values). The obvious alternative is that there are qualitatively different procedures, that is, procedures that contain different processes.

In this article we argue that people can apply multiple procedures of categorization to the same items, perhaps even simultaneously, and that the procedures are qualitatively different from one another. Our specific agenda for the remainder of the paper is as follows. In the next, or second section we select two categorization procedures for examination—applying a rule vs. determining similarity to remembered examples—and characterize each procedure in more detail. In the third sec-

---

[1]We use the terms 'strategy' and 'procedure' interchangeably. However, since 'strategy' suggests the notion of deliberative choice, we favor the term 'procedure' wherever this suggestion would be misleading.

tion we review evidence from cognitive studies that supports the claim that the two procedures of interest are applied to the very same categories. This review will accomplish two goals. Firstly, it will integrate findings from experiments that have used artificial materials with results from studies that have employed natural categories, showing striking convergence between two literatures that have heretofore been kept separate. Secondly, our review will reveal some of the processes that comprise the two procedures of interest, which will show that the procedures are indeed qualitatively different. In the fourth section we consider a different kind of evidence for a qualitative difference between the procedures of interest. Specifically, we will review results from neuropsychology and neuroimaging experiments which indicate that the procedures at issue are mediated by different neural structures. The fifth and final section summarizes our main points, and notes some related research.

2. Rule application and exemplar similarity

2.1. The general distinction

It is time to be more precise about possible categorization procedures. A review of the literature on concepts and categorization (Smith and Medin, 1981) suggests at least three distinct procedures. In deciding whether a test object belongs to a particular category, one may:

1. Determine whether the test object fits a rule that defines the category (the rule specifies the necessary and sufficient conditions for category membership);
2. Determine the similarity of the test object to remembered exemplars of the category; or
3. Determine the similarity of the test object to a prototype of the category.

Subsequent work (e.g. Murphy and Medin, 1985) led to the addition of another strategy to the list:

4. Determine whether the features of the test object are best explained by the 'theory' that underlies the category.

We will focus on just the first two of these classification procedures—which we will refer to as 'rule application' and 'exemplar similarity'—because they are among the most widely discussed in the literature, and because they are sufficiently conceptually distinct that one may readily tell them apart in both cognitive and neuropsychological studies[2].

To illustrate paradigm cases of the procedures of interest, consider the situation in which a dermatologist must decide whether a particular skin lesion is an instance of Disease X. (The following examples are inspired by Brooks et al., 1991). Suppose that our dermatologist knows the additive rule that, 'If the lesion has a sufficient

---

[2]The distinction between rule-application vs. exemplar-similarity mechanisms has also been raised in the category-learning literature (e.g. Shanks and St. John, 1994). In this paper, we focus on mechanisms guiding category use.

number of the following features—elliptical shape, bumpy texture, reddish-brown coloring, etc.—then Disease X is indicated'. If the dermatologist applies this rule in making her diagnosis (categorization), then presumably she will engage in the following sequence of processes:

1. Selectively attend to each critical attribute of the test object (e.g. the shape, texture and color of the lesion);
2. For each attended-to attribute, determine whether the perceptual information instantiates the value specified in the rule (e.g. 'Is this color reddish-brown'?); and
3. Amalgamate the outcomes of Stage (2) so as to determine the final categorization.

This three-stage schematic model of rule application is compatible with numerous discussions of rule following (e.g. Kemler-Nelson, 1984; Smith and Sloman, 1994).

Categorization based on exemplar similarity is a very different matter. Consider, again, our dermatologist attempting to diagnose a particular lesion. In addition to knowing the above rule, if the dermatologist has also seen many patients she will likely have stored in memory numerous exemplars of various skin diseases. Consequently, she may note that the current lesion is very similar to stored exemplars of Disease X, and on this basis categorize the current lesion as an instance of X. Now the sequence of processes presumably include:

1. Retrieve stored exemplars (of various disease categories) that are similar to the test object; and
2. Select that category whose retrieved exemplars are on some measure most similar to the test object.

Note that if the exemplars retrieved in Stage (1) all belong to the same category, then the choice process of Stage (2) is trivial. But if the exemplars retrieved in Stage (1) point to different categories, Stage (2) might require an effortful selection process; for example, computing the similarity of the test object to each retrieved exemplar, combining these similarity scores over members of a category, and choosing the category with the highest similarity score. (Of course, a similarity process is likely the basis of Stage (1) retrieval as well, but presumably it is a more automatic and holistic process). This schematic description of exemplar-based categorization captures some of the key ideas behind the major exemplar-similarity models (e.g. Estes, 1994; Nosofsky, 1986; Medin and Schaffer, 1978).

2.2. Component distinctions

The preceding discussion suggests that the general contrast between rule application and exemplar similarity includes a number of component or correlated distinctions. Specifically, the two categorization procedures differ in the extent to which they involve: (a) analytic vs. holistic processing, (b) differential vs. equal weighting of attributes, (c) instantiation of abstract conditions vs. matching concrete information, (d) high vs. low loads on working memory, (e) serial vs. parallel processing, and (f) strategic vs. automatic processing. We briefly consider each of these component distinctions.

We noted that rule application involves selectively attending to the critical attributes of the test object (and perhaps inhibiting others). This selective-attention component makes rule-application an analytic procedure. In contrast, the retrieval of similar stored exemplars, which comprises the heart of the exemplar-similarity procedure, need not involve any selectivity, and in this sense is often referred to as a holistic process.

Because rule application involves attending to some attributes but not others, the procedure gives different weights to different attributes. In contrast, because exemplar similarity need not assume any selective attention, at least during the critical exemplar-retrieval stage, the procedure may give the same weight to all attributes. A distinction between differential and equal weighting of attributes is, therefore, a natural consequence of the analytic-holistic distinction.

In paradigm cases of rule application, the conditions specified in the rule are more abstract than the representation of the test object. Consequently, rule application typically requires that the categorizer determine whether the information in the test object instantiates the conditions of the rule. In many cases of exemplar similarity, though, the representations of both exemplar and test object are assumed to be at the same level of concreteness, and hence a matching process rather than an instantiation one is needed.

Working memory is often involved in rule application for one of two reasons. In some cases, the rule is sufficiently novel or complex that the categorizer needs to keep it active; in other cases, the rule has numerous conditions, and the categorizer must keep active the outcomes of prior condition tests while performing subsequent ones. Taken together, these reasons could lead to a substantial load on working memory. In contrast, the retrieval of exemplars from long-term memory may impose a relatively small load on working memory, particularly in situations in which only a single exemplar is retrieved.

Note that the distinctions just described are closely related to the three-stage process we used to characterize rule application (see Section 2.1). Being analytic and differentially weighting attributes characterizes the first or selective attention stage, instantiation of abstract-conditions captures the second or instantiation stage, and an involvement of working memory defines the third or amalgamation stage. All of this reinforces the point that rule application is a complex procedure that contains at least three major mechanisms.

The remaining two distinctions do not pick out component mechanisms of rule application or exemplar similarity, but rather characterize the operation of the components. Thus, while exemplar similarity may involve some serial processing (a retrieval process *followed* by a selection process), serial processing seems more pronounced in rule application. This is particularly so when the rule specifics multiple conditions, which may require multiple acts of selective attention and instantiation.

Lastly, paradigm cases of rule application usually involve strategic or controlled processing, whereas paradigm cases of exemplar similarity typically involve more automatic processing. Some aspects of this strategic vs. automatic distinction are captured by previous distinctions, as more strategic processing is more likely to differentially weight information, require working memory, and involve serial processing. Still, there are other aspects of the present distinction that are novel; for example, rule application, being more strategic, is easier to verbalize.

While the preceding distinctions are useful in distinguishing rule application from exemplar similarity, none of them may be perfectly correlated with the rule-similarity contrast. The analytic-holistic contrast seems the most diagnostic; it is difficult to imagine true instances of rule application that do not involve acts of selective attention, whereas such acts play no role in most exemplar-similarity models. Differential weighting of attributes also seems like a necessary feature of rule application, but there are important exemplar-similarity models that include this as well (e.g. Nosofsky, 1986; Kruschke, 1992). Similarly, the instantiation of abstract conditions seems to be true of all clear-cut cases of rule following, but again there are exemplar-similarity models that also include it (e.g. Nosofsky et al., 1994). The extensive involvement of working memory is less useful in telling rule application from exemplar similarity, as many cases of rule application may involve only a single condition and consequently place little load on working memory; also, with sufficient practice, there may be little use of working memory in rule application even when the rule involves multiple conditions. Likewise, extensive practice may result in cases of rule application that involve mostly parallel and automatic processing, which would be hard to distinguish from canonical cases of exemplar similarity. Even these less diagnostic distinctions through, are of some use in contrasting many cases of rule application and exemplar similarity.

3. Cognitive studies of rule application vs. exemplar similarity

The cognitive experiments that have dealt with the issues of interest divide into two sets, depending on whether they have employed artificial or natural categories in their research. In what follows, we consider these two sets in turn.

3.1. Studies with artificial categories

3.1.1. Demonstrating and characterizing the basic mechanisms

A useful starting point is an experiment by Allen and Brooks (1991), which is worth describing in detail because it sets the stage for much of what follows. The subjects' task was to categorize imaginary animals into two categories, referred to as 'Builders' and 'Diggers.' Examples of the animals are given in Fig. 1. There were two phases to the experiment: a training phase, during which subjects learned to correctly categorize a set of ten animals, and a test phase, during which subjects were tested on some novel animals as well as on some that they had learned. In the training phase, one group of subjects was taught an additive rule that would distinguish the Builders from the Diggers: e.g. 'If an animal has at least two of the

Fig. 1. Examples of materials used by Allen and Brooks (1991). The top right cell illustrates a Positive Match because, not only are these animals Builders according to the rule, but they are also most similar to the studied Builders in the top left cell. The bottom right cell illustrates a Negative Match: though the rule specifies that these animals are Builders, they are most similar to the studied Diggers in the bottom left cell.

following three critical (attribute) values—long legs, angular body, spotted covering—it is a Builder; otherwise, it is a Digger'. A second group of subjects was presented the same animals but was not given the rule. They were told that the first time they saw an animal they would have to guess whether it was a Builder or a Digger, but on subsequent trials they would be able to remember what it was. Thus, the first group was induced to use a rule strategy for categorizing the animals whereas the second group was induced to use a memory procedure. Differences between these 'Rule' and 'Memory' groups speak directly to our questions about differences between rule application and exemplar-similarity procedures.

  In addition to the difference between the Rule and Memory groups, the major variation in this experiment concerned the types of items presented during the transfer phase. Two kinds of novel items were of particular interest; it is convenient to illustrate them with respect to the category Builders. One kind of novel item was an instance of Builders according to the rule, and was also extremely similar to an old item that was a known exemplar of Builders (it differed from the known exemplar on only one attribute—see Fig. 1). This kind of item is referred to as a 'positive match'. The other kind of novel item was also a Builder according to the rule, but it was extremely similar to a known exemplar of Diggers (see Fig. 1); this kind of item is a 'negative match'. If the Rule subjects do indeed categorize the test items by the rule, their dominant categorization of both positive and negative matches should be the same: Builders. If the Memory subjects categorize a test object by first retrieving the stored exemplar most similar to it and then selecting the category associated with that exemplar, their dominant categorizations of positive and negative matches should differ, with positive matches being labeled Builders and negative matches Diggers. Thus the Rule and Memory groups should differ on their dominant categorization of negative matches[3].

This is just what happened. For negative matches, such as the one illustrated in Fig. 1, the dominant categorization in the Rule group (55%) was Builders, whereas the dominant categorization in the Memory group (86%) was Diggers. These results support the existence of two distinct categorization procedures that can be applied to the same categories corresponding to rule application and exemplar similarity.

Though Builders was the *dominant* categorization in the Rule group, the fact that this rule-based decision occurred only 55% of the time suggests that rule application was not the only procedure at work. Indeed, further analysis by Allen and Brooks (1991) of just the Rule group showed that exemplar similarity was also involved. The logic of their analysis was as follows. If the Rule subjects always applied their rule and never engaged an exemplar-similarity procedure, they should have performed the same on positive and negative matches. But if the Rule subjects sometimes used exemplar similarity as well as rule application, their performance should have been poorer on negative than positive matches; this is because for negative matches, rule application points to one category whereas exemplar similarity points to the other. The latter pattern of results was obtained: the error rate (where an 'error' means going against the rule) was about 20% for positive matches, but 45% for negative matches.

Given that the Rule subjects sometimes used both procedures, did they apply the two procedures on the same trial? The reaction-time results for correct responses (i.e. categorizations in accordance with the rule) suggest that the answer is, 'yes'. Reaction times were longer to correctly-responded-to negative matches than to correctly-responded-to positive matches. This difference fits with the idea that the two procedures were used on the same trial, because extra time would be needed with negative matches to resolve the conflicting categorizations indicated by the two procedures. These results are further compatible with the idea of parallel application of the two procedures.

The picture that emerges from this experiment is in line with much other research on categorization and reasoning (see, e.g. Smith et al., 1992). Rule application and exemplar similarity seem to be distinct procedures that can operate on the identical contents (perhaps in parallel) and sometimes lead to conflicting categorizations. In

[3]Because each positive or negative match was constructed to be highly similar to just one old item, we assume that only that old item is retrieved. Consequently, categorization should be determined by just that retrieved exemplar.

addition, because the outcome of the exemplar-similarity procedure was able to intrude on the processing due to rule application, the former procedure seems to operate more quickly (at least in some circumstances). This latter claim is further supported by the finding that the Rule group took 250 ms longer to respond than did the Memory group.

3.1.2. Triggering conditions

Given the evidence for two procedures, what aspects of a categorization situation trigger rule application versus exemplar similarity? In the study by Allen and Brooks (1991), it seems obvious that the rule instructions induced in subjects a conscious intention to apply the given rule, but it is difficult to go beyond this rather abstract statement.

We can be more analytic about the triggering conditions for the exemplar-similarity procedure. Because this procedure was used even when subjects were trying to employ a rule, presumably the procedure was automatically activated. That is, as earlier suggested in our schematic model of exemplar similarity and discussion of its components (Section 2), the presentation of a test object automatically activates the representations of similar objects. Hence, the triggering conditions for exemplar similarity should include conditions that foster automatic memory retrieval of the relevant object representations. One such condition is that different aspects of an object be integrated because this will lead to the development of a unitary representation, thereby lessening the demands on retrieval processes. Another such condition is that test objects be perceptually distinct, leading to a reduction in interference from other items during retrieval. Follow-up studies by Allen and Brooks (1991) and Regehr and Brooks (1993) support both of these predictions. When the test objects were made either less integrated or less distinctive, there was a decrease in the difference in errors between negative and positive matches—the litmus test for exemplar similarity.

One obvious determinant of automatic memory retrieval has been explored extensively in the memory literature, namely, sheer familiarity with the items (e.g. Shiffrin and Schneider, 1977). When subjects are still learning to categorize test objects, retrieval of a representation of the entire object and its category label will be imperfect (let alone non-automatic), and consequently exemplar retrieval should play little role in categorization, even if no rule is given and subjects are induced to rely on memory mechanisms. These conditions correspond to the early part of the learning phase of many categorization studies, and under these conditions subjects try to generate simple rules to handle their categorization task. These rules are almost always faulty, yet subjects appear to persist with them until automatic memory retrieval starts to take over (Regehr and Brooks, 1993).

This last observation indicates that we may have found a triggering condition for rule application other than sheer instruction. Suppose that people are given a set of objects that assume different values along the same set of separable and salient attributes (standard operating procedure in categorization studies with artificial materials), and are instructed to categorize these objects into a small number of categories. Subjects may naturally selectively attend to the salient attributes, and seek rules that connect combinations of these attribute values to the different categories.

In summary, the following picture emerges for categorization in a task, such as that of Allen and Brooks (1991) in which subjects have been induced to rely on their memories. Early in learning, subjects search for simple rules that can be used to predict the categorizations. This quest for simple rules typically proves futile because of the structure of the materials (e.g. no single attribute is more than 75% predictive of correct categorization) and because the rule that underlies the desired categorizations typically is not obvious (e.g. 2 of 3 critical attribute values). While the quest continues, subjects inadvertently memorize the exemplars and their associated category labels, and eventually the exemplar-similarity procedure is capable of producing correct categorizations, and takes control of performance. Hence, the similarity procedure takes longer to become effective than the rule procedure, though once both procedures are operative it is not unusual for the similarity procedure to operate faster.

The early reliance on simple rules that we see in categorization tasks also occurs in 'free sorting' tasks. In these tasks, subjects are presented a substantial set of objects and asked to sort them into categories (no mention is made of rules). In the experiments of interest (e.g. Medin et al., 1987; Ahn and Medin, 1992), the materials are such that any simple rule (a single attribute value) will not work, in that some of the items will remain unclassified. Subjects use a simple rule anyway, and then sort the remaining items on the basis of their similarity to the instances already sorted by the rule. Again, classification involves two procedures, rules and similarity, with the rule procedure being applied first.

3.1.3. Other dissociations between rule and memory procedures

Consider again the initial finding by Allen and Brooks (1991) that Rule and Memory subjects categorized negative matches differently, with Memory subjects assigning these objects to the same category as their closest neighbors, and Rule subjects assigning them mostly in accordance with the rule. This finding can be viewed as a *dissociation* between the rule-application and exemplar-similarity procedures. Researchers, particularly in neuropsychology, routinely take dissociations as evidence that distinct processes are involved; we draw the same conclusion here. There are several other findings in the categorization literature as well that can be interpreted as dissociations between these two kinds of procedures.

In a series of studies by Smith and Kemler (1984), test objects were squares that varied on two attributes, brightness and side-length. In one experiment, subjects were presented three such objects and instructed to remove the one that did not belong to the same category as the other two. Referring to the three objects as A, B, and C, A and B were alike in that they had the identical value on one of the attributes; in contrast, A and C were the most holistically similar, i.e. the magnitude of their differences summed over both attributes was less than that of A and B. Thus, there were two means for categorizing the objects, on the basis of a common attribute value (e.g. 'smallest side-length'), or on the basis of overall similarity. During the training phase of the experiment, subjects were given feedback that induced them to categorize by one of these two means. There followed a test phase, during which subjects either had to make their categorizations very rapidly or not. The major result was that at fast speeds the two categorization strategies led to equally accurate performance, whereas at slower speeds categorization based on a common attribute was more accurate. Thus, speed of responding dissociated the two categorization strategies.

The connection of these results to our concerns is straightforward. Categorization based on a common attribute requires selectivity attending to that attribute and determining if the attribute's value instantiates some abstract condition. These are two of the key components of rule application, suggesting that categorization based on a common attribute amounted to applying the rule, 'If two objects have the smallest line length, then they're in the same category'. In contrast, categorization based on overall similarity involved a similarity computation like that used in the first stage of the exemplar-similarity procedure. The dissociation between the strategies further suggests that the successful use of rule application required more time than that needed for exemplar similarity, perhaps because the former procedure involves more time-consuming processes.

Another experiment by Smith and Kemler (1984) involved the same objects and tasks as those described above, except that the rule- and similarity-based categorization strategies were induced by instructions (roughly, 'Respond on the basis of first impressions' versus 'Carefully decide') rather than by feedback. Similarity-based categorizations were faster than rule-based ones. Again, speed of responding dissociated rule and similarity procedures. Still another study in this series varied whether subjects using either rule- or similarity-based strategies had to perform a concurrent task or not. Performing a secondary task interfered with categorization more when subjects were categorizing by rule. So a dual-task requirement also dissociated rule and similarity procedures. Using verbal materials rather than pictorial ones, Smith and Shapiro (1989) have also found that it is easier to perform a secondary task when one is categorizing by similarity than by rule.

3.1.4. Implications of findings

These dissociations fit well with our previous discussion of the components of rule application and exemplar similarity. The findings that a rule-based strategy typically operates slower than a similarity-based one and is more disrupted by a secondary task suggest that the rule strategy demands more of some time- or effort-limited cognitive component than does the similarity procedure. Two such components implicated by the schematic models that we sketched earlier are selective attention and working memory.

These ideas about component processes are summarized in Fig. 2, which fleshes out our earlier schematic models of rule application and exemplar similarity. Note that rule application involves: selective attention (Boxes 2 and 4), making perceptual tests that correspond to conditions of the rule (Box 5), and extensive working-memory operations (Boxes 3, 6 and 7). In contrast, exemplar similarity involves: retrieval from long-term memory (Boxes 2 and 3), and a subsequent similarity-comparison process (Boxes 7 and 8). These models are compatible with the cognitive findings that we have reviewed thus far, and as we will see, with the neurological findings that we present below.

3.2. Studies with natural categories

3.2.1. Studies demonstrating the two categorization mechanisms

In the experiments reviewed thus far, the relevant attribute-values were readily

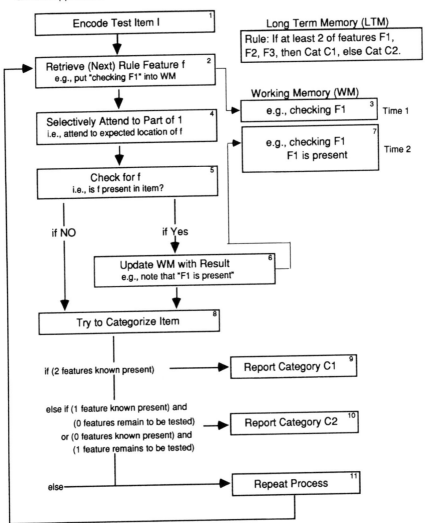

Fig. 2. (a) A model of the rule-application process as applied to Allen and Brooks (1991) categorization task; (b) a model of the exemplar-similarity process as applied to the same task. In (a) the term 'feature' designates an attribute value.

separated from one another and were quite salient. This is typical of studies with artificial categories. In many studies of natural categories, though, the test object is either a picture of a familiar object or a frequent word, and the relevant attribute-values (either in the picture or the word's meaning) seem to be less salient. Hence, most experiments with natural categories are not strictly comparable to most studies with artificial materials. However, a number of researchers have recently empha-sized a new paradigm for studying natural categories that more closely parallels experiments with artificial materials. In this paradigm, subjects are presented with a partial textual description of an object (e.g. 'a small animal that burrows in the earth...') and subjects have to decide whether or not that object is a member of some target category. Because the relevant attribute-values are denoted by distinct words in the description, they are readily separable and salient, just as is the case with artificial materials (though the attributes are semantic rather than perceptual). All of the natural-category studies that we consider are of this type.

A developmental study by Keil and Batterman (1984) speaks to the existence of different categorization strategies. The experiment involved children aged 5–10 years. On each trial, subjects were presented descriptions of two items and had to decide which one belonged to a target category. The categories were natural ones,

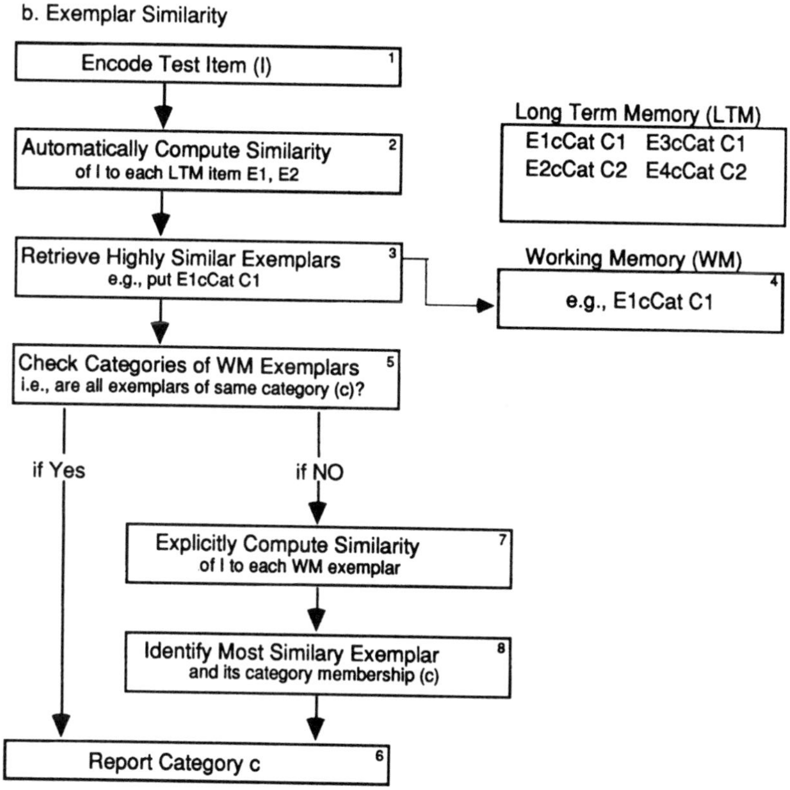

Fig. 2b.

and each contained features (attribute values) that were *necessary* (i.e. true of all members) as well as features that were only *characteristic* (i.e. true of typical members) (Smith et al., 1974). One of the descriptions presented on a trial contained the necessary features of the target category but not the characteristic ones, whereas the other description contained the characteristic features but not the necessary ones. For example, when the category was Robber the two descriptions were:

1. A very friendly and cheerful woman who gave you a hug but then disconnected your toilet bowl and took it away without permission and no intention to return it (necessary but not characteristic); and
2. A smelly mean old man with a gun in his pocket who comes to your house and takes your TV set because your parents didn't want it any more and told him he could have it (characteristic but not necessary).

The major findings were that younger children were more likely to select descriptions with characteristic features, whereas the older subjects favored descriptions with necessary features.

To connect these results to the concerns of the present paper, we note that a description with characteristic features seems more similar to exemplars of its category than does a necessary-feature description. Thus, selection of a characteristic-feature description might well be based on the exemplar-similarity procedure (or on a similarity-to-prototype procedure). In addition, let us assume that selection of a necessary-feature description is often based on noticing the diagnostic status of the necessary feature, selectively attending to it, and then using it as a rule (e.g. 'If someone took someone else's goods without permission..., they're a robber'). Given these assumptions, the results from Keil and Batterman (1984) imply that younger subjects relied more on exemplar similarity than rule application, whereas older subjects did the reverse. This is a dissociation between exemplar-similarity and rule-application procedures, and hence these results converge with those obtained with artificial categories.

However, because these results involve a contrast between two groups of subjects, they do not demonstrate that the same subject applied the two procedures to the same item, as in some of the experiments with artificial materials. A recent report by Hampton (1995) comes closer to offering this demonstration. Hampton's materials were very similar to those of Keil and Batterman (1984), but he used adult subjects. On each trial, subjects were presented a category and a description of an object, and they had to decide whether or not the object was a member of the category. Several kinds of descriptions were used, and four of them are of particular interest. Relative to the category with which it was paired, a description could contain:

1. both the necessary and characteristic features;
2. the necessary but not the characteristic features (like the necessary-feature descriptions of Keil and Batterman, 1984);
3. the characteristic but not the necessary features (like Keil and Batterman's characteristic-feature descriptions); and
4. neither the necessary nor the characteristic features.

Consider first the results for conditions (3) and (4). Because no necessary feature is present in either case, there is no possibility of rule application. If subjects rely on a similarity mechanism (either exemplar similarity or prototype similarity), there should be more positive categorizations ('yes, it's a member') in (3) than (4). This is what Hampton (1995) found. Now consider conditions (2) and (4). Because a necessary feature is present in (2) but not (4), rule application will support a positive categorization only in (2), and hence there should be more positive categorizations in (2) than (4). Again, this is what Hampton found. Neither of these results is surprising. Of greater interest is the contrast between conditions (1) and (2). Because a necessary feature is present in both conditions, rule application will support a positive categorization in both conditions. If only rule application is used, the two conditions should not differ in the frequency of positive categorizations; but if exemplar-similarity is also activated (perhaps automatically), there should be more positive categorizations in (1) than (2). Indeed, this is what Hampton (1995) found, confirming that both categorization procedures could have been active. Note that this pattern of results is very similar to those of Allen and Brooks (1991) who used artificial categories[4].

The convergence of results between studies with natural and artificial materials, however, rests on the assumptions that we have made about when subjects use similarity and rule procedures in natural categorization. It would be useful to 'ground' these assumptions; i.e. to provide evidence that subjects are computing similarity when the described object contains features characteristic of the target category, and are using a rule when focusing on necessary features. A procedure introduced by Rips (1989) provides some empirical confirmation.

Rips (1989) was primarily interested in demonstrating that categorization is not always based on similarity. In his paradigm, on each trial a subject was presented a description of a test object that mentioned only a value of a single attribute (say, the object's diameter). Then the subject had to decide to which of two target categories the object belonged (it had been previously established that the object was between the subject's extreme values for the two categories). For example, one description might be, 'A circular object with a 3-in diameter', with the associated categories being Quarter and Pizza. The description was constructed to be smaller than the smallest pizza in that subject's experience, but larger than the largest quarter. Now, quarters are restricted in size but pizzas are not, and if subjects brought this piece of knowledge to bear they would likely decide that the object is a pizza. All of the items had this structure: one category–the 'variable' category—always allowed more variability on the relevant attribute than did the other category—the 'fixed' category. This variation is similar to varying whether a necessary feature is present or not. What is novel about the paradigm of Rips (1989) is that, in addition to asking subjects for categorization decisions, he also had them rate the similarity of each

---

[4]It is worth noting that Hampton (1995) interpreted his results differently. He took the finding of more positive categorizations in condition (1) than (2) to mean that the so called 'necessary features' present in conditions (1) and (2) were not really necessary, and that category membership is always a matter of degrees. However, Osherson and Smith (1997) present arguments against Hampton's interpretations.

described object to the target categories. This provides a clear indication of which category would be favored by a similarity mechanism.

Rips (1989) found that subjects were more likely to categorize the test objects as members of the variable category (Pizza in our example), but rated the objects as more similar to the fixed categories (Quarter). So we can conclude that categorization was not based on a similarity computation. What was it based on? Presumably, it was based on a rule that focuses on the constraint of the fixed category, e.g. 'If an object is more than 1-in in diameter, it cannot be a quarter.' Given this assumption, Rips' results show a dissociation between similarity- and rule-based judgments. What they do not show, though, is a dissociation between two categorization procedures, because the similarity procedure was operative only in similarity judgments. Also, there is nothing in Rips' results that grounds our assumption about rule use by showing that a focus on a necessary feature involves the application of an explicit rule.

What is needed is a variant of the Rips paradigm—collecting both similarity and categorization responses—that in some cases fosters similarity-based categorizations and in others fosters rule-based categorizations. Smith and Sloman (1994) report just such an experiment. In some conditions of their experiment, they essentially replicated Rips' study—e.g. Is a circular object 3 in in diameter more likely to be a Pizza or a Quarter? Is it more similar to a Pizza or a Quarter? The results in these conditions replicated those of Rips in that subjects judged the objects as more likely to be members of the variable categories but more similar to the fixed categories. In other conditions, the descriptions were enriched so that they contained features characteristic of the fixed categories but not of the variable categories, e.g., 'A circular object with a 3-in diameter that is silver colored'. In these conditions, subjects judged the described objects not only as more similar to the fixed categories, but also as more likely to be members of the fixed categories. That is, categorization judgments tracked similarity judgments. This provides strong evidence that the categorization judgments were indeed based on a similarity procedure.

Finally, consider the evidence for our assumption linking a focus on necessary features to the explicit use of rules. Smith and Sloman (1994) had subjects 'think aloud' while making their decisions, and subsequently analyzed these verbal protocols. In those condition that used the sparser descriptions (e.g. 'A circular object with a 3-in diameter'), on some trials subjects would justify their categorization decision by explicitly stating the relevant rule, e.g. 'Quarter can't be larger than 1-in'. In such cases, subjects chose the variable category (e.g. Pizza) all of the time. The explicit statement of a rule is a standard criterion for rule use (Smith et al., 1992), and the all-or-none responding fits with the all-or-none nature of rule use.

3.2.2. Implications of the findings

These results converge nicely with the findings obtained with artificial materials, particularly the work of Brooks and his colleagues. Even when a rule is present that can be used for categorization, subjects will also invoke a similarity procedure if the test object contains information that is characteristic of one of the target categories.

The results with natural categories are also roughly compatible with the models presented in Fig. 2. Rule application with verbal materials again involves selectively attending to relevant attributes, though now the attributes are semantic (one's knowledge about the categories of interest). In our Pizza-Quarter example, presumably subjects inspect their semantic representations for pizzas and quarters, selectively attending to information about size. Rule application in these semantic cases may also sometimes involve a kind of instantiation process; e.g. one's knowledge about apples includes their distinctive coloring, but one must decide if that distinctive coloring is adequately captured by the word 'red' in the description 'A circular object with a red color.' What is less likely is that working memory plays much of a role in the natural-category experiments. With natural, semantic categories, one does not have to rehearse the rule (necessary feature), nor keep track of how many attributes have been checked thus far, but there may still be a need for keeping some information in an activated state.

With regard to the exemplar-similarity procedure, again the results with natural categories are compatible with the schematic model in Fig. 2. In particular, when a description contains a sufficient number of characteristic features, the category of the described object seems to be automatically activated.

4. Neuropsychological and neuroimaging studies of rule application vs. exemplar similarity

Another way to determine whether rule application and exemplar similarity are qualitatively different strategies is to ascertain whether they are implemented by different neural structures in the brain. In what follows, first we consider some indirect evidence from neuropsychology (i.e. the study of selective deficits due to brain damage), and then present some direct evidence from a neuroimaging experiment from our laboratory.

4.1. Neuropsychological evidence for qualitatively different procedures

The central assumption underlying the exemplar-similarity procedure is that categorization rests on previously stored examples. Consider patients who have damage in regions of the brain known to be involved in storing new items: such patients should have difficulty storing exemplars of a new category, and consequently have difficulty using the exemplar-similarity procedure in future classifications involving this category. This prediction has been assessed by Kolodny (1994). He tested patients with damage in their medial-temporal lobes, which contains the hippocampal system that is known to be critically involved in the consolidation of new memories (e.g. Squire, 1992). Kolodny compared such patients to normal controls on two categorization tasks. One task required subjects to learn to sort novel paintings into two categories that corresponded to two different artists, whereas the other task required subjects to learn to sort dot patterns into two categories that corresponded to two different prototypes. Independent behavioral evidence indicated that only the paintings task typically recruits an exemplar-similarity procedure in normal subjects (the dot-patterns task seems to trigger a reliance on abstract prototypes). The patients learned the dot-pattern categories as readily as the normal controls, but performed far worse than normal on the painting categories. This leads to the inference that damage to the medial-temporal lobe selectively impairs categorization based on exemplar similarity.

With regard to the neural basis of rule following, among the neuroanatomical areas likely to be involved are the frontal lobes. Clinical observations have long suggested that damage to this region is associated with difficulties in thinking analytically and applying abstract rules (e.g. Luria, 1969). Also, there are many experiments which demonstrate that patients with frontal-lobe damage perform substantially less well than normal controls on tasks that require the use of explicit rules. The task of choice is typically the Wisconsin Card Sort Task. On each trial, a card is presented that contains colored geometric forms; from card to card there is a variation in the number, shape, size and background shading of these forms. The subject must learn which one of the four attributes to use as a basis for sorting the cards into four piles. Once subjects have sorted a certain number of cards correctly, the experimenter switches the relevant attribute and subjects now have to discover the new critical attribute. Frontal-lobe patients are strikingly impaired on this rule-based task, not only compared to normal subjects but compared to patients with brain damage outside of the frontal lobes. The frontal-lobe patients may learn the initially relevant attribute as well as other subjects, but they have severe problems shifting to a new rule when the experimenter switches relevant attributes (e.g. Milner, 1964).

The preceding studies are suggestive, but they have definite weaknesses when it comes to providing strong evidence about qualitative differences between rule- and similarity-based categorization. For one thing, these studies deal more with the acquisition of novel categories than they do with categorization using already-learned categories, and it is the latter topic that has been the main concern in this paper. Another matter is that no published experiment has tested two patients of interest—say, a frontal-lobe and a medial-temporal-lobe patient—on two tasks of interest—one that recruits primarily rule application and one that relies mainly on exemplar similarity—showing that one patient is impaired on one task but not the other, whereas the other patient shows the reverse pattern. That is, no neuropsychological double dissociations between rule application and exemplar similarity have been demonstrated.

However, there is a recently obtained neuropsychological double dissociation in the area of lexical processing, and it is relevant here (Ullman et al., 1997). The experiment of interest is based on the prior research of Pinker and colleagues on forming the past tenses of regular and irregular verbs (e.g. Pinker, 1991). This work indicated that generating the past tense of a regular verb (e.g. 'jump'-'jumped') is done by application of a rule (roughly, 'Add -ed to the present-tense'), whereas generating the past tense of an irregular verb (e.g. 'sing'-'sang') is accomplished by retrieving relevant information from memory, including information about similar exemplars (e.g. 'ring'-'rang'). These two procedures have an obvious similarity to rule application and exemplar similarity. Ullman et al. (1997) had patients convert regular and irregular present-tense verbs to their past tenses. They found that patients with Parkinson's disease, who are known to have problems in applying systematic procedures, made more errors on regular than irregular verbs; in contrast, Alzheimer's patients, who have well-documented memory problems, had more difficulty with irregular than regular verbs. This establishes a double dissociation between rule application and exemplar retrieval in a task related to categorization. Furthermore, there is some neuroimaging evidence for this double dissociation, as different brain areas are activated when normal subjects convert regular and irregular present-tense verbs to their past tenses (Jaeger et al., 1996).

4.2. Neuroimaging evidence for qualitatively different procedures

4.2.1. Rationale for the experiment

In an effort to provide more direct evidence for different neural correlates of rule application and exemplar similarity, we conducted an experiment in which normal subjects performed categorization tasks while their brains were scanned using positron emission tomography, or PET (a technique for measuring changes in regional cerebral blood flow as an index of changes in regional neural activity). One group of subjects performed a rule-based categorization task while another performed an exemplar-based task. To the extent that different regions of the brain are activated in the two tasks, we have evidence that qualitatively different cognitive procedures are involved. To the extent that the known functionality of the activated areas in a task corresponds to processes that are thought to be involved in the strategy underlying that task, the PET evidence is strong indeed[5].

The categorization tasks we used were variants of those used by Allen and Brooks (1991). Recall that in that experiment a Rule group and a Memory group first learned to categorize imaginary animals, and then were tested on new animals in a transfer phase. The results from the transfer phase showed that the Memory group relied on an exemplar-similarity procedure, whereas the Rule group relied primarily on rule application. These tasks are well-suited for a PET study for two reasons. Firstly, in a PET study one needs to ensure that differences in brain activity cannot be attributed to differences in the complexity or familiarity of stimuli, and the only difference between Allen and Brooks (1991) two tasks is in the instructions. In all other respects—including amount of training provided prior to testing, the nature of the test items, the number of response alternatives, etc.—the two tasks are identical.

---

[5]Basically, PET works as follows. It is known that regional neural activity in the brain causes regional increases in blood flow. A radioactive substance (^{15}O) is injected into a subject's bloodstream, and flows to the parts of the brain that are neurally activated during the task. As the substance decays in the brain, it emits positrons. Each positron moves only a few mm before it collides with an electron. The annihilation process produces two photons that travel outward from the point of collision in opposite directions. A PET scanner contains rings of photon detectors surrounding the subject's head. When two photons are detected on opposite sides of the detector at nearly the same moment, they are assumed to have come from the same annihilation process. Using tomographic techniques, it is then possible to construct images of where in the brain the annihilations occurred and, by inference, where in the brain there was neural activation.

Secondly, there seems to be little doubt that the Rule and Memory tasks do indeed involve rule application and exemplar similarity, respectively, whereas this difference in procedure is less clear in any of the paradigms that used natural categories.

There is, however, a problem with this choice of tasks. As noted earlier, subjects in the Rule group seemed to make some automatic use of exemplar similarity. This conclusion is based on the fact that, during the transfer phase, the Rule group responded more slowly and less accurately to negative matches—new test animals that were highly similar to an old animal in the wrong category—as compared with positive matches—new test animals that were highly similar to an old animal in the correct category. We, nonetheless, chose to use the Rule task for the following reasons. Firstly, some automatic use of exemplar similarity is unavoidable unless one is willing either to: (a) present different items to the Rule and Memory groups in the transfer phase, such that the Rule subjects see test objects that are highly dissimilar to the training ones and therefore are unable to use exemplar-based processes; or (b) provide different amounts of training to the two groups, such that the Rule subjects would have less practice than the Memory subjects, and therefore have less time to learn the study items in the first place. Either of these changes would seriously compromise our ability to interpret the PET results. Secondly, there is reason to believe that exemplar similarity plays considerably less of a role in the Rule condition than does rule application. In Allen and Brooks (1991), the difference in accuracy between positive and negative matches—the litmus test for the use of exemplar similarity—was approximately 25% in the Rule condition as opposed to approximately 60% in the Memory condition. Hence, even if subjects do engage exemplar-based processes in the Rule condition, the impact of these processes should be relatively small and contribute little to increases in brain activation, especially in the context of the demanding and time-consuming rule-application processes. Finally, even if both memory- and rule-based processes turn out to be responsible for regional blood-flow changes in the Rule condition, those activations that are due to memory processes should be detectable by spotting brain regions active in both the Rule and Memory conditions.

4.2.2. Procedure

We altered the Allen and Brooks (1991) tasks in a number of respects (Smith et al., submitted). Some changes were made to maximize reliance on memory in the Memory condition and time spent on rule application in the Rule condition, thereby improving the chances that these procedures would be captured by PET. To maximize reliance on memory, the imaginary animals were created with more perceptually distinctive features, given that we have already noted that perceptual distinctiveness increases memory use (Regehr and Brooks, 1993). Also, the study period was extended to ensure that the animals were well-learned. To maximize time spent on rule application, we increased the complexity of the rule (it now required matches on at least 3 of 5 attribute-values). Another change was that subjects were given a 2.5-s time window in which to make a response rather than having trials scheduled ad lib. We did this to ensure that the number of categorization decisions was equated across conditions, so that it could not be the cause of differences in PET results. Finally, the experiment was conducted over 2 days. On the first day, subjects performed four blocks of study trials, with two repetitions of the ten study stimuli in each block, followed by one block of transfer trials. In the second session, subjects completed one more block of study trials, and were then scanned while doing three blocks of transfer trials.

In addition to engaging in either the Rule or Memory condition, subjects performed three blocks of a control condition while being scanned. The purpose of this condition was to capture some of the processes that were presumably operative in the Rule and Memory conditions but were not part of categorization per se, and hence not of direct interest. Such irrelevant processes include basic perceptual and response processes. Following standard PET methodology (Posner et al., 1988), the regions activated in this Control task were subtracted from those activated in the Rule and Memory tasks, in order to isolate brain regions associated only with the categorization processes of interest. The Control task was the same for both Memory and Rule subjects, and simply required subjects to push either of two buttons at random whenever a test object appeared. The pictures and response buttons were the same as those used in the categorization conditions.

4.2.3. Results

Consider first the behavioral findings. We focus here on just the results collected during the PET scans, though the results from the first session are quite similar. By and large, the results replicate those obtained by Allen and Brooks (1991). The Rule group took considerably longer than the Memory group to make their responses—an average of 760 ms longer. Furthermore, subjects in the two groups differed in their dominant categorization of negative matches—those items that followed the rule of one category but were most similar to a studied item in the other category. Rule subjects categorized 71% of these items according to the rule, whereas Memory subjects categorized a full 76% in terms of similarity to study items. These results replicate the basic dissociation between the Rule and Memory groups, and suggest that subjects in the two conditions used different processes to categorize the items.

Like Allen and Brooks (1991), we found evidence that the Rule group was also influenced by exemplar-based processes. Specifically, Rule subjects were more accurate on positive (85%) than negative matches (71%). Unlike Allen and Brooks (1991), however, we found no effects of positive vs. negative match on response times. This may have been a result of the time-window procedure employed here; i.e. the procedure may have encouraged subjects to respond at a consistent speed for fear of failing to respond before the deadline. Taken together, these results show that, though there was some use of exemplar similarity in our Rule condition, it was relatively minor; the accuracy difference between positive and negative matches (14%) was small compared to that obtained in the Memory condition (53%), and was even less than that obtained in the Rule condition of Allen and Brooks (25%). These comparisons suggest that Rule subjects mainly did rule processing, which means the PET results should be relatively pure.

The PET results for each condition were computed by subtracting the Control activation data from the Rule or Memory activation data for each subject, and then

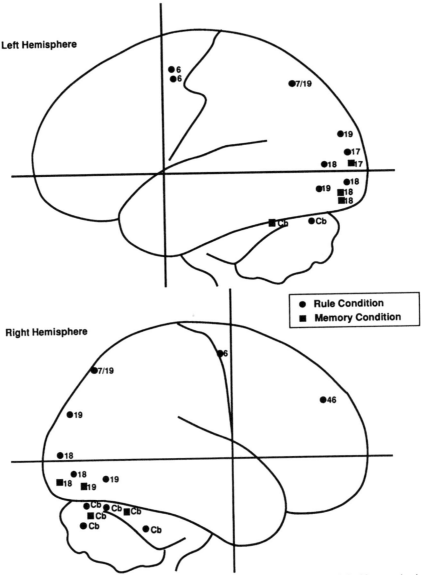

Fig. 3. Marked areas on right and left lateral surfaces of the cortex denote regions of significant activation in Rule- and Memory-condition subtraction images. Numbers correspond to Brodmann's areas; Cb, cerebellum. Active regions not visible from this perspective are: left Brodmann Area 31 (it is on the medial surface of the parietal lobe and is active in the in the Memory condition), and the right thalamus (it is a subcortical structure active in the Rule condition).

averaging the subtraction data across all subjects within each condition. The resulting images revealed numerous areas of significant activation; these are presented schematically in Fig. 3. The main finding is a dissociation: Of the 23 areas activated across both conditions, 14 were activated solely in the Rule condition. Of the remaining nine areas, seven were active in both conditions[6]; only two were active in the Memory condition alone. All of these areas are labeled on the schematic using numbers designated by the physiologist Brodmann to refer to regions of the cortex differing in cytoarchitecture (as well as the designation 'Cb' to refer to areas in the cerebellum).

Areas of activation distinct to the Rule condition are as follows: two areas at the top of the parietal lobes (one in each hemisphere; Brodmann Area 7 in both cases); areas in the frontal cortex, namely, one area in right dorsolateral prefrontal cortex (Brodmann Area 46) and three areas in supplementary motor cortex (two in the left hemisphere and one in the right hemisphere of Brodmann Area 6); four areas in the visual cortex (two in left Brodmann Area 19, one in right Brodmann Area 19, and one in right Brodmann Area 18); three areas in the cerebellum (two in the right and one in the left); and one area in the right thalamus (not shown in the figure because it is a medial structure and only lateral views of the brain are illustrated).

Areas of activation common to both Rule and Memory conditions are: five areas in the visual cortex (one in left Brodmann Area 17, one in each hemisphere of Brodmann Area 18, one in left Brodmann Area 18/31[7], and one in right Brodmann Area 19), and two areas in the right cerebellum. The remaining two areas (one in left Brodmann's Area 18 and one in the left cerebellum) were active only in the Memory condition. At a minimum, the entire pattern of results suggests that there are mechanisms involved in rule-based categorization beyond those involved in exemplar-based categorization, which supports the proposal that rule-based categorization is qualitatively different from exemplar-based categorization. As we are about to see, these additional rule mechanisms are exactly the ones implicated in our previous discussion of the cognitive literature.

Further evidence for qualitative differences between rule and exemplar procedures comes from functional interpretation of the activated areas. Firstly, consider the areas distinctive to the Rule condition. The largest activation is that in the left-hemisphere parietal lobe (Brodmann Area 7). In single-cell studies with non-human primates, neurons in this area of parietal cortex have been found to fire when the organism must selectively attend to certain locations (Bushnell et al., 1981). And studies with human neurological patients show that damage to this region of parietal cortex is associated with impairments in spatial, selective attention. As we have

---

[6]Each area of activation contains a peak—a point of greatest change in activation within the area—that can be specified using an x, y, z coordinate system. An area of activation found in the Rule condition is considered 'common' to an area found in the Memory condition if peaks of the two areas differ by less than 10 mm—the spatial resolution of PET—on each coordinate.

[7]The peak is in Brodmann Area 18 in the Rule condition and in Brodmann Area 31 in the Memory condition. The latter is not shown in figure because Area 31 is a medial structure.

[8]Actually, the evidence about parietal function pertains to selective attention for spatial position, whereas our earlier discussion of rule application emphasized selective attention for different attributes. There is no real conflict here, though. The relevant attributes of the items in our PET study and in other studies of visual categorization consistently occur in different spatial positions (e.g. ears at the extreme left, tail at the extreme right); hence, attending to a particular attribute entails attending to a particular location.

noted repeatedly, selective attention is part of rule application but not exemplar similarity, and hence the activation at issue fits well with our proposals[8].

Another region activated in the Rule condition was in the prefrontal cortex (Brodmann Area 46). As noted in the previous section, damage in the prefrontal cortex in neurological patients is routinely associated with difficulties in applying rules. Thus, the PET data converge with the neuropsychological results in indicating the importance of the prefrontal region in rule application. But what psychological function does this region serve? One possibility, based on other neuroimaging experiments (e.g. Cohen et al., 1994; Smith et al., 1996), is that the prefrontal cortex is activated whenever operations are performed on material currently maintained in working memory. As argued earlier, such working-memory operations should be more frequent in the Rule than the Memory condition[9].

A third area activated in the Rule condition was in supplementary motor cortex (Brodmann Area 6). In general, this area has been shown to play a role in the high-level preparation and planning of movement (Fuster, 1995), including speech (Petersen et al., 1988). Of specific interest here is that activation of supplementary motor cortex has been reported in studies of verbal working memory, and is believed to mediate implicit speech, or rehearsal, of stored verbal information in these contexts (Awh et al., 1995). This region, then, may have been involved in rehearsing both the rule (e.g. 'If an animal has a spotted body...') and the intermediate results of rule application (e.g. 'has spotted body') during categorization in the Rule condition.

The other activated regions in the Rule condition include four visual areas that were not significant in the Memory condition, three cerebellar regions, and one area in the thalamus. The former regions may be involved in processes that generate a percept with a salient part structure, which was needed in the Rule condition but not necessarily in the Memory condition. Alternatively, the visual activations may reflect the analytic perceptual tests made in the Rule condition, e.g. 'Are the legs long?'. Either of these preceding suggestions is speculative (particularly since the areas at issue are somewhat dorsal and posterior to the areas usually associated with the analysis of object parts). We have no firm interpretation of the thalamic or cerebellar activations either, but we note that the latter activations are extremely common in PET studies of working memory (see, e.g. Smith et al., 1996).

Next, consider the seven areas of activation common to the Rule and Memory conditions. Two areas active in both the Rule and Memory conditions were in the right cerebellum; again, we have no firm interpretation of these activations. The remaining five areas were all in the visual cortex. One interpretation of these results is that the region in the visual cortex may be involved in automatic aspects of

---

[9]There are other views of the function of the prefrontal cortex. One is that it is involved whenever the person has to shift attention and processing from one subtask to another (Rubenstein et al., 1994; D'Esposito et al., 1995). Perhaps the need for Rule subjects to shift from one attribute to another is akin to a task shift. Another proposed function of the prefrontal cortex is that it is responsible for inhibition (e.g. Diamond, 1988; Shimamura, 1994). Inhibition may well have played a role in our Rule condition. Whenever a negative match was presented, its close neighbor from the wrong category may have been activated, and consequently subjects would have had to inhibit responding in accordance with this retrieved exemplar.

exemplar retrieval, since this process is occasionally operative in the Rule condition, and of course is prevalent in the Memory condition. That is, the processing revealed may reflect the storage and retrieval of visual memories, namely, animal stimuli. This interpretation is bolstered by recent PET findings about the neural bases of visual imagery (Kosslyn et al., 1993): retrieving a visual image is a paradigmatic case of retrieving a visual memory, and visual-imagery tasks show activation in visual regions close to those activated here (though the imagery regions tend to be more medial).

A second possibility is that, given that these areas of activation were only *roughly* in the same locations for the Rule and Memory conditions, they might be the result of different kinds of processing in each condition. In the Memory condition, the occipital activation might have mediated retrieval of visual memories (as described in the previous paragraph) and perhaps subsequent computations performed on the retrieved representation (e.g. 'Is it sufficiently similar to the test object?'). However, in the Rule condition, the activation may be due to perceptual testing of rule-relevant stimulus features. A third possibility is that more perceptual processing was required in both the Memory and Rule tasks than in the Control condition, and that the occipital regions in question mediate some of this additional processing.

Finally, there are two areas active in the Memory condition only. Because these areas are in the cerebellum and the visual cortex—regions in which common Rule and Memory areas were also found—it is unlikely that the two areas reflect novel cognitive processes. More likely, they (particularly the area in visual cortex) further mediate uniquely Memory-oriented processes such as the retrieval of stored exemplars.

In summary, the most important PET results are:

1. There is a striking dissociation between the neural regions activated in the Rule and Memory conditions (of 23 significant areas, 14 are distinct to the Rule condition); and
2. The known functionality of the activated regions supports the hypotheses that only rule application involves selective attention and working memory, while visual-perceptual and/or visual-memory processes may be common to both procedures of interest.

The results are consistent with the view that rule-application and exemplar-similarity strategies are indeed qualitatively distinct.

5. Summary and other issues

5.1. Summary

Studies with artificial categories provide evidence that rule application and exemplar similarity are qualitatively different categorization procedures (Allen and Brooks, 1991; Regehr and Brooks, 1993). The most straightforward piece of evidence is that subjects instructed to use a rule differ in predictable ways in their dominant categorization of certain items from subjects instructed to rely on their memories. Other experiments with artificial categories provide further dissociations between conditions that foster rule use and conditions that foster reliance on memory; e.g. rule use is more affected by relative emphasis on speed (Smith and Kemler, 1984). The picture that emerges from all these studies is that, compared to exemplar similarity, rule application is a relatively slow and analytic process, presumably because it involves extensive use of selective attention and working memory.

The limitation of the above studies is that they are quite artificial, presenting highly analyzable materials while explicitly encouraging subjects to rely either on rules or memory. However, this limitation is not true of the experiments with natural categories. These studies showed, for example, that under some conditions categorization was likely based on similarity to stored items, whereas in other conditions categorization could not be based on similarity to stored exemplars and instead presumably depended on rule use (Smith and Sloman, 1994). These studies were limited by their lack of independent evidence for rule use. But the fact that the natural-category results converged so well with the data obtained with artificial categories bolsters the case for two distinct categorization procedures.

This pattern of converging results was strengthened by findings from neuropsychology and neuroimaging. The neuropsychological data suggested that selective brain damage can lead to the selective loss of either rule application of exemplar retrieval (Ullman et al., 1997). The neuroimaging experiment provided further evidence for qualitatively different categorization procedures. Not only were many of the areas activated during rule use distinct from those activated during memory-based categorization, but some of the Rule areas were independently known to be involved in selective attention and working memory, processes that characterize rule application but not exemplar similarity.

The overall package of results seems most parsimoniously explained by positing two distinct procedures that can operate independently of one another, perhaps in parallel. While attempts to handle this evidence by a unitary theory—e.g. it's all due to exemplar similarity—might have some success in dealing with the standard cognitive experiments, it is difficult to envision how a unitary approach can encompass the neurological data as well.

5.2. *Other issues*

In addition to the distinction between rule application and exemplar similarity, there are numerous other suggested distinctions between categorization processes and representations. A few of these deserve brief mention.

We noted at the outset that in addition to the two categorization strategies on which we focused, there are at least two others that have a good deal of currency. These are prototype similarity and theory application. With regard to the former, to the extent that one construes a prototype to be the single best example of a category (in the tradition of Rosch, 1973), it may be difficult to distinguish a prototype-similarity procedure from an exemplar-similarity one. Still, the neuropsychological results of Kolodny (1994) suggest that damage to the medial-temporal lobe impairs performance on tasks based on exemplar similarity but not performance on tasks based on prototype similarity. This dissociation clearly supports the distinction between exemplar and prototype similarity, and Squire and Knowlton (1995) have produced a comparable dissociation. With regard to theory application, to the extent one construes it as zeroing-in on just the few core features of a concept and using only them for categorization, it may turn out to be indistinguishable from rule application. But if theory application is instead seen either as providing the best possible explanation of all available features of a test object (as in Rips, 1989), or as a kind of 'proof' of the test object's feature from the category's more abstract attributes (as in Ahn et al., 1992), then it too may turn out to be distinct from other categorization strategies.

While we have focused on the difference between specific categorization procedures, others have considered more abstract processing differences. One such difference is that between analytic and holistic processing. We noted earlier that rule application and exemplar similarity differ with respect to this processing attribute because only the former involves selective attention, but there may be more than selectivity to the analytic-holistic distinction in categorization (e.g. only in analytic processing may an object be decomposed into its parts; see Farah, 1990). Another abstract distinction is that between explicit and implicit categorizations. In the former case, categorization is based on information that is explicitly represented, whereas in the latter case it is based on nonconscious implicit knowledge. Neuropsychological studies have already shown a dissociation between those two kinds of categorization (e.g. Knowlton et al., 1992; Squire and Knowlton, 1995). This explicit-implicit distinction may be relevant in some contrasts of rule- and similarity-based categorization procedures, as a rule is generally assumed to be explicitly represented whereas a retrieved exemplar need not be. However, in some of the tasks we have reviewed, particularly those used in Allen and Brooks (1991) and our PET experiment, the retrieved exemplar may well have been explicitly represented (subjects could readily describe them verbally, for example).

Lastly, there are important categorization distinctions that pertain more directly to representations than processes. The best known of these distinctions come from neurological patients who have a category-specific deficit. Thus, a patient might have an inability to categorize animals while being relatively normal in the ability to categorize artifacts (e.g. Damasio, 1990; Warrington and Shallice, 1984). The dominant account of this dissociation is that animals tend to be represented mainly by perceptual attributes, whereas artifacts are represented as much by functional as perceptual attributes (e.g. Farah and McClelland, 1991). Although this perceptual-functional distinction is intended at the level of representations (or concepts), it might imply a distinction at the level of categorization procedures as well. Different kinds of detectors might be needed to recognize perceptual vs. functional features, and different kinds of detectors might be the starting point for qualitatively different categorization procedures.

But this is getting far ahead of what we know. What we do seem to have evidence for is the claim that rule application and exemplar similarity are very different psychologically and neurologically.

Acknowledgements

Some of the research reported in this paper was supported in part by a grant from the Office of Naval Research and in part by a grant from the National Institute on Aging.

References

Ahn, W., Brewer, W.F., Mooney, R.J., 1992. Schema acquisition from a single example. Journal of Experimental Psychology: Learning, Memory and Cognition 18, 391–412.

Ahn, W., Medin, D.L., 1992. A two-stage model of category construction. Cognitive Science 16 (1), 81–121.

Allen, S.W., Brooks, L.R., 1991. Specializing the operation of an explicit rule. Journal of Experimental Psychology: General 120 (1), 3–19.

Armstrong, S.L., Gleitman, L.R., Gleitman, H., 1983. What some concepts might not be. Cognition 13 (3), 263–308.

Awh, E., Smith, E.E., Jonides, J., 1995. Human rehearsal processes and the frontal lobes: PET Evidence. In: Grafman, J., Holyoak, K.J., Boller, F. (Eds.), Structure and Functions of Human Prefrontal Cortex. New York, NY: The New York Academy of Sciences, Volume 769.

Brooks, L.R., Norman, G.R., Allen, S.W., 1991. Role of specific similarity in a medical diagnostic task. Journal of Experimental Psychology: General 120 (3), 278–287.

Bruner, J.S., Goodnow, J., Austin, G.A. (1956). A study of thinking, Wiley, New York, NY.

Bushnell, M.C., Goldberg, M.E., Robinson, D.L., 1981. Behavioral evidence of visual response in monkey cerebral cortex. I. Modulation in posterior parietal cortex related to selective visual attention. Journal of Neurophysiology 46 (4), 755–772.

Cohen, J.D., Forman, S.D., Braver, T.S., Casey, B.J., Servan-Schrieber, D., Noll, D.C., 1994. Activation of prefrontal cortex in a non-spatial working memory task with functional MRI. Human Brain Mapping 1, 293–304.

Damasio, A.R., 1990. Category-related recognition defects as a clue to the neural substrates of knowledge. Trends in Neuroscience 13 (3), 95–98.

D'Esposito, M., Detre, J., Alsop, D.C., Shin, R.K., Atlas, S., Grossman, M., 1995. The neural basis of the central executive system of working memory. Nature 378 (16), 279–281.

Diamond, A., 1988. The development and neural bases of memory functions as indexed by the AB and delayed response tasks in human infants and infant monkeys. In: Diamond, A. (Ed.), The Development and Neural Bases of Higher Cognitive Functions, The New York Academy of Sciences, New York, NY.

Estes, W.K., 1994. Classification and cognition, Oxford University Press, New York, NY.

Farah, M.J., 1990. Visual agnosia: disorders of object recognition and what they tell us about normal vision, MIT Press, Cambridge, MA.

Farah, M.J., McClelland, J.L., 1991. A computational model of semantic memory impairment: Modality specificity and emergent category specificity. Journal of Experimental Psychology: General 120 (4), 339–357.

Fuster, J.M., 1995. Memory in the Cerebral Cortex, MIT Press Cambridge, MA.

Hampton, J.A., 1995. Testing the prototype theory of concepts. Journal of Memory and Language 34 (5), 686–708.

Hull, C.L., 1920. Quantitative aspects of the evolution of concepts, an experimental study. Princeton, NJ: Psychological review company.

Jaeger, J.J., Lockwood, A.H., Kemmerer, D.L., Van Valin, R.D. Jr., Murphy, B.W., Khalak, H.G., 1996. A positron emission tomography study of regular and irregular verb morphology in English. Language 72 (3), 451–496.

Kahneman, D., Miller, D.T., 1986. Norm theory: comparing reality to its alternatives. Psychological Review 93 (2), 136–153.

Keil, F.C., Batterman, N., 1984. A characteristic-to-defining shift in the development of word meaning. Journal of Verbal Learning and Verbal Behavior 23 (2), 221–236.

Keil, F.C., 1989. Concepts, kinds, and cognitive development, MIT Press, Cambridge, MA.

Kolodny, J.A., 1994. Memory processes in classification learning: An investigation of amnesic performance in categorization of dot patterns and artistic styles. Psychological Science 5 (3), 164–169.

Kemler-Nelson, D., 1984. The effect of intention on what concepts are acquired. Journal of Verbal Learning and Verbal Behavior 23, 734–759.

Knowlton, B.J., Ramus, S.J., Squire, L.R., 1992. Intact artificial grammar learning in amnesia: dissociation of classification learning and explicit memory for specific instances. Psychological Science 3, 172–179.

Kosslyn, S.M., Alpert, N.M., Thompson, W.L., Maljkovic, V., Weise, S.B., Chabris, C.F., Hamilton, S.E., Raunch, S., Buonanno, F.S., 1993. Visual mental imagery activates topographically organized visual cortex: PET investigations. Journal of Cognitive Neuroscience 5 (3), 263–287.

Kruschke, J.K., 1992. ALCOVE: an exemplar-based connectionist model of category learning. Psychological Review 99 (1), 22–44.

Luria, A.R., 1969. Frontal lobe syndromes. In: Vinken, P.J., Bruyn, G.W. (Eds.), Handbook of Clinical Neuropsychology (Vol. 2), North Holland. Amsterdam, Holland.

Milner, B., 1964. Some effects of frontal lobectomy in man. In: Warren, J.M., Akert, K. (Eds.), The frontal granular cortex and behavior, McGraw-Hill, New York, NY.

Medin, D.L., Schaffer, M.M., 1978. Context theory of classification learning. Psychological Review 85 (3), 207–238.

Medin, D.L., Wattenmaker, W.D., Hampson, S.E., 1987. Family resemblance, conceptual cohesiveness, and category construction. Cognitive Psychology 19 (2), 242–279.

Murphy, G.L., Medin, D.L., 1985. The role of theories in conceptual coherence. Psychological Review 92 (3), 289–316.

Nosofsky, R.M., 1986. Attention, similarity, and the identification-categorization relationship. Journal of Experimental Psychology: General 115 (1), 39–57.

Nosofsky, R.M., 1992. Exemplars, prototypes, and similarity rules. In: Estes, W.K. (Ed.), From Learning Theory To Connectionist Theory: Essays in Honor of William K. Estes. Hillsdale, NJ: Lawrence Erlbaum.

Nosofsky, R.M., Palmeri, T.J., McKinley, S.C., 1994. Rule-plus-exception model of classification learning. Psychological Review 101 (1), 53–79.

Osherson, D., Smith, E.E., 1997. On typicality and vagueness. Cognition 64, 189–206.

Petersen, S.E., Fox, P.T., Posner, M.I., Mintum, M., Raichle, M.E., 1988. Positron emission tomographic studies of the cortical anatomy of single-word processing. Nature 331, 585–589.

Pinker, S., 1991. Rules of language. Science 253 (5019), 530–535.

Posner, M.I., Petersen, S.E., Fox, P.T., Raichle, M.E., 1988. Localization of cognitive functions in the human brain. Science 240, 1627–1631.

Regehr, G., Brooks, L.R., 1993. Perceptual manifestations of an analytic structure: the priority of holistic individuation. Journal of Experimental Psychology: General 122 (1), 92–114.

Rips, L.J., 1989. Similarity, typicality, and categorization. In: Vosniadou, S., Ortony, A. (Eds.), Similarity and Analogical Reasoning, Cambridge University Press, Cambridge.

Rosch, E., 1973. On the internal structure of perceptual and semantic categories. In: Moore, T.E. (Ed.), Cognitive development and the acquisition of language, Academic Press, New York, NY.

Rubenstein, J., Evans, J.E., Meyer, D.E., 1994. Task switching in patients with prefrontal cortex damage. Paper presented at the annual meeting of the Cognitive Neuroscience Society, San Francisco, CA.

Shanks, D.R., St. John, M.F., 1994. Characteristics of dissociable human learning systems. Behavioral and Brain Sciences 17, 367–447.

Shiffrin, R.M., Schneider, W., 1977. Controlled and automatic human information processing: II. Perceptual learning, automatic attending and a general theory. Psychological Review 84 (2), 127–190.

Shimamura, A.P., 1994. Memory and frontal lobe function. In: Gazzaniga, M.S. (Ed.), The Cognitive Neurosciences, MIT Press, Cambridge, MA.

Smith, E.E., Jonides, J., Koeppe, R.A., 1996. Dissociating verbal and spatial working memory using PET. Cerebral Cortex 6, 11–20.

Smith, E.E., Langston, C., Nisbett, R.E., 1992. The case for rules in reasoning. Cognitive Science 16 (1), 1–40.

Smith, E.E., Medin, D.L., 1981. Categories and concepts, Harvard University Press, Cambridge, MA.

Smith, E.E., Patalano, A.L., Jonides, J., Koeppe, R.A. (Submitted). Pet evidence for two kinds of categorization.

Smith, E.E., Shoben, E.J., Rips, L.J., 1974. Structure and process in semantic memory: a featural model for semantic decisions. Psychological Review 81 (3), 214–241.

Smith, E.E., Sloman, S.A., 1994. Similarity- versus rule-based categorization. Memory and Cognition 22 (4), 377–386.

Smith, J.D., Kemler, D.G., 1984. Overall similarity in adults' classification: the child in all of us. Journal of Experimental Psychology: General 113 (1), 137–159.

Smith, J.D., Shapiro, J.H., 1989. The occurrence of holistic categorization. Journal of Memory and Language 28 (4), 386–399.

Squire, L.R., 1992. Memory and the hippocampus: a synthesis from findings with rats, monkeys, and humans. Psychological Review 99 (2), 195–231.

Squire, L.R., Knowlton, B.J., 1995. Learning about categories in the absence of memory . Proceedings of the National Academy of Science, USA 92, 12470–12474.

Ullman, M., Corkin, S., Coppola, M., Hickok, G., Growdon, J.H., Koroshetz, W.J., Pinker, S., 1997. A neural dissociation within language: evidence that the mental dictionary is part of declarative memory, and that grammatical rules are processed by the procedural system. Journal of Cognitive Neuroscience 9, 266–276.

Warrington, E.K., Shallice, T., 1984. Category specific semantic impairments. Brain 107, 829–853.

5

Similarity and rules: distinct? exhaustive? empirically distinguishable?

Ulrike Hahn*, Nick Chater

Department of Psychology, University of Warwick, Coventry CV4 7AL, UK

Abstract

The distinction between rule-based and similarity-based processes in cognition is of funda-mental importance for cognitive science, and has been the focus of a large body of empirical research. However, intuitive uses of the distinction are subject to theoretical difficulties and their relation to empirical evidence is not clear. We propose a 'core' distinction between rule- and similarity-based processes, in terms of the way representations of stored information are 'matched' with the representation of a novel item. This explication captures the intuitively clear-cut cases of processes of each type, and resolves apparent problems with the rule/ similarity distinction. Moreover, it provides a clear target for assessing the psychological and AI literatures. We show that many lines of psychological evidence are less conclusive than sometimes assumed, but suggest that converging lines of evidence may be persuasive. We then argue that the AI literature suggests that approaches which combine rules and similarity are an important new focus for empirical work. © 1998 Elsevier Science B.V.

Keywords: Similarity-based process; Rule-based process

1. Introduction

The contrast between rule- and similarity-based accounts of cognition is central to cognitive science. The two approaches correspond to different research traditions, and the contrast between them is the focus of vigorous empirical and theoretical debate across a wide range of cognitive domains.

The idea that cognition involves following mental *rules* lies at the heart of the classical picture of the cognitive system (Newell and Simon, 1990). Mental rules encode general facts about the world and these facts are applied to specific instances

* Corresponding author. e-mail: u.hahn@warwick.ac.uk

in cognitive activity. A paradigm example is language: linguistics aims to specify rules which explicate the structure of language, and it is assumed that these rules are mentally represented and applied in language processing. The same pattern is assumed to hold in knowledge of naive physics (Hayes, 1979), arithmetic (Young and O'Shea, 1981), social conventions (Cheng and Holyoak, 1985), and so on. In all these cases, knowledge is stored in collections of rules, which are organized into *theories*. These are assumed to have the same structure as explicitly-described theories in science: collections of general statements from which predictions and explanations for specific aspects of the everyday world can be constructed. The emphasis on rules is embodied in many formalisms used in psychological modeling, most directly in systems based on production rules (Newell and Simon, 1972; Anderson, 1983; Newell, 1991) or on logical inference (Inhelder and Piaget, 1958; Braine, 1978; Rips, 1994). It is also embodied in much practical artificial intelligence research (within what Haugeland calls GOFAI – good old fashioned AI (Haugeland, 1985)) ranging from early game-playing programs (Newell, 1963) to expert systems (Dayal et al., 1993).

Similarity, in conjunction with sets of stored instances, suggests an alternative model of cognition. Instead of deriving general rules concerning the structure of the world, past situations ('instances' in psychology; 'cases' in AI) are stored in a relatively unprocessed form. Reasoning concerning a new situation depends on its similarity to one or more past situations. Here, we shall call such methods similarity-based reasoning, to emphasise the centrality of similarity. Such theories have been proposed in many contexts: in exemplar theories of concepts (Medin and Schaffer, 1978; Nosofsky, 1984), in instance-based models of implicit learning (Berry and Broadbent, 1984, 1988; Vokey and Brooks, 1992; Redington and Chater, 1996), in theories of reasoning (Ross, 1984, 1987; Ross and Kennedy, 1990), in 'case-based reasoning' in AI (Kolodner, 1991; Aamodt and Plaza, 1994), and 'lazy learning' (Aha, 1997) in machine learning. Moreover, similarity-based approaches to cognition are strongly rooted in behaviorist theories of human learning. The fundamental behaviorist claim is that behavior is mediated by a set of stimulus-response associations. As no stimulus is exactly the same as any previously-encountered stimulus, behavior must depend on some form of *generalization*, depending on the similarity between the new stimulus and previous stimuli. Thus, similarity has been stressed by behaviorists in psychology (Pavlov, 1927) and philosophy (Quine, 1960), as well as being important in cognitive science.

The difference between rule- and similarity-based accounts is clearly of central theoretical importance to cognitive science, but can they be distinguished empirically? There have been many attempts to do so in areas of cognitive psychology as diverse as categorization (Komatsu, 1992), implicit learning (Reber, 1989; Shanks and John, 1994), problem-solving (Gentner, 1989) and the development of reading skills (Goswami and Bryant, 1990). Our own research has concentrated on empirically distinguishing specific rule-based accounts from similarity-based (and other) accounts in the context of language and implicit learning (Redington and Chater, 1994, 1996; Nakisa and Hahn, 1996; Hahn et al., 1997; Nakisa et al., 1998).

However, the interpretation of the empirical evidence is difficult, because both classes of account are very heterogeneous, and hence each can capture a wide range of data. Possibly, these two classes are too broad to really allow an overall empirical assessment. Perhaps, the best empirical research can do is to test particular models of each kind, not 'rules' or 'similarity' generally. Furthermore, the empirical literature contains many confusingly correlated distinctions such as symbolic versus subsymbolic, abstract versus specific or deductive versus inductive. The resulting problems of interpretation which we have encountered in our own work have acted as a personal motivation for developing the ideas in this paper: specifically, to provide a core conceptual distinction between rule- and similarity-based models as a framework for interpreting empirical and computational considerations.

One reaction to the difficulties encountered in distinguishing between such broad classes of account is simply to abandon the attempt. However, we believe that this is at best a last resort: there are strong reasons to attempt to maintain the rule- versus similarity-based distinction. If viable, it allows general theoretical statements to be made about broad classes of account, which are not tied to specific models or implementations. This is important for relating different theoretical proposals, and for unifying what must otherwise remain fractionated literatures on different cognitive domains. Moreover, the viability of a general distinction has been routinely presupposed by the empirical literature, wherever the terms 'rule-' or 'similarity-based' are used without further clarification, such as in the many experimental studies which seek to distinguish rule- and similarity-based reasoning on the basis of their putative effects, without further commitment to more specific models (e.g. Reber, 1989; Shanks, 1995). The issue of whether a general distinction can be maintained is therefore clearly a pressing one. This paper has three main sections. In Section 2, we show how both classes of account appear so general that they seem to collapse into each other. Section 3 provides a core account which successfully separates rule- and similarity-based processes. We show that this core account correctly decides intuitively clear cases of each type more adequately than a range of alternative criteria that might be suggested. In Section 4, we re-assess how empirical and computational evidence can be brought to bear on distinguishing between the two classes of model and, finally, consider implications for future research.

2. Rules and similarity: the problem

The intuitive notions of both rule- and similarity-based processes seem alarmingly general[1]. Almost any aspect of thought may be viewed as determined by

---

[1]Moreover, the very notions of 'rule' and 'similarity' have been attacked in the philosophical literature (Goodman, 1972; Kripke, 1982). However, these problems are so general that they threaten the entire program of cognitive science, rather than providing specific difficulties for the present debate (Hahn, 1996; Hahn and Chater, 1997).

rules, at least in the sense that laws of nature are rules of a kind; and similarity seems an essential ingredient of an extremely wide range of paradigms and phenomena – connectionism, case-based reasoning, exemplar- and prototype-theories, and possibly even metaphor and analogy.

The threat that follows from the generality of both 'rule' and 'similarity' can be illustrated by the apparent possibility of each account 'mimicking' the other.

First, as suggested by Nosofsky et al. (1989), 'rule' can be used to include procedures for computing similarity as special cases. Indeed, specific theories of similarity, such as geometric models (Shepard, 1980) or the contrast model (Tversky, 1977) appear to provide suggestions about what this rule might be.

Second, 'similarity' appears so general that it can include any rule. Suppose we view a rule, R, as a function from inputs to outputs. Define a dissimilarity measure, D, such that

$$D(x, y) = 0 \text{ iff } R(x) = R(y)$$

$$D(x, y) = 1 \text{ otherwise}$$

That is, two inputs are similar when the rule gives the same output for both and dissimilar otherwise.

Therefore, similarity-based reasoning might be viewed as involving a kind of rule; and rule-based reasoning might be viewed as involving a kind of similarity. The notions seem so general that they collapse into each other.

The artificiality of this 'mimicry argument' may lead one to underestimate the extent of the problem. However, more realistic variants abound. Allen and Brooks (1991) discuss 'additive rules of thumb' of the form '*At least two of* (*long legs, angular body, spots*) *then* **builder**.' These rules, however, are equivalent to a special case of a psychological prototype model (Smith and Medin, 1981) – where the prototype is defined by *n* features, of which *m* must be present – which seemingly involves similarity comparison of the new item with the prototype. Moreover, the same behavior can be obtained from a single-layer connectionist network with a linear threshold unit. Therefore, identical behavior appears consistent with rules and similarity, as well as with connectionist networks.

Connectionist networks themselves further illustrate the problem, in that they might be seen to fall in both camps. Back-propagation networks are often described as depending on similarity (Rumelhart and Todd, 1993). However, they are also often described as using 'implicit rules' which can be extracted using appropriate analysis (Bates and Elman, 1993; Hadley, 1993; Andrews et al., 1995; Davies, 1995). Therefore, back-propagation networks appear rule- *and* similarity-based.

These concerns suggest that the intuitively sharp distinction between rule- and similarity-based processing may be illusory. If this conclusion is accepted, then the empirical debate aimed at testing between the two is futile. We will argue that this pessimistic conclusion is not justified, that a core distinction can be made, and that empirical evidence, both from experimental and computational sources, can be brought to bear on whether specific cognitive processes are similarity-based, rule-based, or neither.

3. Rules versus similarity: an explication

An explication of the core distinction between rules and similarity must balance two forces. It must be sufficiently specific that it solves the problems of generality that we have outlined. However, it must also be sufficiently general to take in the great diversity within each type of account. Thus, rule-based processes may invoke symbolic statements with logical connectives, with or without explicit variables (as in classical AI, or some parts of the psychology literature (Nosofsky et al., 1989; Sloman, 1996)); they may operate over banks of connectionist units (Touretzky and Hinton, 1988) or have the form of the additive rules of thumb (Allen and Brooks, 1991) mentioned above. Equally, similarity-based models range from case-based reasoning (CBR) systems in AI, where similarity is assessed between graph structures (Branting, 1991), to spatial and set-theroretic models in psychology where similarity is defined in terms of spatial distance or feature overlap, respectively (Shepard, 1957; Tversky, 1977).

One approach to constructing a core distinction proposes that the two classes can be distinguished because they use *different types of representation*. Perhaps rules contain variables but things entering into similarity comparisons do not; or rules are *general* whereas similarity-based reasoning applies to specific claims (e.g. describing specific instances)[2]; or rules are rigid, whereas representations used in similarity comparison are in some sense fuzzy. Whether explicitly or implicitly, such criteria underlie many definitions of rule-following in cognitive science (e.g. Sloman, 1996).

This focus on different types of representation is undermined by the fact that the *very same representation* can be used both in rule- and similarity-based processing. Consider a representation of the information that monkeys like bananas. This can be used as a rule, on encountering a particular monkey, and classifying it as liking bananas. However, it can also be used in similarity-based reasoning in proposing the generalization that gorillas also like bananas. The core distinction cannot simply be based on different *types* of representation; rather, it must involve the way in which representations are *used*.

To clarify, let us consider a specific scenario. Suppose that we are presented with a new item, which is represented by the features {*large, barks, brown, furry, has-teeth...* }. To classify this item, we must somehow relate its representation to our existing knowledge. Rule- and similarity-based processes differ regarding the way the representation of the new item is integrated with existing knowledge.

A paradigmatic case of rule-based processing runs as follows. Existing knowledge is stored in conditional rules (e.g. 'if something barks and is furry, then it is a dog'). If the antecedent of a rule is satisfied (it barks and is furry), then the category in the consequent applies (it is a dog). A paradigm case of similarity-based processing is as

[2]From a logical point of view, a natural fromulation of this type of claim is that rules involve *universal* quantification, whereas similarity is defined over instances which are represented by *existential* quantification. Aside from the difficulty pointed out below, this approach collapses because of the purely logical result that any representation involving existential quantification can be converted into a sentence involving universal quantification, and vice versa, by applying negation.

follows. Knowledge is stored as a set of past instances, with associated category labels. The new item is classified as a dog if the past instance to which it is most similar was classified as a dog. In both paradigms, there is a 'match' between the representation of the new item and a representation of stored knowledge. Crucially, however, the nature of the matching process differs in two ways.

First, the antecedent of the rule must be *strictly* matched, whereas in the similarity comparison matching may be *partial*. In strict matching, the condition of the rule is either satisfied or not – no intermediate value is allowed. Partial matching, in contrast, is a matter of degree – correspondence between representations of novel and stored items can be greater or less. Notice that there is no restriction on the nature of the representation that is matched, whether strictly or partially. Our example is implicitly a conjunction (the item must be furry *and* a dog for the rule to be satisfied), but the condition of a rule could equally well be disjunction (furry *or* a dog), or have any form whatever.

Second, the rule matches a representation of an instance (large, barks, brown, furry, has-teeth...) with a *more abstract representation* of the antecedent of the rule (barks, furry), whereas the similarity paradigm matches *equally specific* representations of new and past items. The antecedent 'abstracts away' from the details of the particular instance, focusing on a few key properties.

Note, crucially, that abstraction here is *relative*, not absolute. Thus, a similarity-based process could operate over highly abstract representations, such as logical forms of sentences. Rule-based processes can apply to arbitrarily specific representations (e.g. specifying minute detail about the perceptual properties of the objects it applies to) if the representations of new objects are even more detailed. Thus evidence for highly abstract mental representations is not thereby evidence for rule-based processing; and evidence for highly specific mental representations is not evidence for similarity-based processing. This point will be important in our reevaluation of empirical criteria for distinguishing between rule- and similarity-based processes below.

The need for relative abstraction stems from its link with generalization. If the antecedent of a rule were as specific as the representation of the instance, then it would apply to at most this single instance and thus provide no basis for generalizing our knowledge about one case to another. Indeed. a system containing rules of this form is simply a 'memory bank' of instances and their classifications.

Thus our paradigm cases differ along two dimensions, defining a space of possibilities illustrated in Fig. 1.

This space provides a useful framework for differentiating 'rules' and 'similarity' because it allows us to think generally about the different ways in which stored knowledge can be applied to enable the processing of novel items. The paradigm case of processing corresponds to the top right corners 'strict matching/abstraction.' The paradigm case of similarity-based reasoning corresponds to the bottom left corner, 'partial matching/no-abstraction.' Note that these locations are sufficiently general to be compatible with the diverse array of specific instantiations of 'rule' and 'similarity' mentioned at the beginning of this section: strict matching to an abstraction is not a notion which refers to particular rule formats, nor does partial matching

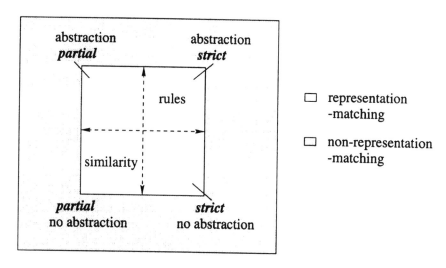

Fig. 1. The space of possibilities for representation matching.

to an instance distinguish between the matching of graph structures, feature overlap or occupying a nearby point in similarity space.

The bottom right corner, 'strict-matching/no-abstraction' corresponds to the 'memory bank.' What about the final corner, at the top left, combining partiality and matching to an abstraction? A candidate for this class are versions of prototype theory, which relax the classic definitional account: i.e. prototypes are construed as lists of core features (hence abstraction) of which only sufficiently many, but not all, must be matched by a new instances (see Komatsu, 1992), thus replacing strict with partial matching. This raises the possibility, which we discuss below, that similarity may encroach into this corner of the space.

Outside the space entirely are processes which do not involve matching the novel instance to stored representations of any kind and, hence, are alternatives to both rule- and similarity-based accounts. For example, generalization might be based on simple failure to discriminate different perceptual stimuli, rather than on stored knowledge. More interestingly, an input-output mapping might be performed without consulting *any* stored representations.

3.1. Why representations matter

We have explained rule- and similarity-based processing in terms of matching between *representations*: of the new item and of stored knowledge. Crucially, it is not sufficient for a process to behave 'as if' it were matching representations. We now illustrate why this is so, considering rules and similarity in turn.

Regarding rules, the issue is the vital distinction between *rule following* and merely *rule describable* behavior (Chomsky, 1980, 1986; Searle, 1980; Dreyfus, 1992; Smith et al., 1992; Marcus et al., 1995). Rule-based reasoning implies *rule-following*: that a *representation* of a rule causally affects the behavior of the system, and is not merely an apt summary description[3]. Thus, only claims about rule-following are claims about *cognitive architecture*. To illustrate with the classic example, the planets exhibit rule-describable behavior, concisely predicted by Newton's laws, but the planets do not rely on mental representations of Newton's laws to determine their orbits; thus, they are not rule-following. By contrast, explaining why a motorist obeys traffic regulations makes reference to mental states, i.e. knowledge of these regulations. Hence, the behavior in question exhibits rule-following. As *any* regularity can be stated in a format which fulfils our intuitions about 'rule', (e.g. as a universally quantified statement) *any* regular behavior would be 'rule-based' if the distinction between rule-following and merely rule-describable were not maintained; the notion of rule-based processing would collapse into triviality.

Analogous considerations apply to similarity. Unless similarity-based models involve comparison between representations, then *any generalization* (rule-based, similarity-based or even non-representational) can be viewed as similarity-based in the sense that items to which generalization applies can, by virtue of this fact, be viewed as 'similar.' However, such post hoc measures of similarity have no explanatory value. If the constraint of representation-matching is relaxed, the splashes of similar rocks thrown into water could be viewed as similarity-based processing on part of the water, given that they cause similar splashes.

For the rule versus similarity debate to be meaningful, matching must apply to actual representations of rules and instances. Consequently, non-representational approaches to cognition, such as situated robotics (Brooks, 1991), stand outside this debate altogether. Furthermore, *mere procedures* cannot constitute rule-based reasoning. Some confusion over this exists with respect to inference rules in cognition, such as *modus ponens*. Smith et al. (1992), for instance, distinguish rule-following and -describable behavior (they call the latter 'conforming' to a rule) and state that they are only concerned with the former (p. 3). When it comes to inference rules, however, they credit a system with rule following, albeit of 'implicit rules', even if a rule is 'only implemented in the hardware and is essentially a description of how some built in processor works' (p. 34). However, for modus ponens to be *followed*, it is not sufficient for modus ponens to be 'built in' to the procedures by which the system operates. Such a proceduralized notion of modus ponens is found in production rule systems. Production rules 'fire' when their antecedent is satisfied and produce a consequent; however, there is no *representation* of modus ponens. In the rule-following sense, modus ponens *itself* is not a rule in a production rule system, any more than the planets implement Newtonian mechanics. If a proceduralized notion of rule and rule-following is allowed, then the distinction between rule-following and rule-describable behavior is lost again, with the consequences outlined above. As elsewhere, the central question of whether human thought can be described by logical rules or norms must be carefully distinguished from the issue of how such inference is realized in the cognitive system.

---

[3]This also means that the philosophical debate on rule-following is of direct relevance here (Kripke, 1982; McDowell, 1984; Collins, 1992; Ginet, 1992).

Finally, these considerations also allow us to clarify the nature of standard back-propagation networks, which, we noted above, are claimed both as rule- and similarity-based. On our analysis these networks neither compute similarity nor apply rules, because they do not involve matching to a stored representation of any kind. What representations could be held to be 'matched' with the input pattern? Past inputs are not stored, so that instance-based comparison seems ruled out. The only candidate appears to be weight vectors, but these are not *matched*, i.e. brought into correspondence with, the input at all. Instead, activation flows through the network as a complex non-linear function of inputs and weights[4].

That the network's behavior can be *described* with rules and that the regularities it uses may be 'extracted' (Andrews et al., 1995) is not to say that the network itself is following rules. Likewise. it is true that networks to some extent *depend* on similarity (Rumelhart and Todd, 1993); similar inputs will tend to produce similar outputs. This, however, is a causal story, due to similarity between inputs in the sense of 'overlap of input representations' and, thus, similar activation flow through the network. It is not due to the fact that similarity is being computed, any more than similar rocks producing similar splashes results from computation of similarity.

In summary, for the debate between rule- and similarity-based accounts to be meaningful, matching must apply to *representations* of rules or instances. Thus important classes of cognitive architecture in which no matching to representations takes place stand outside the rule- versus similarity-based processing debate entirely.

3.2. Exploring representation matching: are rules and similarity exhaustive?

We have outlined a core account of the distinction between rule- and similarity-based processing. We now consider some ways in which these notions may be made more specific, and also whether there are other styles of processing, distinct from rule- or similarity-based processing within the representation matching framework. Leaving aside the 'memory bank' which does not generalize to novel items at all, we consider each of the three non-trivial regions of our space – indicated in Fig. 2 – in turn probing the exhaustiveness of 'rule' and 'similarity'. This analysis also shows why our core distinction does not succumb to the mimicry arguments, which appear to collapse rule- and similarity-based processing.

---

[4]The *inner product* between the input- and the first layer of weights can viewed as a measure of similarity (Jordan, 1986), but only if input vectors are of standard length. If not, our basic intuitions on similarity (Section 3.2.1.) are violated: (1) similarity is not maximal in the case of identity, (2) input vectors – viewed as points in a multi-dimensional input 'feature'-space – which are more distant, i.e. have fewer properties overlapping with the weight vector, can have larger inner products than nearby input vectors due to the effects of length. While normalization is used in some connectionist architectu es such as self-organizing networks (Rumelhart and Zipser, 1985) – and here it may be useful to think of the weight vector is representing a prototypical instance in input space – it is generally not true for back-propagation networks. Even less can we see weight vectors representing rules, and mere procedures, on our account. do not suffice.

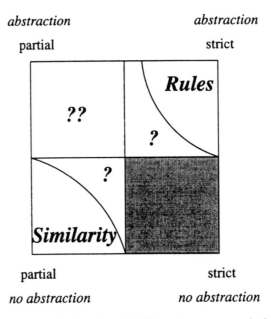

abstraction   *abstraction*

partial   strict

partial   strict

no abstraction   *no abstraction*

Fig. 2. How far do rules and similarity exhaust representation?

3.2.1. Partial matching and no abstraction: relation to similarity

We have argued that paradigmatic similarity-based processes involve partial matching with no abstraction. However, does similarity matching have additional crucial features and hence are there other forms of matching of partial, non-abstract matching? There are many positive examples of measures of similarity, including the geometric (Shepard, 1980) and contrast (Tversky, 1977) models prominent in psychology and a host of measures in the computational literature on instance-based approaches such as case-based reasoning (CBR) (Herbig and Wess, 1992) and nearest neighbor algorithms (Cost and Salzberg, 1993) in machine learning. However, when it comes to delimiting what exactly counts as 'similarity', our underlying intuitions seem remarkably vague. Indeed, they appear to be exhausted by the following criteria:

1. similarity is some function of common properties[5]
2. similarity is graded
3. similarity is maximal for identity

Thus, any function from common properties to a value on a multi-value scale, which is maximal for identity, will fit the bill.

This is vague, but specific enough to defeat one half of the mimicry argument,

---

[5]Where 'property' covers binary attributes, continuous valued dimensions and relations.

because our function D is ruled out: 'common properties' degenerate to one; the function is not graded; nor is it really 'maximal for identity' because, although it returns the maximal value for identical instances, it also returns this value for any other instance which is an instance of the rule.

Are there other types of partial matching with no abstraction, which are not based on similarity? Possible alternatives arise from considering other information which might be included in the matching process in addition to 'common properties'. Information such as frequency or recency might usefully be used in a function performing partial matching, but these do not seem to be aspects of similarity. Hence, it seem that a whole range of 'hybrid' functions is conceivable. Furthermore, to the extent that our vague intuitions (Goodman, 1972; Goldstone, 1994a) about similarity are made more specific, going beyond 'partial matching without abstraction' this automatically means that matching functions in the bottom left corner which do not meet these criteria will not be similarity functions. So it seems that, whatever theory of similarity is ultimately adopted, there will be other types of 'partial matching without abstraction' not classified as involving similarity.

3.2.2. Strict matching with abstraction: relation to rules

Rule-application, we have argued, is a matter of strict matching to knowledge which is more abstract than the new item to be matched. By definition, this means that the set of objects consistent with the representation of the new instance is a proper subset of the set of objects consistent with the antecedent of a rule.

How do we know that the stored information is more abstractly represented than the new item? In some representation languages, different 'types' of representation reflect different levels of abstraction. Many representation schemes make no such overt distinctions, however. Indeed, natural language makes no surface syntactic distinction between the statements: 'the dinosaur is extinct' from 'the dinosaur is in the museum.' Yet the former can be used as a general rule when classifying newly-encountered animals, whereas the latter describes a specific event and cannot be applied to new instances of any kind.

In considering different representational schemes, from natural language state-ments to templates with slots and fillers, semantic networks and production rules, two ways emerge in which the general idea of abstraction is manifest. First, a representation can be more abstract than another by 'underspecification': the more abstract representation simply specifies fewer constraints. This is exemplified, for instance, by the use of variables in production system rules (Anderson, 1983), or unification of feature structures in computational linguistics (Shieber, 1986). It is also present in our 'dog-rule', above, where only 'furriness' and 'barking' matter, and other properties are irrelevant. The second way in which a representation can display greater abstraction is through the use of 'general terms.' This implies a hierarchy of terms (e.g. dog, mammal, animal). A description is more abstract if it contains predicates of which the predicates of the less abstract description are proper subsets. This relationship would hold between our 'dog-rule' and instance descriptions phrased in terms of 'short-fur', 'long-fur' etc. The example also illustrates that underspecification and general terms can be, and frequently are, combined[6].

Therefore, there are many ways in which an internal representation might be more abstract than the instance-representation with which it is matched, but what type of internal representation counts as a rule? Artificial intelligence and cognitive psychology offer a wide range of models for internal representation, from declarative statements in Prolog, through semantic networks, property list, feature vectors to symbolic systems implemented in connectionist hardware. Which of these constitute 'rules'? Must these be propositional or expressed in a language, possibly encompassing symbols and logical connectives? Adopting any such further constraints on the notion of rule restricts the scope of the notion within the top right corner of the space (Fig. 2), making rule-based reasoning non-exhaustive even of strict matching to an abstraction.

Again, however, even the core notion successfully deals with the second half of the mimicry argument, i.e. that similarity comparison is rule-based because any similarity metric can be specified as a rule. First, it is an empirical question whether the similarity metric is in fact *represented* as a rule in specific cognitive processes. although computational systems can contain an explicit representation of their similarity metric, this metric can equally be proceduralized, just as modus ponens can (see e.g. Kruschke's (1992) implementation of Nosofsky's (1988) generalized context model). If the similarity metric *is* explicitly represented, the similarity comparison, strictly speaking, does involve rule-application (of the metric). However, the rule the system is applying is then so general that it is neither an interesting nor useful claim to say that the system is 'rule-based.' In particular, this claim is not the one that cognitive science is concerned with, because it concerns how the matching process itself is implemented, not the crucial issue of what type of representation-matching is used.

How does the core distinction deal with more realistic examples of mimicry? Let us reconsider Allen and Brook's 'additive rule' prototype models and the equivalent connectionist network. Allen and Brook's 'additive rule' *is* a rule, according to the core distinction, because it requires strict matching of its antecedent (i.e. it applies just when at least the specified number of criteria are fulfilled). However, comparison with a prototype involves similarity (assuming that similarity is well-defined between prototypes and exemplars – see below) and hence this model is similarity-based. Although the two processes produce identical results, they involve different kinds of matching to different representations (a declarative specification that m of n features must be fulfilled vs. a prototype). Finally, the equivalent single-layer connectionist network does not involve any kind of matching to stored knowledge and hence it is neither rule- nor similarity-based. Thus, the core distinction preserves the

---

[6]Our notion of abstraction requires *some* loss of information relative to a corresponding specific representation. Hence, we reject the notion of 'ideal abstraction' whcih retains all information (Barsalou, 1990). In fact, information loss is present even in Barsalou's examples where the abstractions contain all the properties of the exemplars but 'centralized'; the centralized, 'abstract', representation no longer contains sufficient information to reconstruct the particular exemplars. As noted, an 'absraction' which retained *all* information about a set of instances could not be used in generalization.

intuitive sense that the three models achieve the same result in very different ways.

The fact that rule- and similarity-based processes can produce equivalent classifications may seem to undermine the empirical testability and even the theoretical importance of the distinction. It is important to stress, however, that these processes do differ in a wide variety of cognitively important 'secondary properties' e.g. in the learning procedures required for acquisition, ease with which modification can be affected, or behavior under noise (see also Hahn, 1996) Thus, the rule/similarity distinction is important for cognitive science, although not always for primary input-output behavior.

In summary, the conclusions on the scope of rules parallel those on similarity. On the one hand, new ways of achieving 'strict matching to an abstraction' may emerge; on the other hand, the notion of rule might be tightened up by adopting further constraints. Consequently, it seems unlikely that 'rules' will ultimately exhaust the space of strict matching with abstraction.

3.2.3. Partial matching to an abstraction

This leaves the 'top-left corner': partial matching to an abstraction. Rules do not seem to spill over into this corner; neither legal rules, physical laws, universally quantified formulae in first order logic, probabilistic rules, nor defeasible rules allow partial matching. However, similarity might extend into this corner, specifically in those versions of prototype theory in which the prototype is an abstraction of typical or core properties that, as neither necessary nor sufficient, need be matched only partially.

Can such partial matching to an abstraction count as a similarity comparison? Current theories of similarity differ on this issue. Tversky's contrast model, for example, allows similarity comparison between *any* two featural representations, even an item and its category.

Geometric models of similarity do *not* allow comparison between an instance and something that is an abstraction relative to this instance; instances are points in similarity space, but abstractions over instances are regions therein, and the notion of 'distance' (and thus, similarity) between a point and a region is not defined. Thus it depends on the choice of similarity theory whether similarity-based processing extends to partial matching with an abstraction. It is not the purpose of this paper to decide such issues and the task of empirically distinguishing rules and similarity can be investigated without legislating terminology on this point. In evaluating empirical evidence for rules or similarity, the existence of this part of the representation-matching space must be born in mind. What it is called is of secondary importance, last but not least, because, here too, it is unlikely that similarity would ultimately exhaust partial matching to an abstraction, even where a theory of similarity allows such matching.

Raised by these issues is the general relationship between similarity- and instance-based reasoning. However, regardless of how the case of partial matching to an abstraction is decided, 'similarity-based' is wider than 'instance-based' if (as is generally the case in psychology (Medin and Schaffer, 1978; Nosofsky, 1988)) 'instance' refers only to actually-encountered exemplars. Alternative notions of prototype such as the central tendency or a modal exemplar (Posner and Keele, 1970; Rosch et al., 1976; Komatsu, 1992; Nosofsky, 1992) are straightforward cases of partial matching between representations of the same level of abstraction and thus constitute similarity-based processing for all similarity theories.

3.3. What the distinction is not

We now examine other criteria that might be viewed as relevant to the distinction between rules and similarity. In contrast to our core distinction, these potential alternatives, although relevant and important in their own right, turn out to cross-classify rules and similarity or, at best, to partially correlate with one or the other.

3.3.1. Types of computational architecture
Similarity-based methods are sometimes associated with highly parallel, distributed computational architectures. Rule-based processes, by contrast, are sometimes associated with serial, symbolic computation.

3.3.1.1. Serial versus parallel. The serial-parallel distinction does not distinguish between similarity- and rule-based approaches. Production rule systems, which are paradigm rule-based systems, have both serial and parallel implementations. On the side of similarity, most CBR systems, paradigmatic similarity-based approaches, have serial implementations, although (partially or completely) parallel implementations are possible e.g. Myllymäki and Tirri, 1993; Brown and Filer, 1995.

3.3.1.2. Symbolic versus connectionist. The border between rule- and similarity-based processes also fails to coincide with the distinction between symbolic and connectionist computation. First, 'symbolic' does not equate to 'rule': similarity-based systems such as CBR systems (Aamodt and Plaza, 1994) and nearest neighbor algorithms in machine learning (Aha et al., 1991; Cost and Salzberg, 1993) are typically symbolic. Second, 'connectionist' does not equate to similarity – indeed, we have seen that the most widely used connectionist networks, back-propagation networks, are neither rule- nor similarity-based.

3.3.2. Structured versus non-structured representations
In psychology, similarity-based methods frequently apply to simple representations, such as vectors of binary feature-values (in Tversky's contrast model) or numerical values (in geometric models), whereas rule-based models typically use structured representations, involving arbitrarily complex symbolic expressions. This distinction, however, is also orthogonal to the division between rule- and similarity-based reasoning. Similarity can be defined over structured representations (Gentner and Markman, 1994; Goldstone, 1994b; Hahn and Chater, 1997) – frequently, this similarity relation is called *analogy*, because structural similarities are of central importance (Gentner, 1983; Gentner and Forbus, 1991). Conversely, rule-based

accounts may be sufficiently simple that structured representations are not required (as in most statistical contexts).

3.3.3. Abstract versus concrete representations

In psychology, similarity-based models are often applied to very concrete, typically perceptual, representations of simple stimuli, such as schematic faces or geometric shapes (Reed, 1972; Nosofsky, 1988). More abstract domains, involving reasoning about social interactions (Cosmides, 1989), norms of behavior (Cheng and Holyoak, 1985) or naive physics (Hayes, 1979) are often viewed as involving general rules. We have seen, however, that the rule/similarity distinction does not relate to absolute level of abstraction. Similarity can operate in highly abstract domains (e.g. using analogy in mathematical or scientific reasoning (Gentner, 1989) or case-based reasoning in law (Ashley, 1990; Aamodt and Plaza, 1994)); and rules may be used to process highly specific representations (as, for example, in 'blackboard' models of perception (Selfridge, 1959)). Crucially, we saw that the same representation in stored knowledge can serve either as a rule or an instance in a similarity comparison, depending on the nature of the matching process with new items.

Thus, psychological evidence concerning the level of abstraction of representations does not thereby provide evidence concerning whether cognitive processes are rule- or similarity-based. We shall see the implications of this in discussing attempts to empirically distinguish the two styles of processing below.[7]

3.3.4. Rigidity and gradedness of classification

The issue of rigid versus graded classification may appear to map on to the distinction between strict versus partial matching. Strict versus partial matching, however, concerns how a new *input* is related to existing knowledge; it does not relate to the gradedness of an *output* such as a classification decision. These two issues are distinct, although connected. Specifically, if we assume that the output is a function of the input, then a strict match to an input implies a rigid output: thus rule-based processes produce rigid, all-or-none classifications. However, a partial match to the input is compatible with both a graded and a rigid output, depending on whether information about degree of match is preserved. Degree of match could be used, for instance, to establish graded category memberships. However, other similarity-based classifiers produce yes/no decisions by using a threshold, or competition between instances. For example, the strict nearest neighbor criterion, the paradigm of similarity-based models, bases the decision on the single most similar known item. Thus, the core distinction is related to, but different from, the distinction between processes producing rigid versus graded classifications.

3.3.5. Deductive versus non-deductive reasoning

The distinction between rule- versus similarity-based reasoning also does not map onto the distinction between deductive (certain) and non-deductive inference. While

[7]Evidence concerning abstraction can, of course, be crucially important in distinguishing between specific theories – either kind, which postulate particular levels of representation.

it is true that similarity-based reasoning is never certain, and, hence, always non-deductive, we find deductive reasoning which is not rule-based and rule-based reasoning which is non-deductive.

Probabilistic rules, as well as the non-monotonic or defeasible inference (see e.g. Ginsberg, 1987) necessary to capture how we actually reason with rules such as 'birds fly,' in the face of countless exceptions such as penguins, broken wings and so on, are not deductive (at least in psychological parlance, see Johnson-Laird and Byrne, 1991; Chater and Oaksford, 1996).

We can also find deductive reasoning which is not rule-based, however. '*Or*-introduction,' for instance, allows the inference from $P(a)$ to $P(a)$ or $Q(a)$. Similarly, we can infer from $P(a)$ that $Exists(x)P(x)$. In either case, such an inference constitutes a case of rule-base reasoning only if the 'inference rule' ('or-introduction') itself is explicitly represented and applied (see Section 3.1.), rather than implemented procedurally.

3.4. Summary

We have explicated the 'core' distinction between rule- and similarity-based processing and argued that this explication is distinct from, and more appropriate than, a range of alternatives. We have also shown that our explication is specific enough to clarify unclear cases such as back-propagation networks, and to block the mimicry argument. Having provided this support for our analysis, we now consider its implications for the problem of distinguishing rule- and similarity-based processes empirically.

4. Re-evaluating the empirical evidence

Empirically distinguishing similarity- and rule-based psychological theories has proved to be extremely difficult. Moreover, there are at least two interpretations of the question.

- *Class distinguishability*. Can empirical data distinguish between the classes of rule-based and similarity-based theories? In other words, can we distinguish between rule- and similarity-based accounts of a task *in general*.
- *Specific distinguishability*. Given fully elaborated, *specific* similarity- and rule-based theories, can these be distinguished empirically? This last question is, of course, many questions, depending on what the specific theories are.

In the literature, doubts about class distinguishability have variously been voiced (e.g. Barsalou, 1990; Koh and Meyer, 1991), and we therefore give this issue particular attention[8]. Note that if the classes of rule- and similarity-based theories

---

[8]However, Barsalou's (1990) argument rests crucially on his notion of 'ideal abstraction', which does not involve any information loss – a notion not allowed in our framework, because information loss is constitutive of what it means to be a.n abstraction, as noted above.

cannot be empirically distinguished, we may nonetheless be able to distinguish fully elaborated, *specific* accounts, i.e. we may be restricted to comparative model fitting.

In terms of our analysis, class distinguishability requires finding empirical evidence which locates a cognitive process in relevant regions of our space of possibilities (Fig. 2) (including, recall, non-representational alternatives, as well as different kinds of matching). Where 'rule' or 'similarity' are given more specific elucidations, they correspond to yet smaller sub-spaces. Thus, empirically establishing a more specific notion also requires eliminating the remaining, rival forms of strict matching to an abstraction or partial matching to an instance. For example, where the use of the term 'rule' is restricted to internal representations which are symbolic and contain variables and logical connectives, an additional empirical case for the symbolic nature of the internal representation has to be made. Likewise, where 'similarity' is restricted to a metric of particular functional form, other forms of partial matching must be ruled out. Hence, dealing only with the broad partitions of the space entailed by our core distinction is the easiest version of the rule/similarity class distiguishability problem and we will focus on how empirical evidence relates here.

Again, the problem is that these classes of account are general, and distinguishing general accounts is difficult in any scientific context. This is because relating general accounts to empirical data requires additional auxiliary (and typically uncertain) assumptions. Indeed, in principle, any theory can be made to fit any data set (Putnam, 1974), by postulating appropriate auxiliary assumptions, requiring additional constraints on what assumptions count as plausible in order to rule out any general account.

In psychology, where any specific mental processes lead to behavior only in conjunction with many other processes which are highly complex but unknown, additional hypotheses which save a theory are particularly easy to provide (Pylyshyn, 1984). Moreover, distinguishing between the classes of rule- and similarity-based accounts of cognition is particularly difficult, because the auxiliary assumptions concern the very essence of the explanation – how instances are encoded, what the actual rule is or what similarities are perceived. This is not a problem of having a single free parameter to tie down: almost the entire predictive content of a rule-based theory depends on what exactly the rules are; almost the entire predictive content of a similarity-based theory depends on what the similarities are.

Perceived similarity depends on which properties of objects are selected as relevant, how they are weighted and what metric is used to compare the resulting representations. The number of possible rules that can be entertained is clearly vast – in principle, there are infinitely many rules which would allow perfect performance in any learning task[9]. Even allowing that this set is restricted by representational and memory limitations, the set of possible rules that an agent might entertain will in most cases still be large. This casts doubt on the possibility of directly distinguishing the classes of rule- and similarity-based theories by a single experimental measure.

[9]For example, in a category learning task, there will be infinitely many rules compatible with the finite set of data (labelled objects) – where the rules differ arbitrarily on the infinite number of unseen examples.

We now consider various suggestions concerning how the classes of theories can, despite the apparent difficulties above, be distinguished, focusing first on experimental criteria and then on computational criteria drawn from AI. Together these will also suggest a different emphasis for future research concerning rule- and similarity-based processing.

4.1. Experimental criteria

We are now in a position to survey empirical evidence which aims to distinguish similarity- and rule-based accounts across various cognitive domains. The literature contains a wealth of potential criteria; we have limited our discussion to those experimental criteria which are widely applicable, i.e. not restricted to a particular question or subject domain.[10] We group this evidence under four headings: effects of instances, effects of rules, generalization beyond the capabilities of instance-based models and patterns of breakdown.

4.1.1. Effects of instances

Similarity-based theories typically assume that new items are compared with representations of old items. If so, then some distinction between performance with genuinely new items (where generalization is required) and old items (which need only be 'looked up' in memory) may be expected.

By contrast, if all items are dealt with using a rule, there seems no reason to suppose that new and old items will be classified differently. This is because the general claim embodied in the rule must be applied to all specific instances; the rule contains no information about which items have been seen before. The ensuing criterion of 'no observable difference between old and new items' is used in many studies (Nosofsky et al., 1989; Allen and Brooks, 1991; Smith et al., 1992) and has been suggested as an 'operational definition' of rule-based performance (Herrnstein, 1990; Shanks, 1995).

4.1.1.1. Old-new recognition. Instance-based accounts, in contrast to rule-based accounts, also require that instances be remembered. Thus, they seem to predict that people should be able to distinguish old from new items, and that their pattern of old-new judgements should relate closely to their categorization performance. Relating categorization and old-new judgements in detail requires a unified psychological account of both. An example of this has been provided by Nosofsky (1988), who obtained a good account of experimental data using simple artificial stimuli. Such a unified account gives strong evidence for similarity-based processing; but failure to find such an account is not equally strong evidence against

---

[10]Thus we do not consider, e.g. arguments for rules based on linguistic analysis (Marcus et al., 1995), or those of the criteria put forth by Smith et al. (1992) which are tailored specifically to identifying rules of inference. We also omit Sloman's S-criterion (Sloman, 1996), which – stemming from a somewhat different interest – uses conflict to establish two cognitive sub-systems, because further, independent evidence is required to identify these as 'rule' or 'similarity' systems. It is only this further evidence, not the S-criterion, which directly applies to our question.

similarity-based processing: old-new discrimination might, for example, draw on a memory store separate from that used in classification. More importantly, the encoding of an instance may be sufficiently abstract that discrimination is not possible (and, of course, *some* abstraction is inevitable, otherwise no item could ever be re-recognized).

4.1.1.2. Manipulations of the instance-space. This approach is mainly used in studies using stimulus sets which pit rule- and similarity-based classification against each other. The interest lies in the classification of 'critical instances' which, although instances of the intended rule, are more similar to instances of another rule or category. Rule-based reasoning seems to suggest that the 'rule' classification should prevail, whereas similarity-based reasoning seems to suggest the opposite. However, sometimes, effects of both rules and similarity are found (Nosofsky et al., 1989; Allen and Brooks, 1991; Vokey and Brooks, 1994).

Generally, a failure to find instance effects is evidence against instance-based reasoning, at least on the experimenter's assumption of instance encoding and instance similarities, and, conversely, instance-effects can be viewed as refuting reasoning with the rules intended by the experimenter. In both cases, however, refutation of one provides only limited support for the other due to the non-exhaustiveness of rule- and similarity-based reasoning. Where instance effects fail, prototype models (both with and without abstraction, see above) must also be ruled out; they provide an important class of alternatives to rule-based accounts in this context, because 'critical instances' by their very construction are peripheral, and, hence, might be misclassified on prototype accounts as well. Where instance effects appear, simple connectionist accounts of the type we have classified as similarity-dependent but not similarity-based, in our usage, must be ruled out. Consequently, the domain most intensely studied with tasks of this kind, artificial grammar learning (see below), has seen a long series of claims and counterclaims (see Redington, 1996 for thorough discussion).

4.1.1.3. Summary. Instance-space manipulations are an effective tool, but the non-exhaustiveness of rules and similarity means that empirical evidence is more powerful in challenging than in supporting, either account. Also, specific assumptions about rules, instances and instance-similarities must be made, so that this criterion does not pertain to entire classes of account. Memory for instances seems indicative only if a 'unified account' succeeds, making it a powerful but demanding tool. Again, specific assumptions about instances and similarities are required.

4.1.2. Effects of rules

4.1.2.4. Rule priming. Throughout cognition, repetition of the same, or a similar, mental process (e.g. recognizing a word or a picture) speeds performance. Smith et al. (1992) suggest that such priming effects might provide evidence concerning the existence of internal rules. Specifically, they suggest that if priming were observed between two cognitive tasks which share the same rule, but correspond to very different instances, the rule-based view would be favored. Once we recognize that similarity-based models may be defined over abstract representations, and not merely superficial features of the stimulus, however, it is difficult to rule out the class of similarity-based models.

Langston et al. (unpublished data), for example, use conditional sentences which express either permission or obligation (see Cheng and Holyoak, 1985). They argue that performance on Wason (1968) selection task using these two rules is primed if the underlying rule-type is repeated, even though the surface form of the rules is altered. They argue that this provides evidence for permission and obligation rules. However, this important empirical result is equally consistent with the suggestion that instances of conditional sentences have abstract codes, which distinguish permission and obligation.

Another example is syntactic priming (H. Branigan et al., unpublished data), where sentence production or comprehension is primed by previous sentences which related syntactic structure. This is evidence for abstract representation of syntactic information. However, again, this information may be embodied in rules or as abstract information about the stored sentence-instances (e.g. sentences may be stored not as strings of words, but as labelled tree structures)[11]. In both examples, priming provides important evidence for a particular kind of abstract representation, rather than evidence between rules and instances.

4.1.2.5. Rule complexity. If cognition is rule-based, then the *number* of rules involved in a cognitive task may explain task difficulty (Smith et al., 1992). The number of rules depends, of course, on the specific set of rules under consideration; and difficulty (e.g. time) will also depend on how rules are implemented. In the same way, task-difficulty predictions can be obtained from specific similarity-based models (for example, reaction-time predictions from a specific model of categorization, e.g. Lamberts, 1995). However, there do not appear to be task-difficulty predictions associated with the classes of rule- and exemplar-based models. Therefore, task-complexity considerations appear to be important in testing specific rule-based accounts, but not suitable for distinguishing the rule- and similarity-based classes of account.

4.1.2.6. Verbal protocols. If people use rules, it is possible that they may express these rules, or aspects of them, in verbal protocols. Many production-rule theories of problem solving and skill-learning are based on an interactive process of building rule-based models and matching these models to verbal protocols and task performance (Newell and Simon, 1972). Equally, protocols mentioning comparison with instances (e.g. analogical reasoning) might also provide evidence for similarity-based processes. Protocol evidence is potentially very important. Crucially, its strength depends on the degree to which protocols tie up with other experimental measures, thus providing evidence that protocols are a reliable

[11]Of course, a similarity-based approach to language processing may seem implausible for other reasons.

indicator of the cognitive processes under study. Hence, production system computer models of learning a computer programming language based on protocols which provide good empirical data fits thereby provide evidence for rules (Anderson, 1983). However, there are also circumstances where independent evidence indicates that reported rules were not followed (see Nisbett and Wilson, 1977).

4.1.2.7. Summary. In short, putative effects of rules might provide useful, but not decisive tests, between the classes of rule- and similarity-based accounts. Priming effects may indicate that particular abstract information is represented, but not whether that information is represented by rules or instances. Effects of rule complexity depend on the specifics of the rule-based account and do not follow from the class of rule-based accounts. Finally, verbal protocols may be suggestive, but require evidence that protocols are reliable indicators of the underlying cognitive mechanisms under study. All three criteria require specific rules, although for protocols, these arise directly from criterion use.

4.1.3. Patterns of generalization

In favor of rules, it has been argued that several types of generalization seem inexplicable by an instance-based approach.

4.1.3.8. Extrapolation. Extrapolation in so-called 'function learning' experiments (Koh and Meyer, 1991) provides a potentially powerful source of evidence for rule-based behavior (Shanks, 1995). For example, imagine subjects learning to press a button with a duration proportional to the size of stimuli; larger stimuli requiring longer durations. Correct performance outside the range of stimuli seen so far (e.g. a very long button-press for a very large stimulus) is argued to be incompatible with an instance-based model as the response is not that of the closest previously seen instance, but a novel, i.e. longer, response. Behavior seems to depend on the application of a rule specifying the function relating stimulus height and response duration (Shanks, 1995).

Finding that people can generalize by extrapolation in this way (Koh and Meyer, 1991; Delosh, 1993) is an important empirical result and it constitutes strong evidence against similarity-based approaches. Notice, however, that it does not show that rules are being used. For example, a single-layer connectionist network, with one input and linear output unit, could trivially learn to extrapolate from increasing input to increasing output.

4.1.3.9. Transfer. A further approach considers the transfer of information learned in one domain to another. Perhaps the paradigm example is transfer in artificial grammar learning (AGL) (Reber, 1989). In AGL, subjects try to memorize a set of letter strings, without being told that they are generated according to a set of rules (typically a simple finite state grammar). They are then told about the existence of the hidden rules, but not what the rules are, and asked to discriminate new test strings which do or do not conform to these rules. Subjects perform significantly above chance in this experiment. One hypothesis is that they have implicitly extracted some of the underlying rules used to generate the items ('implicitly' because subjects typically cannot verbally report any rules they have learned). Another is that they are simply judging the similarity of new items to old, which can also lead to above chance performance. The transfer condition seeks to rule out this possibility by using a different vocabulary of letters in the memorization and discrimination phases. The idea is that the new strings are not at all similar to the memorized strings, and hence similarity cannot mediate generalization. Even here, subjects do show (typically small) above chance transfer performance (Dulaney et al., 1984; Redington and Chater, 1994).

One possible alternative to a rule-based account for this phenomenon is that instance-encoding abstracts away from the specific alphabet used in training, so that instances successfully classify transfer items. Again, we stress that evidence for abstract representations in itself is equally consistent with rule- and similarity-based processes. Abstraction in instance-encoding is perfectly possible, the question is only how much abstraction is *plausible*.

A further alternative is that abstraction occurs only when the stored instances are compared with the transfer stimuli, i.e. at transfer (e.g. Brooks and Vokey, 1991). This is tantamount to analogy and models of this kind equal or surpass human transfer performance without reference to rules (Redington and Chater, 1996). The exact relationship between similarity-based reasoning and analogy is controversial (Seifert, 1989). Thus, analogy presents either a version of similarity-based reasoning or a 'third account'.

Finally, attempts have been made to explain transfer with a connectionist network (Altmann et al., 1995) which appears to involve no matching between input and stored knowledge, and hence falls outside both rule- and similarity-based accounts. Thus, it seems that transfer effects may be explained by rule- and by similarity-based processes and by alternatives in neither framework.

4.1.3.10. Reversal. Another source of evidence comes from reversal of a learned response (Shanks, 1995). In a typical experiment, people or animals are initially trained to associate reliably two distinct responses to two sets of stimuli (Sidman and Tailby, 1982; Vaughan, 1988). Then reversal occurs: it is now the other set which demands the particular response. Subjects are trained to stable performance on the 'reversed' contingency, followed by a second reversal; and so on. After a number of such reversals, both animal and human subjects display the ability to shift almost immediately on new reversed trials, extending their behavior from these first instances to the remaining members of the class. Thus, it is claimed, members of each set are treated as an equivalence class.

This satisfies Shanks' instrumental definition of rule as 'no observable difference between performance on trained items (here, of the reversal trial) and old items' (here, the rest of the class) but it is insufficient on our account. This is because the reversal could be happening solely through a switching of responses *at the response level*. That is, subjects realize that they now have to respond the opposite way from before, e.g. 'yes' now means 'no' and vice versa, but which response to choose (and then reverse) is still determined solely through similarity comparison with past instances. On this account, subjects need only realize that 'responses have gone funny again'; they need not treat the items as belonging to equivalence classes.

4.1.3.11. Summary. The above three criteria all seek to rule out the entire class of instance-based models. The rule models they aim to support have particular rules in mind – i.e. the underlying function, the rules of the underlying grammar, rules describing the equivalence classes – but any rule which delivers the same classification for the data seen will suffice; hence, these experimental criteria can be seen as distinguishing classes of instances from classes of rules. *Transfer* appears consistent with rules, similarity and connectionist alternatives. *Reversal* appears consistent with both rules and similarity, because it can be explained by switching at the response level. More positively, however, *extrapolation* provides strong evidence against similarity-based models, although it is consistent with non-matching models such as neural networks as well as with rules.

4.1.4. Error and patterns of breakdown
    Patterns of breakdown and error provide another potentially valuable source of evidence.

4.1.4.12. Memory failure. Suppose that people learn the rule NOT-RED OR TRIANGLE in an artificial concept learning experiment. Later, they are the tested on generalization to new instances. If their memory is incorrect, they might be expected to classify according to: RED OR NOT-TRIANGLE, or NOT-RED AND TRIANGLE. By contrast, errors on a similarity-based view (based on instances) would not be expected to have this global character. Instead, individual past instances might be misremembered, leading to local misclassifications of nearby novel items. Global errors might, however, result if learning had yielded a single prototype. We are not aware that anyone has aimed to make use of this contrast, but it appears to be a potential direction for future research.

4.1.4.13. Neuropsychology. More dramatically, it is possible that neuropsychological patients may exhibit selective preservation of rules, but loss of exceptions. This appears to occur in reading, with some patients appearing to lose exceptions (surface dyslexia, McCarthy and Warrington, 1986) and others losing the 'rules' of spelling to sound correspondence (phonological dyslexia, Funnell, 1983). This 'double dissociation' has been taken as evidence for rules in reading (e.g. Shallice, 1988).
    This may be over-interpreting the data. While connectionist modeling has made us aware of the fact that a uniform connectionist architecture may not adequately capture the neuropsychological data for reading, i.e. that we might need *dual route architectures*, it has also alerted us to the fact that possibly *neither* route need contain *rules* (Bullinaria and Chater, 1995). Nonetheless this source of evidence may be difficult to account for by a similarity-based account, at least in the case of reading (but for an attempt see Glushko, 1979).

4.1.4.14. Over-regularization. Rule-based accounts of partially regular domains (such as the mapping between spelling and pronunciation or the English past-tense) divide knowledge into two components: a set of rules and a list of exceptions to those rules. Hence, over-extensions of rules might occur, where they should have been blocked by an exception (e.g. the past tense of go is given as goed). Such errors are observed in learning (Ervin, 1964) and have been taken as evidence for rules. Caution is necessary, in that exemplar models overgeneralize both irregular and regular past-tense forms in a manner which depends only on an item's location in phonological space (Hahn et al., 1997). Even where over-regularization does not seem to depend on close similarity to other regular items, connectionist models which are neither rule- nor similarity-based might behave appropriately (e.g. Rumelhart and McClelland, 1986; Plunkett and Marchman, 1991 and Seidenberg and McClelland, 1989; Bullinaria, 1994) although controversy on the (overall) adequacy of *these* models remains (Pinker and Prince, 1988; Forrester and Plunkett, 1994; Westermann and Goebel, 1994; Marcus et al., 1995; Nakisa and Hahn, 1996).

4.1.4.15. Summary. Data from neuropsychology and over-regularization may present problems for similarity-based models in specific contexts (e.g. reading or inflection). These criteria, however, do not appear to distinguish between rule-based and non-matching connectionist accounts. Evidence from 'memory failure' may provide a useful line of evidence, although this has currently not been explored empirically. All of these criteria depend on specific rules and instance-similarities, although in the case of reading and inflection these can be based on large bodies of theoretical and empirical work.

4.1.5. The strength of experimental evidence

We have seen that most experimental criteria distinguish specific, fully elaborated theories in particular domains more effectively than they decide between the entire classes of rule- and similarity-based models. In distinguishing different classes, although individually decisive empirical tests are difficult to provide, *convergence* of several criteria may be persuasive (Smith et al., 1992). Thus, testing between the classes of rule- and similarity-based processes seems possible, but may require integration of a range of sources of data.

4.2. Computational criteria

We have so far focused on experimental evidence and ignored the computational issues concerning the relative merits of rule- and similarity-based processing. Computational considerations are crucial, however, because any viable cognitive theory must be computationally viable.

Moreover, computational constraints provide a general perspective on rule and similarity which contrasts usefully with that from the experimental literature. In experiments such as those considered above, there is typically an inverse relation between experimental precision and generality of the result. Therefore, the construction of ever more specific experimental contexts and tasks runs the risk of contributing relatively little to our understanding of rules and similarity in normal cognition. This does not mean that experimental studies should be abandoned, but it does imply that we should pay close attention to general considerations concerning the *plausibility* of rule- and similarity-based models in normal thought. Computational constraints provide an important class of such general considerations.

Specifically, the debate between rule- and similarity-based processes in cognitive science can draw on the insights and generalizations derived from experience in AI and machine learning of attempting to use each approach in practical contexts. The lessons from computation have been little recognized in psychology. However, we suggest, these lessons provide a vital complementary source of evidence in evaluating the plausibility of rule- and similarity-based accounts of human cognition.

4.2.1. Are theories possible?

Where theories – collections of rules – are available, they can be remarkably effective, as evidenced by spectacular predictive and explanatory successes in many areas of science. The central challenge for a rule-based approach, however, is actually determining rules which adequately capture our common-sense knowledge of the world. The problem has proved to be very hard. It has required enormous intellectual effort even to provide adequate axioms for set theory and arithmetic[12]. Very few aspects of scientific knowledge have been more than partially formalized, and constructing theories for common-sense knowledge appears still more difficult. One problem is that common-sense knowledge does not appear to break up into separate domains. Thus, trying to provide rules for parts of knowledge seems to lead inevitably to the endless task of capturing the whole of human knowledge. This is what Fodor calls the *isotropy* of common-sense knowledge (Fodor, 1983). Another problem is that common-sense rules almost always have exceptions (Reiter, 1980), which raises enormous technical and conceptual difficulties (McDermott, 1987; Oaksford and Chater, 1991, 1993). Moreover, even given a set of rules, there remains the problem of how these rules are applied to specific instances. This too appears to depend on vast amounts of background knowledge, in ways that are not at all well-understood (Oaksford and Chater, 1991; Pickering and Chater, 1995).

For these reasons, AI has not been able to provide a feasibility proof of the claim that knowledge is represented in terms of rules by building general purpose rule-based systems. Although 'expert-systems' based on rules have been developed for highly specialized domains, e.g. DENDRAL (Feigenbaum, 1977), MYCIN (Shortliffe, 1976) or ASSESS (Dayal et al., 1993), 'scaling-up' to real world materials has not been achieved. Thus, it seems that a 'pure' rule-based approach to cognition is unlikely to be viable.

---

[12]Frege's formalization of set theory, which appeared directly to reflect basic intuitions turned out to be inconsistent; and rnoreover Gödel showed that a complete, consistent axiomatization of arithmetic is impossible (Boolos and Jeffrey, 1988). Both results suggest that formalization of human knowledge may also encounter unexpected difficulties in other domains.

4.2.2. The power of similarity-based reasoning

Reasoning by similarity to past instances can be applied even in domains which are little understood and where no theory is available, where theories are partial or there are competing theories (as in law) (Ashley, 1990; Porter et al., 1990). Additionally, re-using entire past 'problem-solutions' in domains such as problem-solving or planning, can lead to faster processing than continually reasoning from first principles (Schank, 1982; Kolodner, 1991, 1992). The ability to cope with 'partial' theories is of central psychological importance, because complete common-sense theories may not be feasible, as outlined above. Indeed, even currently popular 'theory-based views' in psychology, which emphasise the role of general knowledge in categorization, claim only that *partial theories* are brought to bear, thus leaving an important role for similarity-based reasoning (Hahn and Chater, 1997).

Furthermore, similarity-based reasoning can be highly effective. For example, the simplest such algorithm, nearest neighbor, has excellent asymptotic classification accuracy in comparison with other inference methods (Cover and Hart, 1967).[13] The prospect of general and effective reasoning has fuelled enormous interest in similarity-based reasoning in AI.

In practice, however, the situation is not quite so ideal. For example, nearest neighbor methods typically require vast numbers of past instances to achieve good performance on complex problems. Moreover, similarity-based methods are dramatically impaired by redundant or irrelevant features, which have as much effect on similarity computation as the crucial ones, causing inaccurate performance (Wettschereck and Aha, 1995) and slow learning (Langley and Sage, 1994).[14] This has prompted research into so-called 'knowledge-poor' feature-selection algorithms (Aha and Bankert, 1994; Wettschereck and Aha, 1995), to choose or preferentially weight relevant features. No such method can learn optimal weight settings for all tasks, however, (Mitchell, 1990; Wettschereck et al., 1995) and, where there are only few past instances, invoking background knowledge is the only option. Thus, sophisticated CBR systems in AI (Branting, 1989; Ashley, 1990) rely on massive, knowledge-based preprocessing. The situation gets worse, where past cases are so sparse that their solutions require significant *adaptation*, such as in case-based planning (Kolodner, 1991, 1992) – a step which also introduces other forms of inference. Thus, 'scaled-up' similarity-based accounts must be supplemented with accounts of how background knowledge affects feature-weighting, which is currently poorly understood (Hahn and Chater, 1996). It seems certain that such an account will also have to integrate other, non-similarity-based, forms of inference, and that a 'pure' similarity-based account of cognition, like a pure 'rule-based' account is not viable.

---

[13]Asymptotically, the single nearest neighbor algorithm has (assuming smoothness) a probability of error which is less than twice the Bayes probability of error and thus less than twice the probability of error of any *other* decision rule, non-parametric or otherwise, based on the infinite sample set (Cover and Hart, 1967).

[14]The number of instances needed for nearest neighbor to reach a given level of accuracy grows exponentially with the number of irrelevant features (Langley and Sage, 1994).

4.2.3. Knowledge revision

People can clearly learn both from *experience* and from *being told* about the world. These two sources of information fit very differently with the two classes of model.

Rule-based models have the potential of adding new general information directly into the rule-base (i.e. as if the system has been *told* new information) and can interact productively with existing rules. However, this very generality means that learning from *experience* is very difficult, because there are typically many alternative changes to the rule-base that can capture new 'data.' This is analogous to the problem of theory induction or revision in the light of new data, which has notoriously resisted formal treatment. This problem has been profoundly problematic in AI; we already noted that 'expert systems' have been developed successfully only within very restricted domains, but even here, they are not the result of automated learning procedures. Rather, they are based on 'knowledge engineering,' i.e. human compilation of relevant domain knowledge into a computer accessible form. Only very limited versions of the problem of rule-induction have been addressed in machine learning, such as the induction of simple logical conjunctions from instances described as simple property lists (Langley, 1996) although more complex structures have increasingly been studied (Muggleton, 1992). Finally, rule-based systems face the problem of dealing with inconsistency between rules (for instance, as a result of 'noisy data' or of exceptions) which can potentially lead to complete inferential anarchy[15].

Similarity-based models, by contrast, can learn from experience simply by adding new instances to the data base. However, learning from being told information which covers large areas of the domain at a stroke, which is so effective for rule-based systems, is not possible for an instance-based system. On the other hand, by reasoning 'locally' from nearby instances, rather than from the global predictions of an entire system of rules, instance-based systems neither need to be globally revised, nor do they run the risk of logical inconsistency and the resulting inferential chaos. The complementary strengths of both types of system suggest integration of both.

5. Conclusions: integrating rules and similarity

In this paper, we have explicated the core distinction between rule- and similarity-based generalization, based on how representations of novel items are matched to stored representations. This core distinction is what is necessarily implied wherever the terms are contrasted without further specification. In doing so, we have resolved three difficulties with the initial intuitive distinction: we have shown that apparent mimicry arguments do not apply, we have provided clear criteria for deciding intuitively unclear cases and we have provided a clear target for empirical investigation. Moreover, we have provided an organizing framework which positions both

[15]In classical logic, all propositions and their negations can be derived from an inconsistent set of rules. Non-classical, 'para-consistent' logics, which seek to contain inference from contradictions, have therefore become a major topic of research (Touretzky, 1986; Smolenov, 1987).

rule- and similarity-based generalization in a way that shows the alternatives to both and allows visualisation of the effects of adopting further constraints on 'rule' or 'similarity' for the empirical problem of distinguishing between them.

We have also investigated the power of various experimental tests which have frequently been used to distinguish 'rules' or 'similarity' without further specification. This has revealed that these tests are not individually decisive, although convergent evidence from several sources may be compelling. We have also argued, however, that computational considerations drawn from AI provide valuable additional support in evaluating the plausibility of either account. We draw from AI the moral that pure rule- and similarity-based mechanisms appear not to be computationally viable for solving real-world problems and that neither viewpoint accounts for the human ability to learn both by example and from instruction. Both types of computational consideration suggest that the psychological concern with deciding between the two viewpoints may be misguided. Instead, it may be crucial to understand how the two can be integrated, combining the strengths of both.

This view is reflected in an increasing interest in hybrid systems within AI (Rissland and Skalak, 1991; Rissland et al., 1993). It also sits well with the not uncommon finding of both rule and similarity effects in recent experimental work on category learning reported in Section 4.1.1 above. Furthermore, given the difficulties of finding complete theories from which all desired instances can be deduced, it is also the most suggestive interpretation (Hahn and Chater, 1997) of experimental evidence in support of the theory-based view of conceptual structure (e.g. Medin and Wattenmaker, 1987). Finally, the need for interaction between the two processes is suggested by considering the structure of the law, next to science the most elaborate and explicit system we have developed for dealing with everyday life. The law displays both instance- and rule-based reasoning in the form of precedent and statute. While legal systems differ regarding the relative weight they place on each of these factors (e.g. the Anglo-American tradition emphasises similarity to past cases and the continental tradition emphasises rules), the 'blend' of both is common to all western legal systems.

These considerations suggest that rules and similarity both have their respective roles, not just side by side, with similarity covering some domains and rules others, or 'doubling up' in parallel (Sloman, 1996), but in an *active interplay* within a single task. The idea that rules and similarity might operate together is frequently suggested, even by advocates of mental rules (e.g. Smith et al., 1992; Marcus et al., 1995); and where real-world inference has been subjected to psychological explanation (Pennington and Hastie, 1993), a complex interplay of a variety of types of inference has been implicated. This suggests a shift of emphasis in future research, from pitting rules against similarity toward experimental and computational investigation of the potential interplay of rules and similarity in cognition.

Acknowledgements

The authors would like to thank Jacques Mehler, Steven Sloman and three anonymous reviewers for their detailed and valuable comments on an earlier version of this manuscript, and Andreas Schöter, Andrew Gillies and Martin Redington for helpful discussion. Ulrike Hahn was funded by ESRC Grant No. R004293341442. Nick Chater was partially supported by ESRC Grant No. R000236214. The research reported in this article is based on Ulrike Hahn's doctoral dissertation and was, in part, carried out while the authors were at the Department of Experimental Psychology, University of Oxford.

References

Aamodt, A., Plaza, E., 1994. Case-based reasoning: foundational issues, methodological variations, and system approaches. AI Communications 7, 39–59.

Aha, D., 1997. Editorial for the special issue: lazy learning. Artificial Intelligence Review 11, 7–10.

Aha, D., Bankert, R., 1994. Feature selection for case-based classification of cloud types: an empirical comparison. In: Proceedings of the AAAI-94 Workshop on Case-Based Reasoning.

Aha, D., Kibler, D., Albert, M., 1991. Instance-based learning algorithms. Machine Learning 6, 37–66.

Allen, S., Brooks, L., 1991. Specializing the operation of an explicit rule. Journal of Experimental Psychology: General 120, 3–19.

Altmann, G., Dienes, Z., Goode, A., 1995. On the modality independence of implicitly learned grammatical knowledge. Journal of Experimental Psychology: Learning, Memory and Cognition 21, 899–912.

Anderson, J., 1983. The Architecture of Cognition. Harvard University press, Cambridge, MA.

Andrews, R., Diederich, J., Tickle, A., 1995. A survey and critique of techniques for extracting rules from trained artificial neural networks. Knowledge-Based Systems 8, 373–389.

Ashley, K., 1990. Modeling Legal Argument – Reasoning with Cases and Hypotheticals. MIT Press, Cambridge, MA.

Barsalou, L., 1990. On the indistinguishability of exemplar memory and abstraction in category representation. In: Srull, T.K., Wyer, R.S. (Eds.), Advances in Social Cognition, Vol. III, Content and Process Specifity in the Effects of Prior Experiences. Erlbaum, Hillsdale, NJ, pp. 61–88.

Bates, E., Elman, J., 1993. Connectionism and the study of change. In: Johnson, M. (Ed.), Brain Development and Cognition. Blackwell, Oxford.

Berry, D., Broadbent, D., 1984. On the relationship between task performance and associated verbalizable knowledge. The Quarterly Journal of Experimental Psychology 86a, 209–231.

Berry, D., Broadbent, D., 1988. Interactive tasks and the implicit-explicit distinction. British Journal of Psychology 79, 251–271.

Boolos, G., Jeffrey, R., 1988. Computability and Logic, third ed. Cambridge University Press, Cambridge.

Braine, M., 1978. On the relation between the natural logic of reasoning and standard logic. Psychological Review 85, 1–21.

Branting, K., 1989. Integrating generalizations with exemplar-based reasoning. In: Proceedings of the Eleventh Annual Meeting of the Cognitive Science Society Ann Arbor, Michigan. Erlbaum, Hillsdale, NJ, pp. 139–146.

Branting, K., 1991. Integrating Rules and Precedents for Classification and Explanation. Ph.D. thesis, University of Texas at Austin.

Brooks, L., Vokey, J., 1991. Abstract analogies and abstracted grammars: comments on Reber (1989) and Mathews et al. (1989). Journal of Experimental Psychology: General 120, 316–323.

Brooks, R., 1991. Intelligence without representation. Artificial Intelligence 47, 139–159.

Brown, M., Filer, N., 1995. Beauty vs. the beast: the case against massively parallel retrieval. In: First United Kingdom Case-Based Reasoning Workshop. Springer Verlag, in press.

Bullinaria, J., 1994. Internal representations of a connectionist model of reading aloud. In: Proceedings of the Sixteenth Annual Meeting of the Cognitive Science Society. Erlbaum, Hillsdale, NJ.

Bullinaria, J., Chater, N., 1995. Connectionist modelling: implications for cognitive neuropsychology. Language and Cognitive Processes 10, 227–264.

Chater, N., Oaksford, M., 1996. The falsity of folk theories: implications for psychology and philosophy. In: O'Donohue, W., Kitchener, R. (Eds.), Psychology and Philosophy: Interdisciplinary Problems and Responses. Sage, London.

Cheng, P., Holyoak, K., 1985. Pragmatic reasoning schemas. Cognitive Psychology 17, 293–328.

Chomsky, N., 1980. Rules and representations. The Behavioral and Brain Sciences 3, 1–61.

Chomsky, N., 1986. Knowledge of Language: Its Nature, Origin, and Use. Prager, Westport, CT.

Collins, A., 1992. On the paradox Kripke finds in Wittgenstein. Midwest Studies in Philosophy XVII, 74–88.

Cosmides, L., 1989. The logic of social exchange: has natural selection shaped how humans reason? Studies with the Wason selection task. Cognition 31, 187–276.

Cost, S., Salzberg, S., 1993. A weighted nearest neighbour algorithm for learning with symbolic features. Machine Learning 10, 57–78.

Cover, T., Hart, P., 1967. Nearest neighbour pattern classification. IEEE Transactions on Information Theory 13, 21–27.

Davies, M., 1995. Two notions of implicit rule. In: Tomberlin, J. (Ed.), Philosophical Perspectives, Vol. 9, AI, Connectionism, and Philosophical Psychology. Ridgeview, Atascadero, CA.

Dayal, S., Harmer, M., Johnson, P., Mead, D., 1993. Beyond knowledge representation: commercial uses for legal knowledge bases. In: Proceedings of the Fourth International Conference on Artificial Intelligence and Law. ACM, New York, NY.

Delosh, E., 1993. Interpolation and extrapolation in a functional learning paradigm. Purdue Mathematical Psychology Program, Purdue University.

Dreyfus, H., 1992. What computers still can't do - a critique of Artificial Reason (third ed.). MIT Press, Cambridge, MA.

Dulaney, D., Carlson, R., Dewey, G., 1984. A case of syntactical learning and judgement: how conscious and how abstract? Journal of Experimental Psychology: General 113, 541–555.

Ervin, S., 1964. Imitation and structural change in children's language. In: Lenneberg, E. (Ed.), New Directions in the Study of Language. MIT Press, Cambridge, MA.

Feigenbaum, E., 1977. The art of Artificial Intelligence: themes and case studies of knowledge engineering. In: Proceedings of IJCAI-77.

Fodor, J., 1983. Modularity of Mind. Bradford Books, London, UK; MIT Press, Cambridge, MA.

Forrester, N., Plunkett, K., 1994. The inflectional morphology of the Arabic broken plural: a connectionist account. In: Proceedings of the Sixteenth Annual Meeting of the Cognitive Science Society. Erlbaum, Hillsdale, NJ.

Funnell, E., 1983. Phonological processing in reading: new evidence from acquired dyslexia. British Journal of Psychology 74, 159–180.

Gentner, D., 1983. Structure-mapping: a theoretical framework for analogy. Cognitive Science 7, 155–170.

Gentner, D., 1989. The mechanisms of analogical learning. In: Vosniadou, S., Ortony, A. (Eds.), Similarity and Analogical Reasoning. Cambridge University Press, Cambridge, UK.

Gentner, D., Forbus, K.D., 1991. MAC/FAC: a model of similarity-based retrieval. In: Proceedings of the Fifteenth Annual Meeting of the Cognitive Science Society. Erlbaum, Hillsdale, NJ, pp. 504–509.

Gentner, D., Markman, A., 1994. Structural alignment in comparison: no difference without similarity. Psychological Science 5, 152–158.

Ginet, C., 1992. The dispositionalist solution to Wittgenstein's problem about understanding a rule: answering Kripke's objections. Midwest Studies in Philosophy XVII, 53–88.

Ginsberg, M., 1987. Readings in Nonmonotonic Reasoning. Morgan Kaufmann, San Mateo, CA.

Glushko, R., 1979. The organization and activation of orthographic knowledge in reading aloud. Journal of Experimental Psychology: Human Performance and Perception 5, 674–691.

Goldstone, R., 1994a. The role of similarity in categorization: providing a groundwork. Cognition 52, 125–157.

Goldstone, R., 1994b. Similarity, interactive activation, and mapping. Journal of Experimental Psychology: Learning, Memory, and Cognition 20, 3–28.

Goodman, N. (1972). Seven Strictures on Similarity. In: Problems and Projects. Bobbs Merill, Indeanapolis.

Goswami, U., Bryant, P., 1990. Phonological Skills and Learning to Read. Erlbaum, Hillsdale, NJ.

Hadley, R., 1993. The 'explicit/implicit' distinction. Technical report CSS-IS TR93–02. Simon Frasier University, Burnaby BC, Canada.

Hahn, U., 1996. Cases and Rules in Categorization. Ph.D. thesis, University of Oxford, UK.

Hahn, U., Chater, N., 1996. Understanding similarity: a joint project for psychology, case-based reasoning, and law. Artificial Intelligence Review, in press.

Hahn, U., Chater, N., 1997. Concepts and similarity. In: Lamberts, K., Shanks, D. (Eds.), Knowledge, Concepts, and Categories. Psychology Press/MIT Press, Hove, UK.

Hahn, U., Nakisa, R., Plunkett, K., 1997. The dual-route model of the English past-tense: another case where defaults don't help. In: Proceedings of the GALA '97 Conference on Language Acquisition.

Haugeland, J., 1985. Artificial Intelligence: The Very Idea. MIT Press, Cambridge, MA.

Hayes, P., 1979. The naive physics manifesto. In: Michie, D. (Ed.), Expert Systems in the Micro-electronic Age. Edinburgh University Press, Edinburgh.

Herbig, B., Wess, S., 1992. Ähnlichkeit und Ähnlichkeitsmasse. In: *Fall-basiertes Sehliessen – Eine Übersicht*. SEKI Working papers SWP-92–08,, University of Kaiserslautern, Germany.

Herrnstein, R., 1990. Levels of stimulus control: a functional approach. Cognition 37, 133–166.

Inhelder, B., Piaget, J., 1958. The Growth of Logical Reasoning. Basic Books, New York.

Johnson-Laird, P., Byrne, R., 1991. Deduction. Lawrence Erlbaum, Hillsdale, NJ.

Jordan, M., 1986. An introduction to linear algebra and parallel distributed processing. In: Rumelhart, D., McClelland, J. (Eds.), Parallel Distributed Processing:explorations in the Microstructure of Cognition, Vol 1: Foundations. MIT press, Cambridge, MA.

Koh, K., Meyer, D., 1991. Function learning: induction of continuous stimulus-response relations. Journal of Experimental Psychology: Learning, Memory, and Cognition, 17, 811–836.

Kolodner, J., 1991. Improving human decision making through case-based decision aiding. AI Magazine, 52–68.

Kolodner, J., 1992. An introduction to case-based reasoning. Artificial Intelligence Review 6, 3–34.

Komatsu, L., 1992. Recent views of conceptual structure. Psychological Bulletin 112, 500–526.

Kripke, S.A., 1982. Wittgenstein on Rules and Private Language. Blackwell, Oxford.

Kruschke, J., 1992. ALCOVE: an exemplar-based connectionist model of category learning. Psychological Review 99, 22–44.

Lamberts, K., 1995. Categorization under time pressure. Journal of Experimental Psychology: General 124, 161–180.

Langley, P., 1996. Elements of Machine Learning. Morgan Kaufmann, San Francisco, CA.

Langley, P., Sage, S., 1994. Oblivious decision trees and abstract cases. In: Working Notes of the AAAI-94 Workshop on Case-Based Reasoning. AAAI Press.

Marcus, G., Brinkmann, U., Clahsen, H., Wiese, R., Woest, A., Pinker, S., 1995. German inflection: the exception that proves the rule. Cognitive Psychology 29, 189–256.

McCarthy, R., Warrington, E., 1986. Phonological reading: phenomena and paradoxes. Cortex 22, 868–884.

McDermott, D., 1987. A critique of pure reason. Computational Intelligence 3, 151–160.

McDowell, J., 1984. Wittgenstein on following a rule. Synthese 58, 325–363.

Medin, D.L., Wattenmaker, W., 1987. Category cohesiveness, theories, and cognitive archaeology. In: Neisser, U. (Ed.), Concepts and Conceptual Development: Ecological and Intellectual Factors in Categorization. Cambridge University Press, Cambridge, UK.

Medin, D., Schaffer, M., 1978. Context theory of classification learning. Psychological Review 85, 207–238.

Mitchell, T., 1990. The need for biases in learning generalizations. In: Shavlik, J., Dietterich, T. (Eds.), Readings in Machine Learning. Morgan Kaufmann, San Mateo, CA.

Muggleton, S., 1992. Inductive Logic Programming. Academic Press, New York.

Myllymäki, P., Tirri, H., 1993. Massively parallel case-based reasoning with probabilistic similarity metrics. In: First European Workshop on Case-Based Reasoning. Springer Verlag, Berlin.

Nakisa, R.C., Plunkett, K., Hahn, U., 1998. A cross-linguistic comparison of single and dual-route models of inflectional morphology. In: Broeder, P., Murre, J. (Eds.), Cognitive Models of Language Acquisition. MIT Press, Cambridge, MA, in press.

Nakisa, R., Hahn, U., 1996. Where defaults don't help: the case of the German plural system. In: Proceedings of the 18th Annual Meeting of the Cognitive Science Society. Erlbaum, Mahwah, NJ, pp. 177–182.

Newell, A., 1963. The chess machine. In: Sayre, K., Crosson, F. (Eds.), The Modeling of the Mind. Notre Dame University Press, South Bend, IN.

Newell, A., 1991. Unified Theories of Cognition. Cambridge University Press, Cambridge, UK.

Newell, A., Simon, H., 1972. Human Problem Solving. Prentice-Hall, Englewood Cliffs, NJ.

Newell, A., Simon, H., 1990. Computer science as empirical enquiry: symbols and search. In: Bodenz, M. (Ed.), The Philosophy of Artificial Intelligence. Oxford University Press, Oxford, UK.

Nisbett, R., Wilson, T., 1977. Telling more than we can know: verbal reports on mental processes. Psychological Review 8, 231–259.

Nosofsky, R., 1984. Choice, similarity and the context theory of classification. Journal of Experimental Psychology: Learning, Memory and Cognition 10, 104–114.

Nosofsky, R., 1988. Exemplar-based accounts of relations between classification, recognition, and typicality. Journal of Experimental Psychology: Learning, Memory and Cognition 14, 700–708.

Nosofsky, R., Clark, S., Shin, H., 1989. Rules and exemplars in categorization, identification, and recognition. Journal of Experimental Psychology: Learning, Memory, and Cognition 15, 282–304.

Nosofsky, R., 1992. Exemplars, prototypes, and similarity rules. In: Healy, A., Kosslyn, S., Shiffrin, R. (Eds.), From Learning Theory to Connectionist Theory: Essays in Honor of William K. Estes. Erlbaum, Hillsdale, NJ.

Oaksford, M., Chater, N., 1993. Mental models and the tractability of everyday reasoning. Behavioural and Brain Sciences 16, 360–361.

Oaksford, M., Chater, N., 1991. Against logicist cognitive science. Mind and Language 6, 1–38.

Pavlov, I., 1927. Conditional Reflexes. Oxford University Press, London, UK.

Pennington, N., Hastie, R., 1993. Reasoning in explanation-based decision making. Cognition 49, 123–163.

Pickering, M., Chater, N., 1995. Why cognitive science is not formalized folk psychology. Minds and Machines 5, 309–337.

Pinker, S., Prince, A., 1988. On language and connectionism: analysis of a parallel distributed processing model of language acquisition. Cognition 28, 73–193.

Plunkett, K., Marchman, V., 1991. U-shaped learning and frequency effects in a multi-layered perceptron: implications for child language acquisition. Cognition 38, 43–102.

Porter, B., Bareiss, R., Holte, R., 1990. Concept learning and heuristic classification. Artificial Intelligence 45, 229–263.

Posner, M., Keele, S., 1970. Retention of abstract ideas. Journal of Experimental Psychology 83, 304–308.

Putnam, H., 1974. The 'corroboration' of theories. In: Schilpp, P. (Ed.), The Philosophy of Karl Popper, Vol. 1. Open Court Publishing.

Pylyshyn, Z., 1984. Computation and Cognition. MIT Press, Cambridge, MA.

Quine, W., 1960. Word and Object. MIT Press, Cambridge, MA.

Reber, A.S., 1989. Implicit learning and tacit knowledge. Journal of Experimental Psychology: General 118, 219–235.

Redington, M., 1996. What is learnt in Artificial Grammar Learning? Ph.D. thesis, Department of Experimental Psychology, University of Oxford.

Redington, M., Chater, N., 1994. The guessing game: a paradigm for artificial grammar learning. In: Proceedings of the Sixteenth Annual Meeting of the Cognitive Science Society. Erlbaum, Hillsdale, NJ.

Redington, M., Chater, N., 1996. Transfer in artificial grammar learning: a re-evaluation. Journal of Experimental Psychology: General 125, 123–138.

Reed, S., 1972. Pattern recognition and categorization. Cognitive Psychology 3, 382–407.

Reiter, R., 1980. A logic for default reasoning. Artificial Intelligence 13, 81–132.

Rips, I., 1994. The Psychology of Proof. MIT Press, Cambridge, MA.

Rissland, E., Skalak, D., 1991. CABARET: rule interpretation in a hybrid architecture. International Journal of Man-Machine Studies 34, 839–887.

Rissland, E., Skalak, D., Friedman, M., 1993. BankXX: A program to generate argument through case-based search. In: Proceedings of the Fourth International Conference on Artificial Intelligence and Law, ACM, New York, NY.

Rosch, E., Mervis, C., Gray, W., Johnson, D., Boyes-Braem, P., 1976. Basic objects in natural categories. Cognitive Psychology 8, 382–439.

Ross, B., 1984. Remindings and their effects in learning a cognitive skill. Cognitive Psychology 16, 371–416.

Ross, E., 1987. This is like that: the use of earlier problems and the separation of similarity effects. Journal of Experimental Psychology: Learning, Memory and Cognition 13, 629–637.

Ross, B., Kennedy, P., 1990. Generalizing from the use of earlier exemplars in problem solving. Journal of Experimental Psychology: Learning, Memory, and Cognition 16, 42–55.

Rumelhart, D., McClelland, J., 1986. On learning past tenses of English verbs. In: Rumelhart, D., McClelland, J. (Eds.), Parallel Distributed Processing, Vol 2: Psychological and Biological Models. MIT press, Cambridge, MA.

Rumelhart, D., Todd, P., 1993. Learning and connectionist representations. Attention and Performance, pp. 3–30.

Rumelhart, D., Zipser, D., 1985. Feature discovery by competitive learning. Cognitive Science 9, 75–112.

Schank, R., 1982. Dynamic Memory: A Theory of Learning in Computers and People. Cambridge University Press, Cambridge, UK.

Searle, J., 1980. Rules and causation. Behavioral and Brain Sciences 3, 1–61.

Seidenberg, M., McClelland, J., 1989. A distributed, developmental model of word recognition and naming. Psychological Review 96, 523–568.

Seifert, C., 1989. Analogy and case-based reasoning. In: Proceedings: Case-Based Reasoning Workshop. Morgan Kaufmann, San Mateo, CA.

Selfridge, O., 1959. Pandemonium: a paradigm for learning. In: Office, L.H.S. (Ed.), Symposium on the Mechanization of Thought Processes.

Shallice, T., 1988. From Neuropsychology to Mental Structure. Cambridge University Press, Cambridge, UK.

Shanks, D., 1995. Rule induction. In: The Psychology of Associative Learning. Cambridge University Press, Cambridge.

Shanks, D., John, M.S., 1994. Characteristics of dissociable human learning systems. Behavioral and Brain Sciences 17, 367–395.

Shepard, R., 1957. Stimulus and response generalization: a stochastic model relating generalization to distance in psychological space. Psychometrika 22, 325–345.

Shepard, R., 1980. Multidimensional scaling, tree-fitting, and clustering. Science 210, 390–399.

Shieber, S.M., 1986. An Introduction to Unification-Based Approaches to Grammar. Center for the Study of Language and Information, Stanford, CA.

Shortliffe, E., 1976. Computer-based Medical Consultations: MYCIN. Elsevier, New York.

Sidman, M., Tailby, W., 1982. Conditional discrimination vs. matching to a sample: an expansion of the testing paradigm. Journal of the Experimental Analysis of Behavior 37, 5–22.

Sloman, S., 1996. The empirical case for two systems of reasoning. Psychological Bulletin 119, 3–22.

Smith, E., Langston, C., Nisbett, R., 1992. The case for rules in reasoning. Cognitive Science 16, 1–40.

Smith, E., Medin, D., 1981. Categories and Concepts. Harvard University Press, Cambridge, MA.

Smolenov, H., 1987. Paraconsistency, paracompleteness and intentional contradictions. Journal of Non-classical Logic 4, 5–36.

Touretzky, D., 1986. The Mathematics of Inheritance Systems. Morgan Kaufman, Los Altos, CA.

Touretzky, D., Hinton, G., 1988. A distributed connectionist production system. Cognitive Science 12, 423–466.

Tversky, A., 1977. Features of similarity. Psychological Review 84, 327–352.

Vaughan, W., 1988. Formation of equivalence sets in pigeons. Journal of Experimental Psychology: Animal Behavior Processes 14, 36–42.

Vokey, J., Brooks, L., 1992. Salience of item knowledge in learning artificial grammars. Journal of Experimental Psychology: Learning, Memory, and Cognition 18, 328–344.

Vokey, J., Brooks, L., 1994. Fragmentary knowledge and the processing specific control of structural sensitivity. Journal of Experimental Psychology: Learning, Memory and Cognition 18, 1504–1510.

Wason, P., 1968. Reasoning about a rule. Quarterly Journal of Experimental Psychology 20, 273–281.

Westermann, G., Goebel, R., 1994. Connectionist rules of language. In: Proceedings of the Seventeenth Annual Meeting of the Cognitive Science Society. Erlbaum, Hillsdale, NJ, pp. 236–241.

Wettschereck, D., Aha, D., 1995. Weighting features. In Proceedings of the First International Conference on Case-Based Reasoning.

Wettschereck, D., Aha, D., Mohri, T., 1995. A review and comparative evaluation of feature weighting methods for lazy learning algorithms. Technical report AIC-95–012, Navy Center for Applied Research in AI, Washington DC.

Young, R., O'Shea, T., 1981. Errors in children's subtraction. Cognitive Science 5, 153–177.

6

Reuniting perception and conception

Robert L. Goldstone[a],*, Lawrence W. Barsalou[b]

[a]Psychology Department, Indiana University, Bloomington, IN 47405, USA
[b]Psychology Department, Emory University, Atlanta, GA 30322, USA

Abstract

Work in philosophy and psychology has argued for a dissociation between perceptually-based similarity and higher-level rules in conceptual thought. Although such a dissociation may be justified at times, our goal is to illustrate ways in which conceptual processing is grounded in perception, both for perceptual similarity and abstract rules. We discuss the advantages, power and influences of perceptually-based representations. First, many of the properties associated with amodal symbol systems can be achieved with perceptually-based systems as well (e.g. productivity). Second, relatively raw perceptual representations are powerful because they can implicitly represent properties in an analog fashion. Third, perception naturally provides impressions of overall similarity, exactly the type of similarity useful for establishing many common categories. Fourth, perceptual similarity is not static but becomes tuned over time to conceptual demands. Fifth, the original motivation or basis for sophisticated cognition is often less sophisticated perceptual similarity. Sixth, perceptual simulation occurs even in conceptual tasks that have no explicit perceptual demands. Parallels between perceptual and conceptual processes suggest that many mechanisms typically associated with abstract thought are also present in perception, and that perceptual processes provide useful mechanisms that may be co-opted by abstract thought. © 1998 Elsevier Science B.V.

Keywords: Perception; Conception; Perceptual similarity; Symbol systems; Rule-based systems; Similarity-based systems

1. Introduction

Reflecting on the sophistication of human thought, we can be impressed with how

---

* Corresponding author. Present address: Psychology Building, Indiana University, Bloomington IN 47405, USA far we've come, or how we got here. The first perspective emphasizes the distance between starting and final states, whereas the second emphasizes their continuity. In adopting the second perspective, we will describe ways in which conceptual thought is grounded in perceptual similarity. Certainly, many concepts are partially organized around perceptual similarities (Rosch et al., 1976), but we will argue further that perceptual processes guide the construction of abstract concepts even when this direct link may not be so obvious. By adopting a perceptual perspective, we certainly do not mean to deny the use of abstract rules. On the contrary, our position is that abstract conceptual knowledge is indeed central to human cognition, but that it depends on perceptual representations and processes, both in its development and in its active use. Completely modality-free concepts are rarely, if ever, used, even when representing abstract contents. In short, concepts usually stem from perception, and active vestiges of these perceptual origins exist for the vast majority of concepts. Thus, we will argue that *both* similarity and concepts have their roots in perception, and that both rely heavily on perceptual mechanisms for their implementation.

As we shall illustrate throughout this paper, perception's usefulness in grounding concepts comes from several sources. First, perception provides a wealth of information to guide conceptualization. Second, perceptual processes themselves can change as a result of concept development and use. Third, many of the constraints manifested by our perceptual systems are also found in our conceptual systems.

The crux of our argument is that conceptual processing shares important computational resources with perception. For example, we will propose that mechanisms used to represent information in perception perform double duty, also representing information in concepts. Whereas standard theories of concepts assume that different representational systems underlie perception and conception, we assume that a common representational system underlies both, at least to a considerable extent. Thus, mechanisms that represent shape, color and location in perception, also represent shape, color and location in concepts. Analogously, we will argue that processing mechanisms, not just representational mechanisms, are common to perception and conception. For example, we will propose that mechanisms used to scan perceptions and mental images are also used to scan the content of concepts. Various other parallels in processing will be proposed as well. Throughout this paper, when we propose that concepts rely on perception, we will essentially be arguing that concepts share representation and processing mechanisms from perception, rather than using independent mechanisms that work according to fundamentally different principles.

1.1. The allure of the perception/conception distinction

An impressive lineage of theorists has drawn a distinction between perceptual and conceptual systems (for a historical review, see Arnheim, 1969). The Pythagoreans saw a fundamental separation of the 'heaven' of conceptual abstractions and the 'earth' of perceptual experience. Plato believed in 'generic forms' that could not be found by induction across perceptual aspects of specific instances. Parmenides was perhaps the first philosopher to distinguish reasoning from perceiving, on the basis of perceptual illusions (e.g. a straight stick dipped in water appearing bent) that must be overcome by the powers of rationality (Kirk and Raven, 1962).

The Greek tradition has continued into the present day, with the notion that perceptual similarities must be, and at least sometimes are, cast aside when creating categories. Quine (1977) considers it a sign of an advanced science if its theoretical concepts are not based on perceptual qualities. Evidence suggests that scientific conceptualization incorporates increasingly deep, abstract properties, as opposed to perceptual properties, with increasing expertise (Chi et al., 1981). Similarly, part of the notion of the recent 'theory' theory of concepts is that concepts are not organized around clusters of perceptual properties, but rather around organized systems of knowledge (Murphy and Medin, 1985; Medin, 1989; Murphy and Spalding, 1995). Developmental support for this hypothesis indicates that even young children have inchoate theories about concepts that allow them to disregard perceptual similarities. Children can group animals by their names (Gelman and Markman, 1986; Gelman, 1988), hidden internal structure (Carey, 1985), or genetic heritage (Keil, 1989) in manners that conflict with perceptual similarity. In adults, categorization judgments can be dissociated from similarity judgments such that X is judged more similar to Y than to Z, but is still placed in Z's category rather than Y's (Rips, 1989; Rips and Collins, 1993; Kroska and Goldstone, 1996).

Finally, there have been several recent efforts to separate similarity-based from rule-based systems. Whereas similarity-based systems establish concepts on the basis of perceptual similarities between a concept's instances, rule-based systems form concepts from explicit symbolic expressions. Shanks and St. John (1994) and Sloman (1996) review evidence for such a distinction. Evidence for the use of rules comes from occasions when categorization drastically and suddenly changes when a simple instruction is provided, or when superficial similarities can be completely ignored when they are inconsistent with an explicit instruction. According to Sloman, evidence for the existence of both rule- and similarity-based reasoning exists in the form of simultaneous, conflicting judgments in a task, due to contradictory evidence from the separate systems. One hallmark of rules that divorces them from perceptual information is precisely their generality and universal applicability regardless of domain. In discussing criterial evidence for rule use (as opposed to similarity), Smith et al. (1992) argue that when people use rules, they are as accurate with unfamiliar as with familiar material, and with abstract information as with concrete information. All of these researchers believe that they find evidence for the use of such rules in human reasoning.

In short, a wealth of evidence and intuition suggests that superficial perceptual similarity does not always determine categories. According to many philosophers and psychologists, abstract, rule-based reasoning is often at odds with perceptual data and must be marshaled in order to counter the misleading influences of superficial percepts. Still, returning to the Greeks (Kirk and Raven, 1962), Democritus, speaking on behalf of the senses, chastises abstract reasoning thus: 'wretched mind, do you, who get your evidence from us, still try to overthrow us?'

2. Reuniting perception and conception

Like Democritus, we believe that conceptual structures develop from perceptual processes and continue to bear vestiges of this legacy. At one level, this is an uncontroversial statement, given that many of our concepts are clearly characterized by perceptual properties. Perceptual properties are often good indicators of important, concept-defining properties and our perceptual systems have evolved so as to establish useful concepts (Medin and Ortony, 1989). Objects that belong to psychologically important concepts often have similar shapes (Rosch et al, 1976), and our perceptual systems offer a tremendous amount of data that is probably underestimated by the use of overly sparse experimental materials (Jones and Smith, 1993).

Two approaches toward reuniting perception with conception are the *eliminative view* and the *agnostic view*. According to the eliminative view, perceptual representations constitute all knowledge. Human knowledge contains no non-perceptual representations. According to the agnostic view, human knowledge has major perceptual components and may or may not also contain non-perceptual components. One of us has developed the eliminative view elsewhere (Barsalou, 1993; Barsalou et al., 1993; Barsalou and Prinz, 1997; Prinz and Barsalou, 1997). Thus, we do not pursue this view here, except to summarize it briefly as a boundary case in the realm of possibilities. Instead, we focus on the agnostic view that perceptual representations are central to conceptual knowledge, without making a commitment to whether non-perceptual representations exist as well. In making this argument, we address both similarity and rules, demonstrating that each has important perceptual origins.

2.1. The eliminative view

Prior to the twentieth century, theories of mind typically assumed that human knowledge is inherently perceptual. Not only did the British Empiricists believe this, but so did most other theorists of mind thereafter, including philosophers such as Kant in 1787 (Kant, 1965) and Russell in 1919 (Russell, 1956). In the early twentieth century, ordinary language philosophy and behaviorism both attempted to expunge mental states and mechanisms from theories of mind. As part of their strategy to eliminate mentalism, they frequently criticized theories that relied on mental images. When the cognitive revolution occurred 50 years later, theorists were reluctant to view the cognitive mechanisms that they readopted as inherently perceptual. Although theorists once again became comfortable with cognitive mechanisms, they remained wary of mental images. Furthermore, the proliferation of formal languages and the computer metaphor made possible new ways of thinking about knowledge in non-perceptual formats. Whereas earlier approaches assumed that aspects of perceptual states become stored in memory to form concepts, these new approaches assumed that perceptual states are transduced into amodal symbols. Much like the words of a language, amodal symbols are assumed to bear arbitrary relations to perceptions and to their referents in the world. Attractive properties of this approach included the abilities to form propositional representations of the world productively, to represent abstract as well as concrete concepts and to implement these languages on computer hardware.

Early critics in the twentieth century often construed the perceptual view in limited and overly simplistic manners, a tradition many modern critics have continued. For example, critics often construe the perceptual approach as containing images that are only conscious, that are only drawn from sensory states and that are only holistic. Rejection of the perceptual view is typically based on this formulation of the position. Actually, many other formulations are possible, some of which were the theories that the British Empiricists actually proposed. For example, Locke's 1690 (Locke, 1959) theory assumed that images in knowledge could come from internal cognitive states, not only from sensations of the external world. He also argued that images could be analytic and productive, not holistic and unproductive. More recently, a wide variety of researchers across the cognitive sciences, especially in cognitive linguistics, have proposed increasingly sophisticated and powerful theories of perceptually-based knowledge.

As an example of these more modern views, consider *perceptual symbol systems* (Barsalou and Prinz, 1997; Prinz and Barsalou, 1997; Prinz, 1997; (for earlier formulations, see Barsalou, 1993; Barsalou et al., 1993)). This theory begins with the assumption that perceptual representations are not necessarily conscious images but are unconscious states of perceptual systems specified neurally. For example, the representation of a chair might be specified as a configuration of neurons active in the visual system rather than as a conscious mental image. These perceptual representations are not necessarily holistic. Instead, a perceptual representation can be a schematic aspect of a perceptual state extracted with selective attention and stored in long-term memory. For example, selective attention might focus on the form of an object, storing only its shape in memory and not its color, texture, position, size and so forth. This schematic extraction process not only operates on sensory states, it also operates on internal mental events, extracting aspects of representational states, cognitive operations, motivational states and emotions. Once these schematic perceptual representations become established in memory, they can function as symbols. They can refer to entities in the world, they can combine productively using combinatoric and recursive mechanisms and they can implement propositional construals of situations. Furthermore, they can represent abstract concepts such as *truth*, *negation* and *disjunction* by capitalizing on perceptual symbols for internal mental events and simulated external events. Note that this very brief review simply serves to provide a sense of the theory's coverage. We do not present it more fully here, because our goal is not to explicate and defend the eliminativist view. This theory is pursued further by Barsalou and Prinz (1997).

One purpose of developing the eliminativist position is to establish an existence proof that a completely perceptual approach is sufficient for establishing a fully functional symbolic system. If this approach can implement reference, productivity, propositions and abstract concepts, it would be comparable with amodal symbol systems in expressive power. As a result, amodal symbols could be eliminated because they are not necessary. Of course, many sorts of evidence must be considered to determine whether eliminativism is justified, but, again, the primary purpose of this theory is to serve as an existence proof that one *can* develop a fully functional symbolic system that is inherently perceptual.

If one were to push for the eliminativist view, additional sources of evidence could be brought to bear, besides the argument that perceptual symbol systems have sufficient expressive power. First, the amodal view suffers serious problems. These include lack of accounts of how amodal symbols become transduced from perceptual states and, conversely, for how reference from amodal symbols to perceptual states is established (Searle, 1980; Harnad, 1987). Furthermore, there is no direct empirical evidence that conceptual symbols are inherently amodal. Instead, the primary evidence for amodal symbols is indirect, namely, systems having sufficient expressive power can be constructed from them. Finally, the amodal view is too powerful. It can explain virtually any finding post hoc, yet fails to predict many perceptually-based phenomena a priori or provide insight into them. In contrast, the perceptual symbols view does not suffer from these problems. It provides natural accounts of how conceptual symbols are linked to perceptual states and there is considerable evidence that conceptual symbols are perceptual (as we review shortly). Furthermore, the perceptual view is falsifiable, given that it predicts close parallels between conceptual and perceptual processing. Indeed, it makes the strong prediction that the human conceptual system shares representational mechanisms with perception. If this view is correct, then perceptual mechanisms should become engaged when people perform conceptual processing.

This, then, is the flavor of the eliminative position. Clearly, theories of perceptual symbols and the evidence for them remain to be developed considerably in many regards. At this time, this approach primarily attempts to provide an existence proof that, in principle, perception and conception can be united in a way that does not require amodal symbols.

2.2. *The agnostic view*

A more moderate approach to reuniting perception and conception is to propose that perceptual information plays a major role in conceptual knowledge, which may or may not also include amodal symbols. Our primary purpose is to convince the reader of this and *only* this point. In the remaining sections, we review a large diversity of empirical phenomena that implicate perception in conception. One might wish to follow these phenomena to the stronger eliminativist conclusion, but we will not take that route here. Instead, we will remain content to conclude that conceptual processing at all levels reflects perceptual mechanisms in unexpected ways.

3. The many roles of perception in conception

The distance between percepts and many of our concepts may seem insurmountable. However, several properties of perception prove very useful, in fact irreplaceable, in constructing concepts. In the remaining sections, we demonstrate how

concepts rely on implicit information in perceptual representations, how perceptually-based holistic similarity plays important roles in cognition, how learned
perceptual similarities become conceptual biases, how various abstractions (including rules) originate in perception, how perceptual simulation can underlie conceptual processing and how various perceptual mechanisms enter into higher cognition.

3.1. Freeloading with analogical systems

Systems that reflect perceptual similarities in their conceptual structures have a
major advantage over those that only incorporate amodal representations – the same
advantage that analog systems have over digital systems. Perceptual and analogical
representations, because they preserve aspects of the external object in a relatively
direct way, can represent certain aspects of the represented object without explicit
machinery to do so (Palmer, 1978). For example, to decide that a particular couch
belongs to the category, *things that will fit through the front doorway*, a good
strategy is to manipulate an analog representation of the couch's shape in reference
to an analog representation of the doorway. If shape and relative size are preserved
in one's representation, then one can be confident that conclusions drawn from
mental manipulations will be applicable to the real-world couch.

The alternative to computing with perceptually-based representations is to reason
from symbolic representations that either completely remove perceptual information
or start with a symbolic representation. One prominent example of the latter
approach is Lenat's CYC project, an attempt to build common sense reasoning
into a computer by having 'knowledge engineers' input symbol-level knowledge
(Lenat and Guha, 1994). The main problem with this approach is that a tremendous
number of facts is needed to represent the same information conveyed efficiently by
shape. A picture is indeed worth a thousand symbols, provided that there are processes (such as rotating, scanning and zooming) that take advantage of the picture's
analog format.

Representations that preserve physical properties are often more efficient than
purely symbolic representations because they do not require external constraints to
ensure proper inferences. With amodal systems, symbol manipulation must be controlled through external means such as inference rules. The relation 'next to' is
symmetric but not transitive, whereas 'taller than' is transitive but not symmetric.
These facts can be represented in an amodal systems so that it does not infer that
Rich is next to Jerry upon being informed that Rich is next to Julie and Julie is next
to Jerry, but precluding this inference would require devising and applying explicit
rules to be used for inferring 'next to' relations. The alternative is to represent the
locations and heights of Rich, Julie and Jerry in a spatial medium, whereupon the
proximity and height relations can be read off directly (Johnson-Laird, 1983). The
logical inferences that are admissible depend on the physical properties of described
world, and, accordingly, it makes good sense to preserve these physical properties in
the first place rather than try to mimic their effect with specially-designed rules that
add constraints back to those stripped by amodal representations. Notably, percep-

tual representations are required to identify the content of these specially-designed rules.

Furthermore, it is surprising how many seemingly abstract properties can be computed by analog devices. For example, many people would assume that if one wished to find the correlation between two variables (e.g. the heights and weights of a sample of college students), it would be necessary to symbolically represent the variables by numbers and use mathematical equations to derive a measure of correlation. Dewdney (1985) describes an analog alternative (shown in Fig. 1). Partially drive in a nail on a wood surface at each point representing an individual height-weight pair. Fit a single, thin rod approximately into place between the nails, and attach a rubber band to each nail and the rod (an incorrect placement of the rod with respect to a nail can be diagnosed by complete slackness of the connecting rubber band). When the rod is released, it quickly falls into an equilibrium position such that the angle of the rod represents the best fitting linear regression of height on weight, and total slackness of the rubber bands represents the correlation between height and weight. The overall slackness of the rubber bands, measured by strumming them or by feeling how much force is necessary to jiggle the rod, can be used to guide decisions about the relatedness between the variables without ever using numeric symbols. As another example, the shortest connecting path between points can be found by pounding nails between slightly separated, clear boards and dipping the boards into a soap solution. When lifted from the solution, the trapped soap film will form a minimal spanning tree that could be used to efficiently lay cables between cities.

Analog representations such as these are often efficient representations, because properties 'ride for free' within the representation without explicitly being computed

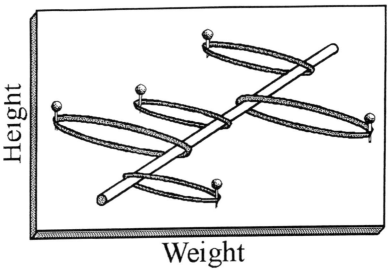

Fig. 1. Although normally computed by amodal mathematical systems, properties such as the correlation between height and weight can also be computed by an analog device consisting of a rod, rubber bands, tacks, and a cork board.

(e.g. correlation, slope and intercept). Analog representations are particularly useful when one does not know what properties will be needed at a later point, or explicitly how to compute the needed properties. As such, ironically enough, analogical representations are often most useful for more complex concepts – those without simple definitions. Although it is unclear what class of object properties are well handled by analog representations, we suspect that many of the properties useful for categorizing objects (e.g. shape, size, pattern of motion, texture, density and curvature) are good candidates. Certainly, other researchers have gotten mileage from analog representations that preserve in a direct form many of the properties and spatial relations present in visual percepts (Shepard, 1984; Finke, 1986).

3.2. The primitive appeal of overall similarity

To the extent that concepts can be characterized thoroughly by simple rules or verbal definitions, the role of perceptual similarity in structuring concepts is weakened. If 'unmarried male human' adequately captures the concept *bachelor*, then sophisticated perceptual representations seem unnecessary.[1] Alternatively, similarity might be said to explain the concept *bachelor*, because members of the *bachelor* category are similar in all being unmarried men, but this hardly salvages similarity as useful for explanation. As Goodman (1972) criticizes similarity: 'when to the statement that two things are similar we add a specification of the property that they have in common, [...] rather than supplementing our initial statement, we render it superfluous' (pp. 444–445). That is, if the similarity of concept members that determines categorization is only with respect to particular properties of commonality, why not just dispense with similarity altogether and discuss the common properties instead?

Our reply to this is to deny the premise. Similarity often involves not only single properties, but integration across many properties. Many of the most important disputes in the field of categorization concern exactly how to integrate across several properties when calculating similarity. Some approaches list features of the two objects, and integrate the overlapping features and the distinctive features to determine overall similarity (Tversky, 1977). Other approaches represent objects as points in a multidimensional space and calculate similarity as an inverse function of the points' distances (Ashby, 1992; Nosofsky, 1992). Still other approaches posit that similarity is proportional to the degree to which the parts of the two compared objects can be aligned with one another (Markman and Gentner, 1993; Medin et al., 1993; Goldstone, 1994a). In all of these approaches, several sources of information (features, dimensions, or parts, respectively), not single criterial properties, are the basis for determining similarity.

Similarity assessments may typically integrate across many properties because it is natural for people to form impressions of overall similarity. In fact, evidence suggests that in many situations, it is easier for people to base similarity and cate-

[1] Although *bachelor* is often presented as one of the clearest cases of an easily definable concept, Lakoff (1986) argues that even here, the definition cannot account for cases such as seven-year old boys or popes being extremely poor examples of *bachelor*, if they are examples at all.

gorization judgments on more, rather than fewer, properties (Kemler, 1983; Goldstone, 1994b). For example, Sekuler and Abrams (1968) report cases in which people are faster to respond that two displays are identical along all their elements than that two displays have a single common element. Nickerson (1972) reviews evidence in favor of a fast, 'sameness detector' that allows people to quickly assess overall similarity between displays before being able to respond to particular dimensions. Individuals whose cognitive judgments are impeded, because they are young (Smith and Kemler, 1978; Kemler, 1983; Smith, 1989), inexperienced (Foard and Kemler Nelson, 1984), hurried (Ward, 1983), or distracted (Smith and Kemler Nelson, 1984), seem to rely on 'holistic' rather than 'analytic' processes. Thus, responding on the basis of overall, undifferentiated similarity may be a more primitive computation than responding on the basis of particular properties.

In a similar vein, Brooks (1978) argued that judging category membership by overall similarity is an often-used strategy, particularly when the category members are rich and multi-dimensional and the category rules are complicated (see also Allen and Brooks, 1991). Determining overall similarity across many properties is efficient relative to determining similarity with respect to a particular property when it is difficult to break an object down into separate features or aspects. Such a state of affairs is likely to occur for many real-world objects. Laboratory stimuli often 'wear their featural compositions on their sleeves,' but natural objects are seldom so obliging (Goldstone and Schyns, 1994; Schyns et al., 1998).

As all of this work illustrates, people have a strong disposition to process overall similarity, and doing so appears to serve a number of important cognitive functions. This is *not* to say that people do not also process similarity more analytically, a topic to which we turn shortly. Nevertheless, people do appear to process similarity holistically on many occasions. We propose that this basic tendency has its origins in perception, and that perception places important constraints on it, thereby mitigating Goodman's problem of unconstrained similarity. The perceptual system is geared toward providing overall similarity because of the importance of parallel comparison in object categorization. Rapid categorization is possible when multiple perceived properties can be matched in parallel to potentially corresponding properties in category knowledge. If processing were serial, processing would probably not be as efficient, and survival might be compromised. Thus, overall similarity may have evolved in perception to aid categorization, having the additional result of producing a comparison mechanism that is used broadly across many other cognitive tasks as well.

Overall similarity seems to be more efficiently processed by perceptual systems than amodal symbolic systems. First, the processes that allow simple features to be registered in parallel without a capacity limit are found widely throughout perceptual systems. For example, the features *red* and *horizontal line* can be detected simultaneously across an entire visual display (Treisman and Gelade, 1980), whereas non-visual semantic features cannot be detected in parallel with unlimited capacity (Mullin and Egeth, 1989). Second, perceptual systems often respond to multiple sources of information by blending them together without individuating the sources. For example, people can combine light from two spatial locations so that light detection depends on their summed energy (Bearse and Freeman, 1994). Amodal symbols are separately individuated, and thus require explicit combination of symbols in order to produce overall similarity responses. Overall responding can be achieved by analytically combining separated sources of information, or by never differentiating the sources in the first place; perceptual systems do both whereas amodal systems have profound difficulties with the second.

Overall similarity is computed efficiently by perceptual systems, but is useful for concepts more generally. Categories that permit many inductive inferences typically have members that share many features (Rosch and Mervis, 1975). In contrast to the members of metaphor-based categories (such as 'situations that are 'time bombs' waiting to go off' (Ortony, 1979; Glucksberg and Keysar, 1990)) or ad-hoc categories ('things to take from a burning house' (Barsalou, 1991)), our standard taxonomic categories, such as *chair*, *trout*, *bus*, *apple*, *saw* and *guitar*, are structured by overall similarity across many attributes. They are characterized by their effective compromise between within-category similarity and between-category dissimilarity (Rosch, 1975). If we know that something belongs to the category *bird*, then we know that it probably has two legs and two eyes, nests, flies, is smaller than a desk and so on. These inductive inferences are admissible because of the high overall similarity between members of the *bird* category. If we want to rapidly learn and deploy these taxonomic categories, it behooves us to pay attention to overall similarity.

3.3. Learned perceptual similarities

One reason why perceptual similarity is more powerful than might be thought is that it is not inflexible and insensitive to contextual factors. Although similarity certainly affects categorization, there is also an influence, albeit attenuated, in the reciprocal direction. Lassaline (1996) reports that judgments of induction across categories (e.g. if horses have property X, how likely is it that cows do?) have an influence on subsequent similarity assessments involving the same items. Kelly and Keil (1987) find that exposure to metaphors can even influence similarity judgments to different materials. For example, subjects who received the metaphor 'The New Yorker is the quiche of newspapers and magazines' gave higher similarity ratings to food-periodical pairs that had similar values on a *tastefulness* dimension (e.g. *steak* and *Sports Illustrated*) than did subjects who were not given these metaphors. In short, impressions of similarity are educated by the more sophisticated tasks that use them.

In the above examples, one could charge that the similarity assessments are influenced by high-level tasks simply because they are quite sophisticated judgments themselves. While similarity ratings do certainly seem sophisticated and cognitively penetrable, effects of categorization have also been found on tasks that tap more perceptually-based similarities. Goldstone (1994c) first trained subjects on one of several categorization conditions in which one physical dimension was relevant and another was irrelevant. Subjects were then transferred to same/different judgments (e.g. 'are these two squares physically identical?'). Ability to discriminate between squares in the same/different judgment task, measured by signal detection theory's d'(sensitivity) was greater when the squares varied along dimensions that were relevant during categorization training. In one case, experience with categorizing objects actually decreased people's ability to spot subtle perceptual differences between the objects, if the objects belonged to the same category. Similarly, work in categorical perception indicates that discriminations involving pairs of stimuli that straddle category boundaries are more easily made than are discriminations involving stimuli that fall within the same category, equating for physical dissimilarity between the pairs (Harnad, 1987).

Research in perceptual learning indicates influences of tasks on perceptual systems that are surprisingly early in the information processing sequence. For example, practice in discriminating small motions in different directions significantly alters electrical brain potentials that occur within 100 ms of the stimulus onset (Fahle and Morgan, 1996). These electrical changes are centered over the primary visual cortex, suggesting plasticity in early visual processing. Karni and Sagi (1991) similarly find that the primary visual cortex exhibits adaptation in simple discrimination tasks. In general, similarities are adapted to promote the categories or responses required for performing a task, and these adaptations often occur at an early stage of processing.

The argument that perceptual similarity is powerful because it can be tuned to an organism's needs is a two-edged sword. Turned around, similarity's critic can argue, 'the flexibility of similarity only exposes its inadequacy as a solid ground for explaining cognitive processes'. Certainly, similarity's explanatory value is attenuated if it is based on exactly those processes that it attempts to explain (similar arguments are presented by Goodman, 1972; Shanon, 1988; Rips, 1989). However, our position is that perceptual processing is slower to change than higher-level conceptual processing. New conceptualizations, such as categorizing a chair as a device suitable for reaching a light bulb, when the current tasks demand this (Barsalou, 1991), are not immediately transformed into modifications of the perceptual system. Perceptual learning is typically a prolonged process requiring thousands of trials of practice (Shiffrin and Lightfoot, 1997). Transitory conceptions or task-specific needs will not typically modify perceptual systems permanently. However, if a task-dependent categorization is frequently made, or is particularly promising for its organizing power, then it may eventually change perceptual similarities that are noticed. Experts eventually come to see the objects in their domain of expertise in a different way than novices (Biederman and Shiffrar, 1987; Burns and Shepp, 1988), and perceptual development in children may involve spotting new perceptual commonalities (Schyns et al., 1998).

In general, then, perceptual similarity may change, but over a small range with a relatively protracted time course. As such, it can serve as a point of departure for highly context-dependent cognitive process such as goal-driven categorization, metaphorical comparison and analogical reasoning. Since perception is flexibly tuned, the departure point itself moves, making often-traveled points more accessible (Goldstone, 1995a). Similarities that were once effortfully constructed, become second nature to the organism. In this manner, perceptual similarity can provide a useful starting-off point for specialized cognitive processes – useful because it has been tuned, although perhaps slowly, to the tasks that use it.

The distinction between slowly-changing perceptual processes and more labile conceptual processes is closely related to the associative/rule distinction (Smith and Sloman, 1994; Sloman, 1996). We suspect that associative mechanisms are, in general, a large class of relatively automatic processes, and that rule mechanisms are, in general, a large class of relatively controlled processes (Shiffrin and Schneider, 1977). Associative mechanisms tend to be those that process bursts of features made available automatically, either through parallel processing in perception or automatic activation in long-term memory. Rule mechanisms tend to be those that process individual features selectively through serial processing in working memory, using limited attentional resources. Whereas associative mechanisms require much practice to develop, rules can be constructed in an ad hoc manner to produce large immediate changes in performance.

3.4. Abstractions from perception

Until now, we have concentrated on the usefulness of perceptual information in conceptual representations. However, we underestimate the importance of perceptual information in concepts if we restrict ourselves to situations in which it is represented directly. In this section, we consider situations in which perception less directly, but not necessarily less strongly, 'jump starts' concepts, by motivating, informing and providing procedures for abstract thoughts.

If we focus on the current state of an abstract concept, we risk ignoring the simpler, less sophisticated starting point that was necessary for its development. Developmental evidence provides several examples of abstractions evolving out of what appear to have been perceptually-based concepts. For example, infants appear biased to treat parts of a display that move together as belonging to the same object (Spelke, 1990). Once spatially separated parts of a display are joined together in the same object because of their common motion, other object properties, such as edges, smoothly varying contours and uniform coloration, can be detected. The detection of motion is also instrumental in acquiring the distinction between living things and artifacts (Keil, 1989; Gelman, 1990; Mandler, 1992). Not all living things move, and not all artifacts are static, but Keil, Gelman and Mandler suggest that the original inspiration for this latter distinction may be based on movement patterns. In fact, children often treat human-made objects with irregular patterns of motion as being alive. This distinction has a significant impact on concepts, determining how extensively we infer properties from one member of a category to others, and whether we believe the categories are organized around essences. This elevated role in inductive reasoning belies the 'lowly' motion-based origin of the natural kind/artifact distinction.

We do not necessarily disagree with theorists who argue that biological categories are organized around 'theories' that involve genetic heritage, internal structure, birth, death and reproduction (Carey, 1985; Keil, 1989; Rips, 1989). For example, Carey's finding that children and adults are more likely to extend an unfamiliar property from humans to worms than from humans to toy monkeys may derive from knowledge concerning internal organs. However, we suggest that, in many cases, the original inspiration for constructing the theory comes from relatively simple, perceptual cues such as motion, the presence of internal fluids and so forth. Moreover, perceptual representations of events may underlie many abstract concepts (Barsalou, 1993; Barsalou and Prinz, 1997). In the spirit of the earlier section (Section 3.1) perceptual representations of reproductive events, such as mating and giving birth, may provide large amounts of implicit information that underlie biological theories. Without perceptual knowledge of these events, we suspect that people would have little understanding of biological concepts.

The evolution of abstract concepts from perceptual roots has other applications. Pure mathematical concepts are often originally inspired by perceptual evidence. In the development of number concepts, there is strong evidence that children rely on perceptual representations. (Stigler, 1984; Huttenlocher et al., 1994). Similarly, mathematicians frequently report first creating a visual 'proof' of a theorem, and only subsequently derive the symbolic, and publishable, version, written out in theorems and lemmas (Hadamard, 1949; Barwise and Etchemendy, 1990, 1991; Anderson, 1997). In problem solving, one of the most effective ways of deriving an abstract schema, such as 'overcoming an object by converging weak intensity forces from several pathways onto the object' is to use several concrete examples (Gick and Holyoak, 1983). Categorizations that are based on a complex abstract rule may initially be solved by using perceptual similarity between items to be categorized and known category members (Brooks, 1978; Allen and Brooks, 1991).

Another body of evidence indicates that experimentally-noticed perceptual similarities alter more abstract processes. Requiring subjects to perform similarity judgments on pairs of scenes makes subjects more likely to treat the scenes in an abstract manner subsequently (Markman and Gentner, 1993). For example, early similarity judgments promote responses based on common roles (e.g. 'these two things correspond to each other because they are both donors') rather than on superficial attributes (e.g. 'these go together because they are both men'). As another example, when people are shown an object to be categorized, they are often reminded of a superficially similar object. Once reminded, they try to come up with an abstract description for the category that encompasses both objects (Ross et al., 1990).

In sum, even when concepts eventually come to be characterized by abstractions, these abstractions owe their existence to perceptual similarity. Two consequences follow. First, conceptual end states do not imply an absence of perceptual origins. Even if the end-state of a concept were free of perceptual information, perceptual processing may have been required to build it. Second, perceptually-inspired abstractions can provide a mechanism for developing abstractions not currently within the abstract system's powers. New expressive capacities arise when abstractive processes create new uses and descriptions for concepts that have been established perceptually.

To borrow an example from evolution, where we have good reasons to think that genuinely new structures and functions arise, mammalian ear bones probably evolved from jaw bones (Gould, 1993). The sound-transmitting function of the jaw/ear bones was only selected for once the biting function of the jaw had already established the jaw bone's basic shape. Likewise, the starting shape of our concepts may be perceptually-specified initially, but can be transformed in quite different directions once developed. Later structures (ear bones and abstractions) depend on and grow out of earlier structures (jaw bones and perceptually-based concepts) for their very existence even as they acquire radically different functions.

In Section 3.6 we suggest several examples of conceptual mechanisms (highlighting, structuring, productivity) that may have evolved from perceptual mechanisms (e.g. selectivity, binding, juxtaposition). Although Fodor (1975) has argued that it impossible for a symbolic representation system to learn concepts that have expressive powers not already present in the system, we propose that perceptual mechanisms have lead the conceptual system to entertain hypotheses that it would not otherwise have entertained. Our view stresses the evolution of concepts from perception, through processes that can eventually achieve abstract end states.

3.5. Perceptual simulation in conceptual tasks

Standard conceptual tasks that lack pictorial materials offer a means of assessing how far perception extends into conceptual processing. In the feature-listing task, for example, subjects receive the word for a concept and verbally list features typically true of its instances (e.g. list features typically true of 'watermelons'). Similarly, in the property-verification task, subjects receive the word for a concept and verify whether a second word specifies a property true of the concept (e.g. for 'watermelon' is 'seeds' a property?). In neither task do subjects receive pictures, nor are they asked to use imagery. Instead, they receive only linguistic materials with neutral instructions.

Perceptual mechanisms play no role in standard theories of these tasks. Instead, these theories assume that subjects access feature lists, frames and semantic nets that only contain amodal symbols. Recent evidence, however, strongly implicates perceptual mechanisms (for a review, see Barsalou et al., 1997). Rather than accessing amodal representations, subjects appear to simulate referents of the concepts perceptually and then scan these simulations to produce the required information.

For example, Wu's (1995) dissertation found evidence of perceptual simulation in the feature listing task. Subjects produced features for nouns (e.g. 'watermelon') and related noun phrases (e.g. 'half watermelon'). Two sources of evidence indicated that subjects simulated the referents of these nouns and noun phrases in order to list features. First, subjects who received neutral instructions produced essentially the same features as subjects asked to construct and describe images, suggesting that the neutral subjects adopted images spontaneously. Second, the visibility of features in real-world referents (not encountered in the experiment) predicted their likelihood of being produced. For example, the feature *seeds* is occluded in the perception of a whole watermelon but is visible in the perception of a half watermelon. Across four experiments, noun phrases, for referents with non-occluded internal properties (e.g. 'half watermelon') produced much higher rates of internal feature listing than nouns for referents with occluded internal properties (e.g. 'watermelon'). These results strongly suggest that subjects simulated referents of the concepts perceptually in order to produce features.

Perhaps subjects in Wu's experiments performed perceptual simulation because feature listing is a deliberate, recall-oriented task that allows time for such simulations. If so, then we shouldn't observe such effects in faster, recognition-oriented tasks that produce reaction times under 1 s. To explore this issue, Solomon's (Solomon, 1997) dissertation explored the role of perceptual simulation in the property verification task (for a preliminary report, see Olseth and Barsalou, 1995).[2] Although Kosslyn (1976, 1980) found no evidence of perceptual simulation when neutral subjects performed property verification, the easy false trials in his experiments made such simulation unnecessary. Like Kosslyn, Solomon found that when the false trials were easy (e.g. does a *crab* have a *brick*?), subjects adopted a linguistic associative strategy that bypassed conceptual knowledge and perceptual simulation. However, when the false trials were difficult (e.g. does a *crab* have a *fin*?), subjects could not use the linguistic associative strategy and had to use conceptual knowledge instead. Under these conditions, perceptual factors, such as property size, provide the best prediction of reaction time. Thus, when subjects were forced to perform conceptual processing, they resorted to perceptual simulation to find and verify property information about concepts.

Further evidence for this conclusion comes from the second half of Solomon's 1997 dissertation. In these experiments, the perceptual similarity of parts was manipulated across trials. Whereas one subject might first verify the concept-property pair, *PONY-mane*, and later the pair, *HORSE-mane*, another subject might first verify *LION-mane* and later *HORSE-mane*. If subjects perceptually simulate the concepts to verify the parts, then they should be faster for the *PONY-HORSE* sequence than for the *LION-HORSE* sequence, because pony manes are more similar to horse manes than are lion manes. When subjects process the *HORSE-mane* pair, they are reminded of the earlier pair involving *mane*, which either facilitates or inhibits processing. Across three experiments, Solomon observed this result, suggesting that subjects perceptually simulated the concepts to perform verifications. One could argue that this effect results from *HORSE* being more similar to *PONY* in general than to *LION*. To assess this possibility, all experiments included materials in which the part is equally similar to all three concepts. For example, the part, *back*, is roughly the same across *PONY*, *HORSE*, and *LION*. For these materials, there is no difference between sequences such as *PONY-HORSE* and *LION-HORSE*, indicating that part similarity, not concept similarity, is the important factor.

Together, the results from these three projects indicate that perceptual simulation is central to conceptual processing. Even when subjects receive no pictorial materials and are not asked to use imagery, they nevertheless perform perceptual simulation spontaneously.

3.6. Parallels between perceptual and conceptual processing

Contrary to the Greek philosophers' polarized dichotomy between perception and
_____
[2]Karen Olseth is now Karen Olseth Solomon.

cognition, we have seen that there is good reason to believe that cognitive processes borrow from perceptual ones. Cognitive economy and evolutionary considerations (large frontal lobes being a relatively recent evolutionary advance) encourage the co-option (borrowing) of perceptual processes for symbolic cognition. Thus, although some symbolic reasoning operations appear to have no perceptual equivalent (e.g. deduction and modus tollens; but see Johnson-Laird (1983) for concrete models of these abstract operations, and Rips (1986) for a reconsideration), many suggestive parallels can nevertheless be drawn elsewhere. The points to be taken from these parallels are: (a) that properties typically associated with abstract cognition are often present in perceptual systems, (b) perceptual systems have mechanisms that are useful for more abstract cognition and provide new insights into how higher-order cognition may operate and (c) patterns of correlations between perceptual and conceptual processes suggest that they share common mechanisms. While the evidence for (c) is admittedly correlational rather than causal, additional considerations with respect to the evolution and development of mental abilities suggest that these correlations may often be due to conceptual processes borrowing from perceptual ones. Table 1 lists several parallels, which we consider next.

3.6.1. Selectivity

A hallmark of abstract, rule-like, cognition is that it emphasizes certain properties over others. To apply the rule 'an island is any piece of land completely surrounded by water' to a particular plot of land, one must emphasize this *criterial* attribute and ignore characteristic island features such as *tropical* and *sandy* (Keil, 1989). This selective highlighting of important attributes has a clear parallel in the considerable body of work on selective attention (for a review, see Johnston and Dark, 1986). Many properties of perceptual attention make it a promising candidate for subserving situations where more abstract highlighting of properties is needed, and indeed recent theories of knowledge and language have incorporated it centrally (e.g. Talmy, 1983; Langacker, 1986; Mandler, 1992; Barsalou, 1993). First and most basically, perceptual selection of relevant information is highly effective. Researchers have found that when people are instructed to respond to one of two overlapping shapes, there is very little processing of the irrelevant shape (Garner, 1974, 1978; Rock and Gutman, 1981; also Melara and Marks, 1990), and very little performance decrement compared with when just one shape is shown (Neisser and Becklen, 1975). Second, attention can be directed to particular stimulus properties (Treisman

Table 1
Parallels between cognitive and perceptual processes.

Cognition	Perception
Highlighting	Selective attention
Abstraction	Blurring, filtering
Structuring	Binding
Differentiation	Dimensionalization
Analogy	Cross-modal matching
Productivity	Image juxtaposition

and Gelade, 1980), and properties automatically capture attention if they have been important during prolonged training (Shiffrin and Schneider, 1977; Logan and Etherton, 1994). This latter capacity could underlie people's ability to learn new criterial, abstract definitions. Third, attention is not only directed by simple stimulus properties, but also by semantic coherence and context (Triesman, 1960). If perceptual selection processes were not capable of being driven by higher-level properties, then it would have had limited application to more strategic cognition.

From this description of perceptual selection, it is clear that, at a minimum, we cannot use selectivity as evidence for symbolic, rule-like cognition. Perception also benefits from a sharp, efficacious form of selectivity.[3]Our critic then continues, 'just because both abstract reasoning and perception have mechanisms for highlighting relevant properties does not mean that the abstract ability derives from the perceptual ability'. Although far from definitive, evidence exists for the co-option of perceptual selective attention by cognitive selective attention. One line of evidence comes from an examination of individual differences and mental disorders. For example, schizophrenic patients have characteristic attentional and cognitive deficits that parallel each other in interesting ways. Cognitive correlates of schizophrenia include abnormal word associations, problems with developing coherent discourses and difficulties with abstract thought that stem from intrusions of superficial information (Schwartz, 1982). Perceptual correlates of schizophrenia include problems with allocating attention to relevant stimulus attributes, driving attention by informative cues and inhibiting irrelevant attributes (Liotti et al., 1993).

The parallel between these high- and low-level deficits is that both involve problems with selective attention. The pattern of correlations is well explained if the same selective attention processes are at work for surprisingly different levels of processing, among tasks that many have claimed to be handled by special modules (e.g. for language and visual information). Although the evidence above is principally correlation, there is further suggestive evidence that perceptually-based selective attention is borrowed for more conceptual selective attention, rather than vice versa. Schreiber et al. (1992) found that schizophrenic patients show impairments on a visual selection task before cognitive impairments arise, even when the tasks are roughly equated for their sensitivity at diagnosing abnormalities. The implication of this result is that if perceptually-based selective attention processes go awry, then more general cognitive impairments of selective attention may follow.

The perceptual and cognitive deficits of schizophrenics seem to be attributed to attentional processes that are insufficiently selective (Beech et al., 1989). That is, schizophrenics have particular difficulty inhibiting inappropriate thoughts and irrelevant perceptions. Conversely, many of the perceptual and cognitive symptoms of childhood autism, including minimizing sensory stimulation, focused attention on a single environmental cue, abnormally narrow generalizations from training and lack of productive language, may be traced to an overly selective attentional process

---

[3]This is not inconsistent with the earlier argument for a primitive sense of overall similarity. We seem to have both effective routines for processing overall similarity and routines for selectively overruling this primitive process, consistent with the automatic versus controlled distinction that we applied earlier to the associative-rule distinction.

(Lovass et al., 1979). A narrowing of attention characterizes both autistic perceptual behavior and autistic use of words and concepts. Sensations and semantic meanings outside of a tightly restricted range are ignored.

Another example of surprising correlations between superficially dissimilar perceptual and conceptual tasks is found in individual differences in 'field (in)dependence' (Wapner and Demick, 1991). Field dependent individuals have difficulty selectively attending to one component of a stimulus while ignoring its context. In the canonical test for field dependence, people locate hidden figures that are embedded in a scene. Most importantly, proficient performance on this perceptual task is correlated with conceptual tasks, such as making fine semantic categorizations, drawing sharp boundaries between concepts, verbal coding strategies and constrained analogical reasoning. In reviewing the evidence for field (in)dependent personalities, Miller (1987) concludes that there are selective attention (and its converse, holistic integration) operations that are shared by a wide array of perceptual and conceptual processes.

Selective attention to important stimulus aspects may emerge from one of two processes – a process that focuses on important, criterial, or goal-based aspects, or a process that actively suppresses irrelevant aspects. While many theories of abstract reasoning focus on the former, recent perceptually-based work has found a strong presence of the latter. For example, research on 'negative priming' (Neill, 1977; Tipper, 1992) has shown that people are slower to respond to a target if it was a distractor on previous trials. Again, non-perceptual equivalents are available. Processes exist to inhibit irrelevant memories (Anderson and Spellman, 1995) and words (Gernsbacher and Faust, 1991), depending on how much they compete with other, potentially more appropriate items.

In short, there appear to be strong correlations between classes of cognitive and perceptual behavior that stem from shared processes of selective attention to relevant properties, and selective inhibition of irrelevant properties. If this speculation is correct, then we might expect interference between cognitive and perceptual tasks that both make demands on the same selective attention process. Focusing on a target location or property (as with Flanker and Stroop tasks) should interfere with focusing on criterial properties in a categorization task. Regardless of the empirical outcome, given the functional similarities between perceptual and conceptual processes for highlighting relevant information, it is plausible that some of the early (phylogenetically and developmentally) processes for allocating perceptual attention would be co-opted for later processes.

3.6.2. Blurring and filtering

Turning to some of the other parallels in Table 1, it is somewhat surprising to note a link between abstraction, often considered the epitome of cognition that has transcended perception, and the 'lowly' processes of blurring and filtering. By blurring, we are referring to any process that removes detailed information from further processing. To abstract is to distill the essence from its superficial trappings. The conventional way to do this is by developing a 'schema' that is tuned to the essence (Gick and Holyoak, 1983). Another way is to blur over the irrelevant aspects. Blurring has the advantage that it can operate even when the essential schema cannot be formulated. One does not need to know what makes something a dog in order to categorize the neighbor's poodle as a dog, as long as one knows that a beagle is a dog, and is able to ignore (blur over) the differences between poodles and beagles. Visual agnosias provide support for the notion of categorizing by blurring. Often brain damage in visual processing areas results in preserved ability to make coarse categorizations (e.g. 'I know this is some kind of animal'), despite an inability to use narrower categories (Farah, 1990). An agnosic patient may be able to perceive that a photograph depicts some sort of animal without recognizing the animal to be a cat. Similarly, 18-month old children show sensitivity to broader categories such as *vehicle* and *animal* without showing sensitivity to narrower categories like *dog* and *car* (Mandler et al., 1991). Thus, people who have not yet learned how to, or have lost their ability to, categorize at relatively narrow levels, may still be able to make broad categorizations. This suggests that broad categorizations can be obtained simply by not registering within-category differences.

Blurring is a particularly appropriate technique when the superficial aspects are details, and the global structure is correlated with important abstractions. Furthermore, *strategic* blurring may cause only particular features to be ignored, thereby permitting features known to be irrelevant to exert little influence on behavior, even if the relevant features have not been identified. Strategic blurring is probably instantiated by attentional, rather than visual, means, given that the attentional system shows flexibility in allocating intermediate degrees of attention to stimulus features. At times, attention given to a stimulus feature nearly optimally matches the feature's diagnosticity for a task (Shaw, 1982; Nosofsky, 1986). Thus, ignoring is not necessarily all-or-none. Whereas amodal abstractions must either represent or not represent a property, an advantage of incorporating perceptual attention in high-level cognition is that it provides a mechanism for partially representing a property.[4]

3.6.3. Structure and binding

The binding of arguments to values is often proposed as a structure that distinguishes high-level cognition from its lower-level counterpart. The proposition *Loves(John, Mary)* means something different than *Loves(Mary, John)*, much to John's dismay. The predicate *Loves* takes arguments that are ordered by their roles, with the 'agent' role bound to John, and the 'patient' role bound to Mary. This binding of objects to roles establishes a structure in propositions that goes beyond the representational capacities of 'flat' representations such as feature lists (Barsalou, 1992, 1993; Barsalou and Hale, 1993). Although structured representations are necessary for orderly thought, abstract thought is not alone in this regard.

---

[4]The typical solution to representing partially diagnostic information in amodal representations is to attach numeric weights such as (Bird (lays eggs 0.95) (flies 0.76)). However, this solution requires the semi-diagnostic features to be represented as fully as the diagnostic features. In many cases, it is desirable to have the quality or size of the actual feature representation correspond to its diagnosticity.

Detailed mechanisms are now available to describe the role of binding in perception. Elements from a person's left-eye image are bound to their corresponding elements from the right-eye image, such that globally harmonious structures, and the perception of depth, are established (Marr and Poggio, 1979). Similarly, elements from one 'frame' of an event are bound to their corresponding elements from the subsequent frame on the basis of local similarity and their respective roles within frames, in order to establish the perception of motion (Dawson, 1991). Finally, models of object recognition work by binding the parts of a perceived object to the parts of an internal object model (Hummel and Biederman, 1992). Thus, a suitcase is recognized by binding one part of an image to a 'handle' role and the rest of the image to a 'container' role. Bindings are created by first passing inhibitory and excitatory signals between image elements so that elements belonging to a single part are activated in phase with each other. Bindings, thus, can be implemented by synchronized patterns of activity between the elements. In the case of Hummel and Biederman's model, these bindings may connect amodal symbols such as the 'handle' role to a part, but also occur between perceptually-grounded representations such as two image parts.

While these models of perceptual binding offer mechanisms for the structuring of abstract thought (for an application to analogical reasoning, see Hummel and Holyoak, 1997), they also offer the exciting possibility of intermediate degrees of binding. This possibility is neglected by standard propositional representations because of their explicit, all-or-none assignment of arguments to roles. In contrast, most perceptually-motivated models of binding provide a dynamic and temporally extended mechanism for establishing structures, with completely unambiguous, one-to-one bindings as only a special case. For example, in Goldstone and Medin (1994; Goldstone, 1994a) model of similarity assessments, parts of two scenes are gradually placed into alignment to the extent that they are similar and play the same role in their respective scenes. Until the alignments are fully established, a particular part may be bound 70% to another part. Such an approach holds promise for abstract cognition as well. Even in the abstract domains of analogical reasoning and problem solving, the determination of abstract correspondences is imperfect (Gentner and Toupin, 1986), and is sensitive to superficially misleading features (Holyoak and Koh, 1987; Ross, 1987). In reading comprehension, fast processing is characterized by minimal inferences that can be established by unstructured priming rather than thoroughly worked out conceptual assignments (McKoon and Ratcliff, 1992). People's primitive preferences also seem to use imperfect bindings. Drinks labeled 'not poisonous' are rated as undesirable, presumably because 'poisonous' is somewhat free-floating, not completely bound to 'not' (Rozin et al., 1990). In sum, perception requires structured binding as much as does abstract cognition, and mechanisms of perceptual binding may better explain cases of intermediate degrees of binding than do amodal propositions.

3.6.4. Differentiation, subcategories and dimensions

A primary method for refining thought is to differentiate – to take a rough category and sub-divide it into smaller categories. Researchers frequently describe the development of children's concepts as differentiation. Children, who originally confuse weight and density (Smith et al., 1985), or goats and dogs (Mandler and McDonough, 1991; Mandler et al, 1991), develop cognitively by creating distinct concepts for the originally confounded entities. Interestingly, child development also involves a parallel process of dimensionalization – breaking apart dimensions that were originally fused. Evidence suggests that dimensions easily separated by adults, such as the brightness and size of a square, are fused together for children (Kemler, 1983; Smith, 1989). For example, children have difficulty identifying whether two objects differ on their brightness or size, even though they can easily see that they differ in some way. Both differentiation and dimensionalization occur throughout one's lifetime. Tanaka and Taylor (1991) show that experts in a domain become increasingly adept at making subordinate-level categorizations. Dog experts, for example, can distinguish between German shepherd and golden retrievers as fast as they can distinguish between dogs and cats; non-experts are much faster at the latter discrimination. Likewise, dimensions that are psychologically fused for most adults, such as the chroma and hue of a color, can become separated with practice (Goldstone, 1994c). Artists and scientists who deal with colors regularly are better than non-experts at extracting dimensional information about chroma while ignoring hue differences (Burns and Shepp, 1988).

The primary reason to think that cognitive differentiation and perceptual dimensionalization share fundamental mechanisms is that it is simply hard to make a principled distinction between dimensions (features) and concepts. Many of the features that have been proposed for describing concepts (e.g. 'nests' and 'lays eggs' for 'bird,' 'has wheels' and 'has engine' for 'car' and 'sit on, and 'legs' for 'chair') are concepts in their own right (Schyns et al., 1998). If we dispense with the traditional division between concepts and dimensions, then we can potentially take advantage of the interesting work on computational mechanisms that ground conceptual differentiation in perceptual dimensionalization (de Sa and Ballard, 1997; Smith et al., 1997). For example, in the neural network model of Smith et al., the network's ability to assess specific similarities and differences between objects depends on the network's first creating separate perceptual dimensions along different units. Furthermore, this link also explains why the left hemisphere appears specialized for both fine perceptual discriminations, such as when stimuli have high spatial frequencies or when subjects are told to use a strict criteria for identification (Robertson and Lamb, 1991), and relatively differentiated language use, such as choosing the appropriate meaning of an ambiguous word (Burgess and Simpson, 1988). Conversely, the right hemisphere seems better tuned to relatively global, multi-dimensional perceptual aspects and relatively broad linguistic categories (Brownell et al., 1990). Thus, it is at least plausible to believe that the processes that split percepts into dimensions and more abstract categories into sub-categories may be related.

3.6.5. Cross-modal matching

In the spirit of speculative inquiry, we include two additional parallels between conceptual and perceptual processes. An ability to reason analogically may borrow from perceptual processes that underlie cross-modal matching, which is characterized by people's naturally tendency to link distinct sensory domains. The most publicized example of this phenomenon is the synesthesia experienced by rare individuals who experience, for example, vivid auditory percepts when shown visual stimuli and vice versa. However, even normal adults seem predisposed to directly perceive relations between separate sensory modalities such as loudness, pitch and color (Melara, 1989).

3.6.6. Productivity

The operation of productivity (combining atomic units together to create larger structures) is important for abstract thought because it produces mundane creativity; a potentially infinite number of new thoughts can be generated by recombining existing thoughts in new arrangements. Although productivity is typically associated with amodal systems, perceptual representations can support an equivalent operation: spatio-temporal juxtaposition (Barsalou, 1993; Barsalou and Prinz, 1997; Prinz, 1997; Prinz and Barsalou, 1997). Separate images can be juxtaposed to produce new images. Furthermore, evidence exists that new interpretations can accompany these juxtapositions. When asked to rotate an imagined 'D' counterclockwise 90°, and then intersecting an imagined 'J' such that the top of the 'J' touches the top of the rotated 'D,' subjects often are able to reinterpret their concatenation as an umbrella (Finke et al., 1989). Fodor and Pylyshyn (1988) argue that amodal symbols are required for compositionality, which is required, in turn, for productivity; our point is that images, not merely amodal symbols, can and do function as the atomic units that are combined.

3.6.7. Summary

The significance of these parallels is two-fold. The first point is that many properties of abstract cognition, when explored from the perspective of processes that could furnish them, are also found in perceptual systems (for other parallels between perceptual and conceptual categories, see Medin and Barsalou, 1987). Claims that abstract cognition is special because it highlights relevant properties, is abstractive, has argument structure, permits analysis into components, or allows productivity are weakened by the presence of perceptual equivalents. In several cases, much more is known about the mechanisms of these perceptual processes than is known about their conceptual counterparts (Ullman, 1984), and, pragmatically speaking, we would be well-advised to use this knowledge to guide our understanding of abstract thought. The second, more speculative, point is that these parallels are hardly coincidental but arise because important mechanisms are common to perception and cognition. An extreme version of this position is unlikely, but an examination of individual differences, task manipulations and neuropsychological data provides enough evidence for correlations between perceptual and conceptual tasks to encourage exploration of the possibility that some of the process pairs of Table 1 are linked by process-overlap rather than by mere analogy.

4. Remaining issues

In an attempt to reunite perceptual and conceptual processing, we have argued that perceptual mechanisms provide unexpectedly rich and useful resources for implementing a conceptual system. First, perceptual representations are powerful, because they can implicitly represent properties of the external world in an analog fashion. Fairly abstract properties, such as the regression coefficient and minimal spanning distance, can be represented in analog systems without being calculated explicitly. Second, impressions of overall, undifferentiated similarity seem to be perceptually primary and to be exactly the perceptually-constrained type of similarity that is useful in creating many common categories. Third, perceptual similarity is not static, but changes as a function of the categorization demands confronting an organism. This flexibility reduces the gap between perception and sophisticated analytic concepts. Fourth, even when concepts seem to have little perceptual basis, their origins can often be traced to perceptual processing. Fifth, people appear to perform perceptual simulation in conceptual tasks that have no perceptual demands. Sixth, striking commonalities exist between the mechanisms that process abstract information and those established for perception. Correlations between cognitive tasks (e.g. problem solving, language and reasoning) and perceptual tasks suggest that shared mechanisms underlie them.

4.1. The perceptual/conceptual distinction

Is there a continuum from perceptual to conceptual representations, and, if so, what varies along this continuum? Given the top-down influences of concepts on perception (e.g. Goldstone, 1995b) and the surprisingly far-reaching influences of expectations on low-level perceptual judgments (e.g. Peterson and Gibson, 1994), searching for *the* boundary between perception and conception is most likely futile. However, it may be useful to describe a *continuum* from perceptual to conceptual. What varies along this continuum is how much and what sort of top-down processing has been done to bottom-up input information. Specifying exactly where expectations and conceptual pressures influence processing along the perception/conception continuum is a real, although highly empirical, question. The general principle that conceptual processes can more readily be tuned to particular demands than perceptual processes probably has some validity. When we categorize 'T's and tilted 'T's as belonging to the same letter category, it increases their rated similarity (here, similarity ratings, despite 'similarity' in their name, are relatively conceptual tasks!). However, categorizing 'T's and tilted 'T's has little influence on more perceptual measures of similarity, such as our ability to quickly spot the borderline between a group of 'T's and a group of tilted 'T's (Beck, 1966). Similarly, one's momentary goals have clear and large influences on cognitive processes such as description and inference (Barsalou and Sewell, 1984), but less influence on perceptual processes such as figure/ground segmentation, color afterimages, edge detection, and same/different discrimination, (or it is more surprising when they do have an influence (Moscovici and Personnaz, 1991)).

We also assume that conception differs from perception in degree of productivity. In conception, one can combine perceptual representations in ways that go far beyond perception. In imagining the Cheshire Cat from *Alice in Wonderland*, productivity is freed from the constraints of actual perception. Real cats don't have human smiles, and their bodies don't fade in and out while their smiles remain. Although conception may have fundamental underpinnings in perception, its ability to manipulate schematic perceptual representations productively allows it to go considerably further.

4.2. The perceptual/abstract distinction

We are less sanguine about the usefulness of a perceptual/abstract continuum. Perception often involves the abstraction of certain elements. Concrete details are often blurred over, ignored or actively suppressed. Similarly, selective attention can focus analytically on a perceptual dimension, extracting information about that aspect of experience. As Arnheim (1969) points out, the difference between realistic and abstract art is not one of concreteness or relevance of perception. Abstract art is, of course, concrete. An understanding of perceptual processes is often of fundamental importance for creating and appreciating abstract art. The abstractions at work in a piece of music or painting are often not the same sort of abstractions present in a novel. For example, in a painting, abstractions often deal with spatial relations, relations between colors and the manner of dividing and integrating different areas on the canvas. Often, it is notoriously difficult to verbally describe these perceptual abstractions (e.g. those in the works of Picasso). The representations in a particular perceptual domain (hearing or seeing) may be highly abstract even though they are constrained by concrete qualities of the particular domain.

A corollary to the notion that abstractions can be abstract even when tied to their particular perceptual domain, is that it is misleading to equate 'perceptual' and 'superficial.' A traditional assumption, particularly in research on analogical reasoning, is that comparisons based on perceptual aspects are superficial. Accordingly, the *deep* similarity between time bombs and cigarettes is that they both cause delayed damage; the fact that they both involve fire is deemed superficial (and hence less interesting or important). In contrast, following Bassok (Bassok and Olseth, 1995; Bassok et al., 1995), we believe that perceptual aspects typically are at least cues for the abstraction that is built, and often are never removed from the abstraction. The similarity between diving boards and bed springs depends on perceptual aspects (a bouncing motion with gradual deceleration and acceleration). These perceptual aspects are 'deep' in the sense that they permit widespread causal inferences between highly dissimilar objects, and that they result from general physical laws. Many physical, biological and psychological principles that are discussed in everyday life produce perceptual effects, and our perceptual systems have been refined to make this apparent. Given this, perceptually-based comparisons probably yield more reliable inferences than those produced by analogies that are completely stripped of their perceptual grounds.

4.3. Concluding remarks

In endorsing the perceptual/conceptual distinction, we essentially argue that being conceptual is being abstract. In not endorsing the perceptual/abstract distinction, we implicitly deny the requirement that abstract knowledge be amodal. Instead, we argue that abstract knowledge can be constituted from perceptual bases.

There is a certain tension between two of our arguments. On the one hand, we have argued that perceptual representations are useful because of the constraints and mechanisms inherent in their unprocessed, image-like representations. On the other hand, we have also argued that perceptual systems provide abstractive and selective processes that allow perception to distort or transform sensory inputs. These positions can be reconciled. Perceptual processes vary in how much they transform the original sensory input, yet concrete aspects of the input are rarely, if ever, discarded completely. The special case of completely amodal symbols can be approximated by highly-transformed perceptual representations. There is a continuum of distance from sensory input, with amodal symbols constituting an ideal endpoint. Recognizing this continuum allows us to imagine thought processes that highlight, structure and abstract information, without discarding all perceptual contents. Rather than implicating dichotomies between bound versus unbound representations, holistic versus analytic processes and abstract versus concrete thought, the reviewed evidence suggests continua instead. In developing future theories of cognition, it may be fruitful to design architectures capable of implementing a wide variety of special cases along these continua, as required under varying task demands.

We are left with the question of what role, if any, do amodal symbols play in conceptual knowledge? We have seen that perceptual mechanisms can accomplish many of the functions that are well-known for amodal symbol systems. On the basis of such observations, one might be inclined to adopt the eliminativist view that amodal symbols are unnecessary. We can think of two reasons why one might want to maintain amodal symbols. First, if there is some necessary function of intelligence that amodal symbols can accomplish that perceptual ones cannot, then this is an obvious reason for maintaining amodal symbols. Second, we might find that amodal symbols deliver certain conceptual functions more efficiently that perceptual symbols. Even though perceptual symbols could implement the same functions, amodal symbols may do so more optimally.

Regardless of where one comes down on the eliminative/agnostic distinction, we believe that perceptual mechanisms underlie conceptual processing to a considerable degree. From overall similarity to analytic rules, many sources of evidence implicate perception in conception.

Acknowledgements

We would like to thank Douglas Medin and Linda Smith for useful comments. This research was supported by National Science Foundation grant SBR-9409232, a

Gill Fellowship and a James McKeen Cattell Award to Robert Goldstone and by National Science Foundation grant SBR-9421326 to Lawrence Barsalou.

References

Allen, S.W., Brooks, L.R., 1991. Specializing the operation of an explicit rule. Journal of Experimental Psychology: General 120, 3–19.

Anderson, J.A., 1997. Seven times seven is about 50: learning arithmetic with a neural network. In: S. Sternberg (Ed.), Invitation to Cognitive Science. MIT Press, Cambridge, MA, in press.

Anderson, M.C., Spellman, B.A., 1995. On the status of inhibitory mechanisms in cognition: memory retrieval as a model case. Psychological Review 102, 68–100.

Arnheim, R., 1969. Visual Thinking. Faber and Faber, London.

Ashby, F.G., 1992. Multidimensional Models of Perception and Cognition. Erlbaum, Hillsdale, NJ.

Barsalou, L.W., 1991. Deriving categories to achieve goals. In: Bower, G.H. (Ed.), The Psychology of Learning and Motivation: Advances in Research and Theory, Vol. 27. Academic Press, New York.

Barsalou, L.W., 1992. Frames, concepts, and conceptual fields. In: Kittay, E., Lehrer, A. (Eds.), Frames, Fields, and Contrasts: New Essays in Semantic and Lexical Organization. Erlbaum, Hillsdale, NJ, pp. 21–74.

Barsalou, L.W., 1993. Flexibility, structure, and linguistic vagary in concepts: manifestations of a compositional system of perceptual symbols. In: Collins, A.C., Gathercole, S.E., Conway, M.A., (Eds.), Theories of Memories. Erlbaum, London, pp. 29–101.

Barsalou, L.W., Hale, C.R., 1993. Components of conceptual representation: from feature lists to recursive frames. In: Van Mechelen, I, Hampton, J., Michalski, R, Theuns, P (Eds.), Categories and Concepts: Theoretical Views and Inductive Data Analysis. Academic Press, San Diego, CA, pp. 97–144.

Barsalou, L.W., Prinz, J.J., 1997. Mundane creativity in perceptual symbol systems. In: Ward, T.B., Smith, S.M., Vaid, J. (Eds.), Creative Thought: An investigation of Conceptual Structures and Processes. American Psychological Association, Washington, DC, pp. 267–307.

Barsalou, L.W., Sewell, D.R., 1984. Constructing categories from different points of view. Emory Cognition Report No. 2. Emory University, Atlanta, GA.

Barsalou, L.W., Solomon, K.O., Wu, L.L., 1997. Perceptual simulation in conceptual tasks. In: Hiraga, M.K., Sinha, C, Wilcox, S. (Eds.), Cultural, Typological, and Psychological Perspectives in Cognitive Linguistics: the Proceedings of the 4th Conference of the International Cognitive Linguistics Association, Vol. 3. John Benjamins, Amsterdam, pp. 337–346.

Barsalou, L.W., Yeh, W., Luka, B.J., Olseth, K.L., Mix, K.S., Wu, L., 1993. Concepts and meaning. In: Beals, K, Cooke, G., Kathman, D., McCullough, K.E., Kita, Testen, D. (Eds.), Chicago Linguistics Society 29: Papers from the Parasession on Conceptual Representations. Chicago Linguistics Society, University of Chicago, pp. 23–61.

Barwise, J., Etchemendy, J., 1990. Information, infons, and inference. In: Cooper, R., Mukai, K., Perry, J. (Eds.), Situation Theory and its Applications. University of Chicago Press, Chicago, pp. 33–78.

Barwise, J., Etchemendy, J., 1991. Visual information and valid reasoning. In: Zimmerman, W., Cunningham, S. (Eds.), Visualization in Mathematics. Mathematical Association of America, Washington, pp. 9–24.

Bassok, M., Olseth, K., 1995. Object-based representations: transfer between cases of continuous and discrete models of change. Journal of Experimental Psychology: Learning, Memory, and Cognition 21, 1522–1538.

Bassok, M., Wu, L., Olseth, K., 1995. Judging a book by its cover: interpretative effects of content on problem-solving transfer. Memory and Cognition 23, 354–367.

Bearse, M.A., Freeman, R.D., 1994. Binocular summation in orientation discrimination depends on stimulus contrast and duration. Vision Research 34, 19–29.

Beck, J., 1966. Effect of orientation and of shape similarity on perceptual grouping. Perception and Psychophysics 1, 300–302.

Beech, A., Powell, T., McWilliam, J., Claridge, G., 1989. Evidence of reduced 'cognitive inhibition' in schizophrenia. British Journal of Clinical Psychology 28, 109–116.

Biederman, I., Shiffrar, M.M., 1987. Sexing day-old chicks: a case study and expert systems analysis of a difficult perceptual-learning task. Journal of Experimental Psychology: Learning, Memory, and Cognition 13, 640–645.

Brooks, L.R., 1978. Non-analytic concept formation and memory for instances. In: Rosch, E., Lloyd, B.B. (Eds.), Cognition and Categorization. Erlbaum, Hillsdale, NJ. pp. 169–211.

Brownell, H.H., Simpson, T.L., Bihrle, A.M., 1990. Appreciation of metaphoric alternative word meanings by left and right brain-damaged patients. Neuropsychologica 28, 375–383.

Burgess, C., Simpson, G.B., 1988. Cerebral hemispheric mechanisms in the retrieval of ambiguous word meanings. Brain and Language 33, 86–103.

Burns, B., Shepp, B.E., 1988. Dimensional interactions and the structure of psychological space: the representation of hue, saturation, and brightness. Perception and Psychophysics 43, 494–507.

Carey, S., 1985. Conceptual Change in Childhood. MIT Press, Cambridge, MA.

Chi, M.T.H., Feltovich, P., Glaser, R., 1981. Categorization and representation of physics problems by experts and novices. Cognitive Science 5, 121–152.

Dawson, M.R., 1991. The how and why of what went where in apparent motion: modeling solutions to the motion correspondence problem. Psychological Review 98, 569–603.

Dewdney, A.K., 1985. Analog gadgets that solve a diversity of problems and raise an array of questions. Scientific American, June, 18–29.

de Sa, V., Ballard, J., 1997. Learning Perceptual Dimensions. In: Medin, D.L., Goldstone, R.L., Schyns, P. (Eds.) Psychology of Learning and Motivation. Academic Press, San Diego, pp. 309–352.

Fahle, M., Morgan, M., 1996. No transfer of perceptual learning between similar stimuli in the same retinal position. Current Biology 6, 292–297.

Farah, M.J., 1990. *Visual Agnosia: Disorders of Object Recognition and What they tell us about Normal Vision.* MIT Press, Cambridge, MA.

Finke, R.A., 1986. Mental imagery and the visual system. Scientific American, March, 98–104.

Finke, R.A., Pinker, S., Farah, M., 1989. Reinterpreting visual patterns in mental imagery. Cognitive Science 13, 51–78.

Foard, C.F., Kemler Nelson, D.G., 1984. Holistic and analytic modes of processing: the multiple determinants of perceptual analysis. Journal of Experimental Psychology: General 113, 94–111.

Fodor, J., 1975. The Language of Thought. Crowell, New York.

Fodor, J.A., Pylyshyn, Z.W., 1988. Connectionism and cognitive architecture: a critical analysis. Cognition 28, 3–71.

Garner, W.R., 1974. The Processing of Information and Structure. Wiley, New York.

Garner, W.R., 1978. Aspects of a stimulus: features, dimensions, and configurations. In: Rosch, E., Lloyd, B.B. (Eds.), Cognition and Categorization. Erlbaum, Hillsdale, NJ.

Gelman, S.A., 1988. The development of induction within natural kind and artifact categories. Cognitive Psychology 20, 65–95.

Gelman, S.A., Markman, E.M., 1986. Categories and induction in young children. Cognition 23, 183–209.

Gelman, R., 1990. First principles organize attention to and learning about relevant data: number and the animate-inanimate distinction as examples. Cognitive Science 14, 79–106.

Gentner, D., Toupin, C., 1986. Systematicity and surface similarity in the development of analogy. Cognitive Science 10, 277–300.

Gernsbacher, M.A., Faust, M.E., 1991. The mechanism of suppression: a component of general comprehension. Journal of Experimental Psychology: Learning, Memory, and Cognition 17, 245–262.

Gick, M.L., Holyoak, K.J., 1983. Schema induction and analogical transfer. Cognitive Psychology 15, 1–39.

Lakoff, G., 1986. Women, Fire and Dangerous Things: what Categories tell us about the Nature of Thought. University of Chicago Press, Chicago.

Glucksberg, S., Keysar, B., 1990. Understanding metaphorical comparisons: beyond similarity. Psychological Review 97, 3–18.

Goldstone, R.L., 1994a. Similarity, interactive activation, and mapping. Journal of Experimental Psychology: Learning, Memory, and Cognition 20, 3–28.

Goldstone, R.L., 1994b. The role of similarity in categorization: providing a groundwork. Cognition 52, 125–157.

Goldstone, R.L., 1994c. Influences of categorization on perceptual discrimination. Journal of Experimental Psychology: General 123, 178–200.

Goldstone, R.L., 1995a. Mainstream and avant-garde similarity. Psychologica Belgica 35, 145–165.

Goldstone, R.L., 1995b. Effects of categorization on color perception. Psychological Science 6, 298–304.

Goldstone, R.L., Medin, D.L., 1994. The time course of comparison. Journal of Experimental Psychology: Learning, Memory, and Cognition 20, 29–50.

Goldstone, R.L., Schyns, P., 1994. Learning new features of representation. Proceedings of the Sixteenth Annual Conference of the Cognitive Science Society. Erlbaum, Hillsdale, New Jersey, pp. 974–978.

Gould, S.J., 1993. Eight Little Piggies. Norton, New York.

Goodman, N., 1972. Seven strictures on similarity. In: Goodman, N. (Ed.), Problems and Projects. Bobbs-Merrill, New York, pp. 35–41.

Hadamard, J., 1949. The Psychology of Invention in the Mathematical Field. Dover Books, New York.

Harnad, S., 1987. Categorical Perception. Cambridge University Press, Cambridge.

Holyoak, K.J., Koh, K., 1987. Surface and structural similarity in analogical transfer. Memory and Cognition 15, 332–340.

Hummel, J.E., Biederman, I.,1992. Dynamic binding in a neural network for shape recognition. Psychological Review 99, 480–517.

Hummel, J.E., Holyoak, K.J., 1997. Distributed representations of structure: a theory of analogical access and mapping. Psychological Review 104, 427–466.

Huttenlocher, J., Jordan, N., Levine, S., 1994. A mental model for early arithmetic. Journal of Experimental Psychology: General 123, 284–296.

Johnston, W.A., Dark, V.J., 1986. Selective attention. Annual Review of Psychology 37, 43–75.

Johnson-Laird, P.N., 1983. Mental Models. Harvard University Press, Cambridge, MA.

Jones, S.S., Smith, L.B., 1993. The place of perception in children's concepts. Cognitive Development 8, 113–140.

Kant, I., 1965. The Critique of Pure Reason (N.K. Smith, Trans.). St. Martin's Press, New York. (Original work published in 1787.).

Karni, A., Sagi, D., 1991. Where practice makes perfect in texture discrimination: evidence for primary visual cortex plasticity. Proceedings of the National Academy of Sciences of the United States of America 88, 4966–4970.

Keil, F.C., 1989. Concepts, Kinds and Development. Bradford Books/MIT Press, Cambridge, MA.

Kelly, M.H., Keil, F.C., 1987. Metaphor comprehension and knowledge of semantic domains. Metaphor and Symbolic Activity 2, 33–51.

Kemler, D.G., 1983. Holistic and analytic modes in perceptual and cognitive development. In: Tighe, T.J., Shepp, B.E. (Eds.), Perception, Cognition, and Development: Interactional Analyses. Erlbaum, Hillsdale, NJ, pp. 77–101.

Kirk, G.S., Raven, J.E., 1962. The Presocratic Philosophers. Cambridge University Press, Cambridge.

Kosslyn, S.M., 1976. Can imagery be distinguished from other forms of conceptual representation? Evidence from studies of information retrieval times. Memory and Cognition 4, 291–297.

Kosslyn, S.M., 1980. Image and Mind. Harvard University Press, Cambridge, MA.

Kroska, A., Goldstone, R.L., 1996. Dissociations in the similarity and categorisation of emotions. Cognition and Emotion 10, 27–45.

Langacker, R.W., 1986. An introduction to cognitive grammar. Cognitive Science 10, 1–40.

Lassaline, M.E., 1996. Structural alignment in induction and similarity. Journal of Experimental Psychology: Learning, Memory, and Cognition 22, 754–770.

Lenat, D.B., Guha, R.V., 1994. Enabling agents to work together. Communications of the ACM 37, 203–215.

Liotti, M., Dazzi, S., Umilta, C., 1993. Deficits of the automatic orienting of attention in schizophrenic patients. Journal of Psychiatric Research 27, 119–130.

Locke, J., 1959. An essay concerning human understanding, first ed. (Vols. I and II). Dover, New York. (Original work published in 1690.).

Logan, G.D., Etherton, J.L., 1994. What is learned during automatization? The role of attention in constructing an instance. Journal of Experimental Psychology: Learning, Memory, and Cognition 20, 1022–1050.

Lovass, O.I., Koegel, R.L., Schreibman, L., 1979. Stimulus overselectivity in autism: a review of research. Psychological Bulletin 86, 1236–1254.

Mandler, J.M., 1992. How to build a baby: II. Conceptual primitives. Psychological Review 99, 587–604.

Mandler, J.M., Bauer, P.J., McDonough, L., 1991. Separating the sheep from the goats: differentiating global categories. Cognitive Psychology 23, 263–298.

Mandler, J.M., McDonough, L., 1991. Concept formation in infancy. Cognitive Development 8, 291–318.

Markman, A.B., Gentner, D., 1993. Structural alignment during similarity comparisons. Cognitive Psychology 25, 431–467.

Marr, D., Poggio, T., 1979. A computational theory of human stereo vision. Proceedings of the Royal Society of London 204, 301–328.

McKoon, G., Ratcliff, R., 1992. Inference during reading. Psychological Review 99, 440–466.

Medin, D.L., 1989. Concepts and conceptual structure. American Psychologist 44, 1469–1481.

Medin, D.L., Barsalou, L.W., 1987. Categorization processes and categorical perception. In: Harnad, S., (Ed.) Categorical Perception. Cambridge University Press, Cambridge, pp. 455–490.

Medin, D.L., Goldstone, R.L., Gentner, D., 1993. Respects for similarity. Psychological Review 100, 254–278.

Medin, D.L., Ortony, A., 1989. Psychological essentialism. In: Vosniadou, S., Ortony, A. (Eds.), Similarity and Analogical Reasoning. Cambridge University Press, Cambridge, pp. 179–195.

Melara, R.D., 1989. Similarity relations among synesthetic stimuli and their attributes. Journal of Experimental Psychology: Human Perception and Performance 115, 212–231.

Melara, R.D., Marks, L.E., 1990. Dimensional interactions in language processing: investigating directions and levels of crosstalk. Journal of Experimental Psychology: Learning, Memory, and Cognition 16, 539–554.

Miller, A., 1987. Cognitive styles: an integrated Model. Educational Psychology 7, 251–268.

Moscovici, S., Personnaz, B., 1991. Studies in social influence: VI. Is Lenin orange or red? Imagery and social influence. European Journal of Social Psychology 21, 101–118.

Mullin, P.A., Egeth, H.E., 1989. Capacity limitations in visual word processing. Journal of Experimental Psychology: Human Perception and Performance 15, 111–123.

Murphy, G.L., Medin, D.L., 1985. The role of theories in conceptual coherence. Psychological Review 92, 289–316.

Murphy, G.L., Spalding, T., 1995. Knowledge, similarity, and concept formation. Psychologica Belgica 35, 127–144.

Neill, W.T., 1977. Inhibition and facilitation processes in selective attention. Journal of Experimental Psychology: Human Perception and Performance 3, 444–450.

Neisser, U., Becklen, R., 1975. Selective looking: attending to visually specified events. Cognitive Psychology 7, 480–494.

Nickerson, R.S., 1972. Binary Classification reaction time: a review of some studies of human information-processing capabilities. Psychonomic Monograph Supplements 4 (6), 275–317.

Nosofsky, R.M., 1986. Attention, similarity, and the identification-categorization relationship. Journal of Experimental Psychology: General 115, 39–57.

Nosofsky, R.M., 1992. Exemplar-based approach to relating categorization, identification, and recognition. In: Ashby, F.G. (Ed.), Multidimensional Models of Perception and Cognition. Erlbaum, Hillsdale, NJ, pp. 207–225.

Olseth, K.L., Barsalou, L.W., 1995. The spontaneous use of perceptual representations during conceptual processing. Proceedings of the seventeenth annual meeting of the Cognitive Science Society. Erlbaum, Hillsdale, NJ, pp. 310–315.

Ortony, A., 1979. Beyond literal similarity. Psychological Review 86, 161–180.

Palmer, S.E., 1978. Structural aspects of visual similarity. Memory and Cognition 6, 91–97.

Peterson, M.A., Gibson, B.S., 1994. Must figure-ground organization precede object recognition? An assumption in peril. Psychological Science 5, 253–259.

Prinz, J.J., 1997. Perceptual Cognition: an Essay on the Semantics of Thought. Dissertation, Department of Philosophy, University of Chicago.

Prinz, J.J., Barsalou, L.W., 1997. Acquisition and productivity in perceptual symbol systems: an account of mundane creativity. In: Dartnall, T.H. (Ed.), Creativity, Computation, and Cognition. MIT/AAAI Press, Cambridge, MA, pp. 231–251.

Quine, W.V.O., 1977. Natural kinds. In: Schwartz, S.P. (Ed.), Naming, Necessity, and Natural Kinds. Cornell University Press, Ithaca, NY, pp. 35–59.

Rips, L.J., 1986. Mental muddles. In: Brand, M., Harnish, R.M. The Representation of Knowledge and Belief. University of Arizona Press, Tuscon, pp. 258–286.

Rips, L.J., 1989. Similarity, typicality, and categorization. In: Vosniadu, S., Ortony, A. (Eds.), Similarity, Analogy, and Thought. Cambridge University Press, Cambridge, pp. 21–59.

Rips, L.J., Collins, A., 1993. Categories and resemblances. Journal of Experimental Psychology: General 122, 468–486.

Robertson, L.C., Lamb, M.R., 1991. Neuropsychological contributions to theories of part/whole organization. Cognitive Psychology 23, 299–330.

Rock, I., Gutman, D., 1981. The effect of inattention on form perception. Journal of Experimental Psychology: Human Perception and Performance 7, 275–185.

Rosch, E., 1975. Cognitive representations of semantic categories. Journal of Experimental Psychology: Human Perception and Performance 1, 303–322.

Rosch, E., Mervis, C.B., 1975. Family resemblance: studies in the internal structure of categories. Cognitive Psychology 7, 573–605.

Rosch, E., Mervis, C.B., Gray, W., Johnson, D., Boyes-Braem, P., 1976. Basic objects in natural categories. Cognitive Psychology 7, 573–605.

Ross, B.H., 1987. This is like that: the use of earlier problems and the separation of similarity effects. Journal of Experimental Psychology: Learning, Memory, and Cognition 13, 629–639.

Ross, B.H., Perkins, S.J., Tenpenny, P.L., 1990. Reminding-based category learning. Cognitive Psychology 22, 460–492.

Rozin, P., Markwith, M., Ross, B., 1990. The sympathetic magical law of similarity, nominal realism and neglect of negatives in response to negative labels. Psychological Science 1, 383–384.

Russell, B., 1956. Logic and Knowledge. Routledge, London. (Original work published in 1919.).

Schreiber, H., Stolz-Born, G., Kornhuber, H.H., Born, J., 1992. Even before cognitive effects emerge, there are visual differences: event-related potential correlates of impaired selective attention in children at high risk for schizophrenia. Biological Psychiatry 32, 634–651.

Schwartz, S., 1982. Is there a schizophrenic language? Behavioral and Brain Sciences 5, 579–626.

Schyns, P.G., Goldstone, R.L., Thibaut, J-P., 1998. The development of features in object concepts. Behavioral and Brain Sciences (in press).

Searle, J.R., 1980. Minds, brains, and programs. Behavioral and Brain Sciences 3, 417–424.

Sekuler, R.W., Abrams, M., 1968. Visual sameness: a choice time analysis of pattern recognition. Journal of Experimental Psychology 77, 232–238.

Shanks, D.R., St. John, M.F., 1994. Characteristics of dissociable human learning systems. Behavioral and Brain Sciences 17, 367–447.

Shanon, B., 1988. On similarity of features. New Ideas in Psychology 6, 307–321.

Shepard, R.N., 1984. Ecological constraints on internal representations: resonant kinematics of perceiving, imagining, thinking, and dreaming. Psychological Review 91, 417–447.

Shaw, M., 1982. Attending to multiple sources of information: I. The integration of information in decision making. Cognitive Psychology 14, 353–409.

Shiffrin, R.M., Lightfoot, N., 1997. Perceptual learning of alphanumeric-like characters. In: Goldstone, R.L., Schyns, P.G., Medin, D.L. (Eds.), Psychology of Learning and Motivation, Vol. 36. Academic Press, San Diego, CA, pp. 45–82.

Shiffrin, R.M., Schneider, W., 1977. Controlled and automatic human information processing: II. Perceptual learning, automatic attending, and a general theory. Psychological Review 84, 127–190.

Sloman, S.A., 1996. The empirical case for two systems of reasoning. Psychological Bulletin 119, 3–22.

Smith, C., Carey, S., Wiser, M., 1985. On differentiation: a case study of the development of the concepts of size, weight and density. Cognition 21, 177–237.

Smith, E.E., Langston, C., Nisbett, R., 1992. The case for rules in reasoning. Cognitive Science 16, 1–40.

Smith, E.E., Sloman, S.A., 1994. Similarity- versus rule-based categorization. Memory and Cognition 22, 377–386.

Smith, L.B., 1989. From global similarity to kinds of similarity: the construction of dimensions in development. In: Vosniadou, S., Ortony, A. (Eds.), Similarity and Analogical Reasoning. Cambridge University Press, Cambridge, pp. 146–178.

Smith, L.B., Gasser, M., Sandhofer, C. 1997. Learning to talk about the properties of objects: a network model of the development of dimensions. In: Goldstone, R.L., Schyns, P.G., Medin, D.L. (Eds.) Psychology of Learning and Motivation, Vol. 36. Academic Press, San Diego, CA, pp. 219–256.

Smith, L.B., Kemler, D.G., 1978. Levels of experienced dimensionality in children and adults. Cognitive Psychology 10, 502–532.

Smith, J.D., Kemler Nelson, D.G., 1984. Overall similarity in adults' classification: the child in all of us. Journal of Experimental Psychology: General 113, 137–159.

Solomon, K.O., 1997 The Spontaneous use of Perceptual Representations during Conceptual Processing. Dissertation, Department of Psychology, University of Chicago.

Spelke, E.S., 1990. Principles of object perception. Cognitive Science 14, 29–56.

Stigler, J.W., 1984. 'Mental abacus': the effect of abacus training on Chinese children's mental calculation. Cognitive Psychology 16, 145–176.

Talmy, L., 1983. How language structures space. In: Pick, H., Acredelo, L (Eds.), Spatial Orientation: Theory, Research, and Application. Plenum Press, New York, pp. 225–282.

Tanaka, J.W., Taylor, M., 1991. Object categories and expertise: is the basic level in the eye of the beholder? Cognitive Psychology 23, 457–482.

Tipper, S.P., 1992. Selection for action: the role of inhibitory mechanisms. Current Directions in Psychological Science 1, 105–109.

Triesman, A.M., 1960. Contextual cues in selective attention. Quarterly Journal of Experimental Psychology 12, 242–248.

Treisman, A.M., Gelade, G., 1980. A feature-integration theory of attention. Cognitive Psychology 12, 97–136.

Tversky, A., 1977. Features of similarity. Psychological Review 84, 327–352.

Ullman, S., 1984. Visual routines. Cognition 18, 97–159.

Wapner, S., Demick, J., 1991. Field Dependence-Independence: Cognitive Style across the Life Span. Erlbaum, Hillsdale, NJ.

Ward, T.B, 1983. Response tempo and separable-integral responding: evidence for an integral-to-separable processing sequence in visual perception. Journal of Experimental Psychology: Human Perception and Performance 9, 103–112.

Wu, L., 1995. Perceptual Representation in Conceptual Combination. Doctoral dissertation, University of Chicago.

7

Similarity and the development of rules

Dedre Gentner[a],*, José Medina[b]

[a]*Department of Psychology, Northwestern University, 2029 Sheridan Road, Evanston, IL 60208, USA*
[b]*Department of Philosophy, Northwestern University, Evanston, IL 60208, USA*

Abstract

Similarity-based and rule-based accounts of cognition are often portrayed as opposing accounts. In this paper we suggest that in learning and development, the *process of comparison* can act as a bridge between similarity-based and rule-based processing. We suggest that comparison involves a process of structural alignment and mapping between two representations. This kind of structure-sensitive comparison process – which may be triggered either by experiential or symbolic juxtapositions – has a twofold significance for cognitive development. First, as a learning mechanism, comparison facilitates the grasp of structural commonalities and the abstraction of rules; and, second, as a mechanism for the application and extension of previously acquired knowledge, comparison processes facilitate the application of abstract knowledge to new instances. © 1998 Elsevier Science B.V.

Keywords: Similarity-based processing; Rule-based processing; Analogical learning; Structure-sensitive comparison

We are **far** cleverer than anybody else, and that we are cries out for explanation.
(Fodor, 1994).

1. Introduction

Adult humans are formidable thinkers. We routinely carry out feats of abstract reasoning that are beyond the capabilities of other species. And as Rips (1994), notes, 'much of the deductive work that we carry out from day to day consists of... 'steps so routine that they seem not to require deduction at all.' For example, when given two options, we know that if we reject one, we are committed to the other; and this reasoning appears to us so natural that we are not aware of invoking the abstract inference schema of modus tollendo ponens (P or Q, not P; therefore Q). Yet, as

* Corresponding author. fax: +1 847 4917859; e-mail: gentner@nwu.edu

Fodor (1990) has pointed out, our ability to reason across contexts in a content-independent way is, or should be, deeply puzzling. How do these abstract cognitive abilities develop?

Accounts of the development of abstract thought can be grouped into four broad categories. According to the empiricist tradition, abstract cognition evolves through experiential learning and complex ideas are compounded out of simple ideas. Behaviorism, the heir to empiricism in this century, proposed the mechanisms of association and stimulus generalization to explain learning. However, its refusal to deal with mental representations and its reliance on purely perceptual similarity restricted this account to only the most rudimentary forms of learning. A second approach is Piagetian constructivism, which postulates increasingly complex mental representations learned through the child's own interactions with the experiential world (Piaget, 1951). A third, related approach was Vygotsky's (1962, 1987) theory of the social formation of mind: that abstract cognition develops through interaction with cultural and linguistic systems. The theories of Piaget and Vygotsky offered a richer and more appealing view of cognitive development, but the processes by which learning occurs – assimilation, accommodation, acculturation, internalization – are not closely defined. The inadequacy of learning mechanisms powerful enough to explain the development of abstract cognition was all the more apparent in light of increasingly persuasive evidence of the sophistication and generativity of human cognition and language. Cognitive developmental research such as Gelman's (1990) findings on early number concepts and Spelke's (1988, 1990) and Baillargeon's (1987) research on infants' knowledge of objects was revealing early capabilities far beyond what had been envisioned. This gap lent force to an extremely influential fourth view: that higher-level cognition is guided by innate constraints. The strong nativist approach postulates that the mind comes endowed with abstract principles, though perhaps in nascent form. In strong versions, development is seen as the maturation or unfolding of innate potentialities, with learning playing a distinctly minor role.

The fortunes of similarity as an explanation of development have risen and fallen with these tides. (Although we have laid these out historically, all four views exist in various degrees in current theorizing.) In behaviorist approaches, similarity is a major engine of learning. However, because similarity is conceived of narrowly as stimulus and response generalization, its success in this arena does little to address issues of abstract thought. Perhaps as a reaction to the simplistic reliance on perceptual similarity in behaviorist accounts, similarity has been relegated to a minor role in most current accounts of intellectual development. Similarity is seen as a distraction from the important principles, or at best as a fallback when theory fails. There are exceptions, of course: similarity figures in many information-processing views (e.g. Klahr, 1984; Siegler, 1989; Halford, 1993) and in some moderate forms of nativism that emphasize innate specific processing capacities, rather than innate declarative knowledge. However, our point is that in rejecting similarity processes along with the behaviorist account of learning, our field has thrown the baby out with the bathwater.

Our goal in this paper is to argue for a reconsideration of similarity-based learning as a major force in development. We propose that similarity, viewed as a *process of comparison*, is a key mechanism in experiential learning and in linking experiential learning to cultural learning. We will suggest (1) that the comparison between two representations can be understood as a process of alignment or structure-mapping; (2) that these kinds of alignment processes display the kind of structure-sensitivity that could facilitate rule-learning; and (3) that comparison processes can be invited not only by experiential juxtaposition but also by *symbolic* juxtaposition through the learning of common linguistic labels. Our research suggests that similarity comparisons, guided by cultural and linguistic patterns, can lead the child from concrete comparisons to abstract, rule-like regularities.

A proposal to reconsider similarity-driven mechanisms of abstraction may seem perverse in light of the wealth of philosophical and developmental literature that casts doubt on the explanatory power of similarity. As Quine (1969) puts it, there is little reason to think that 'the muddy old notion of similarity' has anything to contribute to the development of abstract capacities. Similarity has been viewed as too context-dependent and too narrowly perceptual (or if not too perceptual, then too unconstrained) to account for abstract, rule-governed capacities such as reasoning and categorization, either in adults (Goodman, 1972) or in children (Keil, 1989). Goodman's arguments that similarity is uninformative (because any two things can be similar in some respect) or superfluous (once the respects are specified) have been taken as particularly damning to similarity-driven accounts. We will return to Goodman's challenge later, after we lay out our proposal. For now we merely preview our argument: that similarity becomes both more constrained and more powerful if we shift from considering similarity as a cognitive *state* or *product* to similarity as the *process* of comparison. We will argue that there are natural structural constraints on similarity when similarity is viewed as a process of alignment and mapping (e.g. Gentner, 1983; Markman and Gentner, 1993a,b, 1996; Medin et al., 1993; Gentner and Markman, 1994, 1995, 1997; Goldstone, 1994b).

1.1. A note on terminology

Before going further, we need to clarify the key terms, since both 'rules' and 'similarity' are used in different ways. Rules can be transformations, as in $S \rightarrow NP + VP$, or simply expressions that specify a particular set of relations; they can be concrete, as in 'dial 9 for an outside line' or abstract; and they can be implicit or explicit. Smith et al. (1992) propose several criteria for rule use such as that rule-following should be unaffected by the familiarity or concreteness of the material, that application of a rule should prime subsequent uses and that rules may be mentioned in a verbal protocol. We will adopt Smith et al.'s construal of *rule* as an explicit, abstract schema that contains variables. As in their treatment, we will be liberal in our interpretation of 'explicit'. We will not require that a schema be explicitly mentioned on each use in order to count as a rule, rather, it must seem readily capable of being stated. (We are aware that this is a loose description, but to count only fully-articulated principles would be unrealistically restrictive.) We will include not only abstract rules of reasoning such as modus ponens but also abstract conceptual representations. This extension is fairly standard, Rips (1989) comments that concepts are in many ways akin to rule-governed explanations, and Murphy and

Medin (1985) argue that concepts are theory-governed, and not arbitrary collections of features. Smith and Sloman (1994) note evidence for rule-based categorization, in that adults often focus on certain criterial features, such as 'has the correct DNA,' in judging category membership. Under this construal, there is abundant evidence for abstract rules and concepts in adults.

'Similarity' is a another pluralistic term. The most serious ambiguity is between similarity as a *process* of comparative reasoning and similarity as a *product* – e.g. a sense of closeness or representational unity. We will avoid this ambiguity by using process language to talk about the first sense, reserving 'similarity' for the product. The second polysemy occurs at the product level. There is a persistent ambiguity in the use of 'similarity' to mean sometimes overall similarity (common perceptual and functional characteristics) and sometimes purely perceptual or surface similarity. This is a dangerous ambiguity that obscures important distinctions. For one thing, overall similarity is a good predictor of further commonalities and surface similarity is not. As Goldstone (1994b) has shown, this ambiguity can distort the interpretation of similarity data.

In our research we distinguish three classes of similarity – analogy, literal similarity and mere-appearance (object similarity). These similarity types are not strict categories, but rather continua. In *analogy* – e.g. comparing the atom with the solar system – there is substantial relational overlap with very little object similarity: objects correspond not because of inherent similarity but by virtue of playing like roles in the relational structure. As object-similarity increases, the comparison shifts towards *literal similarity* – e.g. comparing one stellar system with another – which involves both relational and object commonalities. In the opposite direction, *mere-appearance* matches – e.g. comparing a planet with a round ball – share object descriptions but not relations. Mere-appearance matches are the quintessential 'dumb similarity' matches; they have virtually no predictive utility. Nonetheless, they are important to consider, because they often occur among children and other novices, and may interfere with learning. Finally, *surface similarity* is another polysemous term. It is used contrastively with some better or deeper form of similarity and typically means either *perceptual similarity* or *mere-appearance (object-based) similarity*. For our purposes, the major interest is in literal (overall) similarity and purely structural similarity (analogy). Though both can yield useful inferences, they have different psychological profiles. Overall similarity comparisons are far easier to notice and map than analogies, especially for novices (Holyoak and Koh, 1987; Keane, 1988; Ross, 1989; Gentner et al., 1993; Ross and Kilbane, 1997). As we will discuss, analogies occur later in learning and development.

Focusing on mapping process, we suggest that there is a continuum between similarity-based and rule-based processes. More fundamentally, we suggest that the process of structural comparison acts as a bridge by which similarity-based processes can give rise to abstract rules. There are two parts to this second claim. The first is that comparison can render domain representations more abstract, in two senses: Carrying out an analogy can lead to a schematic structure in which (a) the domain objects are replaced by variables, while retaining the common relations[1].

[1]Whether relations can also turn into variables is debatable; we think this is possible but rare.

(Winston, 1982); and (b) the domain relations are more abstract or general than the original domain relations (i.e. they contain fewer conceptual features). So far, these ideas are not new. Our second major claim is a bit newer and results from our recent empirical work: It is that carrying out a fully concrete mapping – even one in which the objects transparently match their intended correspondents – makes it easier to subsequently carry out an analogical mapping, in which relational structures must be matched with no support (or even with conflict) from the object matches. Putting this together, the comparison process offers a mechanism for moving from highly-similar pairings of concrete representations to gradually less similar pairings. With repeated comparisons, the resulting common system becomes more abstract, until it can be represented as a schema containing variables rather than objects. Such a schema can be applied as a rule.

Our main contention is that the process of comparison constitutes an important bridge between similarity-driven and rule-governed processes. We suggest that the developmental significance of a structurally-sensitive comparison process is two-fold. In the first place, as just described, structural alignment is a central learning mechanism enabling the child to notice and store abstract relational commonalities. Second, structure-mapping acts as a mechanism for the extension and application of knowledge. We will argue that for adults as well as children, structure-mapping processes can provide both a means of deriving abstract knowledge from instances and a means of extending it to new cases.

We also want to be clear about what we are *not* claiming. We do not claim that comparison is the only force in development, or the only kind of learning. We also do not claim that comparison processes are the chief or only source of knowledge representations. On the contrary, we assume that knowledge is initially derived in a number of ways – from direct experience, social interaction, and so forth. Our point is that comparisons among these various representations act to enrich, abstract, or otherwise modify them to create new representations. We will show that such modifications can result in meaningful changes in knowledge.

2. Structure-mapping

We briefly lay out the theoretical framework. We propose that comparison takes place via a structure-mapping process of alignment of conceptual representations. According to this view, the commonalities and differences between two situations are found by determining the maximal structurally-consistent alignment between their representations (Gentner, 1983, 1989; Falkenhainer et al., 1989). A *structurally consistent* alignment is one that obeys *one-to-one mapping* (i.e. an element in one representation corresponds to at most one element in the other representation) and *parallel connectivity* (i.e. if elements correspond across the two representations, then the elements that are linked to them must correspond as well). A central characteristic of analogy and similarity comparisons is *systematicity*: a preference for matching *connected systems of relations* (Gentner, 1983, 1989). A matching system of relations interconnected by higher-order constraining relations makes a better analogical match than an equal number of matching relations that are unconnected to each other. People are not much interested in analogies that merely capture a set of coincidences. The systematicity principle captures a tacit preference for coherence and causal predictive power in analogical processing.

Arriving at a deep structural alignment might seem to require advance knowledge of the point of the comparison. Such a mechanism would be implausible as a developmental learning process. In fact, however, structural alignment can be realized with a process that begins blind and local. The structure-mapping engine (SME) utilizes an alignment process that begins with purely local matches and culminates with one or a few deep, structurally consistent alignments (Falkenhainer et al., 1989; Forbus et al., 1995; see also Keane and Brayshaw, 1988; Holyoak and Thagard, 1989; Hummel and Holyoak, 1997). SME carries out its mapping in three stages. In the first stage, it detects possible matches between all pairs of identical predicates at any level (attribute, function, relation, higher-order relation and so on) in the two representations. At this stage, there are typically many mutually-inconsistent $(1 \rightarrow n)$ matches. In the second stage, these local matches are coalesced into structurally-consistent connected clusters (called *kernels*). Finally, in the third stage, these kernels are merged into one or a few maximally structurally-consistent interpretations (i.e. mappings displaying *one-to-one corre-spondences* and *parallel connectivity*). SME then produces a structural evaluation of the interpretation(s), using a cascade-like algorithm in which evidence is passed down from predicates to their arguments. This method is used because it favors deep systems over shallow systems, even if they have equal numbers of matches (Forbus and Gentner, 1989). Finally, predicates connected to the common structure in the base, but not initially present in the target, are proposed as *candidate inferences* in the target. This means that structural completion can lead to spontaneous unplanned inferences.

Taken as a process model, SME has testable psychological implications. First, as mentioned above, it begins rather blindly with a mass of mutually-inconsistent local matches; the overall interpretation emerges out of the alignment through a preference for systematicity and structural consistency in the common system. Second, although SME often produces one interpretation, it can produce two or three alternative interpretations of an analogy. This, we believe, captures the occasional human experience of alternative possible interpretations. Third, inference projection occurs as a natural outcome of comparison, without special intention. This capacity to produce unanticipated inferences fits with human patterns: inferences often arise unbidden from an analogy and may even surprise the reasoner. Fourth, SME can save the common schema that results from carrying out a comparison. For example, Skorstad et al. (1988) simulated category learning by allowing SME to sequentially compare instances and retain the common system as a category abstraction. This fits the human phenomenon of spontaneous schema abstraction as a natural outcome of the comparison process (Gick and Holyoak, 1983; Catrambone and Holyoak, 1989; Ross et al., 1990).

SME's process of structural alignment also suggests limitations on the human comparison process, that are relevant to children's processing. First, because the alignment process operates simultaneously over objects and relations, we should find that the easiest, most natural form of similarity to process is *literal similarity* (*overall similarity*), in which the object matches and the relational alignment are correlated. In this case the matching information is mutually supporting and there is one dominant interpretation. Pure analogies, in which the matching relations are unsupported by matching objects, should be more difficult to process. This prediction fits the human pattern. Adults normally prefer relational interpretations but will select object matches when under time pressure (Goldstone et al., 1988). Furthermore, children can correctly carry out overall similarity mappings before purely relational mappings (Gentner and Toupin, 1986; Gentner and Rattermann, 1991; Rattermann and Gentner, 1998). Second, the most difficult case for both adults and children should be a *cross-mapping* (Gentner and Toupin, 1986): an analogical match in which similar objects play different relational roles in two analogous scenarios: e.g. *grandmother: mother::mother:daughter.* This prediction is also supported for both adults and children, as discussed below.

3. The career of similarity in development

Developmentally, these assumptions interact with considerations of change of knowledge. When domain theories are weak, as for very young children, the representations typically contain relatively sparse knowledge of relations, but often contain rich knowledge of objects. Gentner and Rattermann (1991) proposed a knowledge-driven account of the 'career of similarity',[2] as follows. Very young infants can notice highly specific, massively overlapping literal similarity comparisons, but at this stage they are limited to strong similarity matches (Foard and Kemler-Nelson, 1984; Smith, 1989). For example, infants show that they can remember a mobile that they have seen before (by later kicking a similar mobile in the same way to make it move) but only if the new one is a very close perceptual match to the original (Rovee-Collier and Fagen, 1981). As infants gain in stable knowledge, they become able to make partial matches. Object matches, such as the similarity between one shoe and another, occur very early. As children's domain knowledge becomes richer and deeper, purely relational matches become possible: e.g. the similarity between a shoe *covering* a foot and a mitten *covering* a hand. There is a domain-specific relational shift with experience (Gentner, 1988). Thus, the career of similarity runs from overall matches to object matches to relational matches to higher-order relational matches (Gentner and Rattermann, 1991; see Halford, 1987, 1993 for a related proposal).

These predicted patterns are illustrated in a study of children's ability to map a plot structure from one set of actors to another (Gentner and Toupin, 1986). Two factors were varied: (1) *object similarity (transparency)*, the degree to which corre-

---

[2]The claim that the relational shift is driven by increases in domain knowledge has wide support (Gentner, 1977a,b, 1988; Ortony et al., 1978; Gentner and Toupin, 1986; Vosniadou, 1987; Brown and Kane, 1988; Brown, 1989; Chen and Daehler, 1989; Goswami, 1992) although changes in processing capacity have also been argued to be important (Halford, 1987, 1993).

sponding actors resembled one another and (2) *systematicity*, whether children were given an explicit statement of the higher-order relational structure that governed the plot. The story plots were identical across the object-similarity conditions. However, in the systematic condition, two additional statements were given – one at the beginning and one at the end of the story – that provided an overarching causal or moral summary. Both age-groups were affected by object similarity: They were more accurate in retelling the story when *squirrel* mapped onto *chipmunk* than when it mapped onto *moose*. In contrast, the systematicity of the relational structure appeared to influence only the older children: 9-year-olds, but not 6-year-olds, were far more accurate when given a higher-order structure that constrained the plot. In fact, 9-year-olds in the systematic condition were able to transfer the story accurately regardless of the transparency (or degree of object similarity) of the correspondences. Although we cannot be sure, we suspect that the young children's failure to profit from systematic structure stemmed from lack of sufficient knowledge of social and causal regularities, rather than from inherent processing limitations.

These results fit the predictions of the career of similarity account. Children gradually shift from object-dominated to relation-dominated similarity matches as their domain knowledge increases. Other studies of analogical transfer have found a similar early reliance on object matches, (e.g. Holyoak et al., 1984; Daehler and Chen, 1993; Chen et al., 1998; Rattermann and Gentner, 1998).

4. Learning

We can now be more specific about our central claim that comparison promotes learning, and, more specifically, that children's comparison processes can lead to the development of abstract rules. Structure-mapping suggests three[3] ways in which the alignment and mapping process brings about learning. First, by *highlighting common systems* of features and relations, thereby promoting the noticing and extraction of subtle and possibly important commonalities (especially common relational systems), and facilitating schema-abstraction. Second, by *projecting inferences* from the base to the target (Clement and Gentner, 1991; Gentner et al., 1997; Gentner and Wolff, 1998; Markman, 1998). Third, by *inviting re-representation* to improve the match, thereby promoting representational uniformity. Crucial to our position is the claim that comparison acts to promote *systems of interrelated knowledge*.[4] If the comparison process resulted in isolated feature matches, it would hardly qualify as a candidate for abstracting causal laws and other principled regularities. One way to observe the effects of structure in comparison is to use cross-mappings, which put structural commonalities in conflict with object matches (Gentner and Toupin, 1986;

---

[3]A fourth way in which analogy can promote learning is by inviting the re-structuring of one domain in terms of the other (Gentner et al., 1997). This mechanism is beyond the scope of this paper.

[4]This may seem to contradict our earlier assertion that young children often focus on object matches. However comparison can promote relational commonalities only relative to the learner's existing knowledge base.

Ross, 1987; Markman and Gentner, 1993b; Goldstone and Medin, 1994). For example, Markman and Gentner (1993b) showed people two scenes. In one, a women was shown *giving* food to a squirrel; in the other, the women was shown *receiving* food from a man. One group of participants rated how similar the two scenes were to each other, while another group simply rated the two scenes' aesthetic value (to control for time spent looking at the pictures). All participants were then asked to say which thing in the second picture the *woman* should map to. Participants who first rated the similarity of the scenes made significantly more relational mappings (i.e. woman to squirrel) (69%) than those who did not (42%). It appears that the very act of carrying out a similarity comparison can induce a structural alignment, increasing people's likelihood of making matches on the basis of shared relations instead of simple object similarities.

More specifically, there is evidence that which information is selected by a comparison is determined by *systematicity*: the presence of higher-order connections between lower-order relations. For example, Clement and Gentner (1991) showed people analogous scenarios and asked them to say which of two lower-order assertions shared by base and target was most important to the match. People chose the assertion that was connected to matching causal antecedents: that is, their choice was based not only on the goodness of the local match, but on whether it was connected to a larger matching-system. A second study showed that inferences from one scenario to the other were also governed by systematicity; people made the inference that completed a causal system. (See also Bowdle and Gentner, 1998). We now consider highlighting, re-representation and inference projection, showing developmental evidence that these processes operate to promote learning.

4.1. Highlighting common systems

We suggested above that comparison acts to promote common systems. If such highlighting of common structural systems occurs in development, then comparison could act to orient children towards *systems of interconnected knowledge* – e.g. systems linked by higher-order causal, mathematical or perceptual relations. Kotovsky and Gentner (Gentner et al., 1995; Kotovsky and Gentner, 1996) investigated the possibility that comparison processes might promote children's learning about higher-order perceptual relations such as *symmetry* or *monotonic increase*. We focused on perceptual relations for four reasons: (a) the materials – objects in simple configurations – are familiar to children; (b) prior work indicates a relational shift in children's sensitivity to perceptual relational structure (Chipman and Mendelson, 1979; Smith, 1984) and, most importantly; (c) perceptual patterns permit independent manipulation of different levels of relational commonality (Chipman, 1977; Smith, 1984, 1989, 1993; Halford, 1987, 1992), in contrast to rich causal situations, in which object similarity and relational similarity are typically correlated; and (d) we wished to extend the evidence for systematicity beyond causal relations.

We asked when and how children become able to perceive cross-dimensional relational matches. The task was a triads-similarity task: The child was shown a standard geometric pattern (e.g. oOo) and two choice alternatives and was asked to

Within dimension (size)

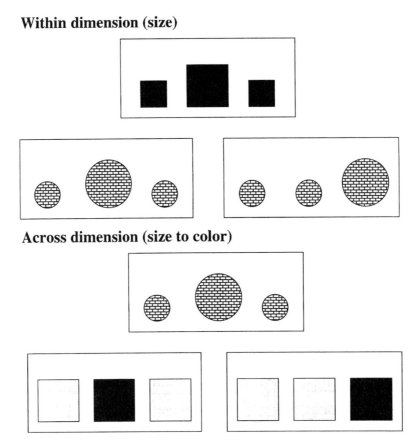

Across dimension (size to color)

Fig. 1. Results of Kotovsky and Gentner's (Kotovsky and Gentner, 1996) progressive alignment study. Given mixed triads, 4-year-olds were at chance (47%) on cross-dimension triads, even when they chose relationally on the within-dimension triads. However, when given the within-dimension triads first – inviting easy alignment – those 4-year-olds who chose relationally on within-dimension triads also chose relationally on cross-dimension triads. Those who scored above median on within-dimension triads chose 80% relationally on the cross-dimension triads.

say with which alternative the standard 'goes best'.[5] Each triad had a relational choice that shared a higher-order relation with the standard – either *symmetry* or *monotonicity*. The other alternative was a foil. It was composed of the same elements as the relational choice, rearranged to remove the higher-order pattern (see Fig. 1). Since the relational choice and the foil were made up of the same objects, this task is a pure test of children's appreciation of relational similarity. The key manipulation

[5]We avoided the term 'most similar' as we feared it might lead children to seek concrete matches (See Goldstone, 1994b). We oriented them towards similarity by giving them pre-training with clear similarity choices. During the task, although no feedback was given, the children showed that they construed the task as a similarity task by choosing correctly on filler triads designed to be easy similarity matches as well as on most of the within-dimension triads.

was whether the higher-order relation occurred over the *same* dimension or over *different* dimensions (as shown in Fig. 1). The logic was, first, to verify that the cross-dimensional task is difficult for young children and, second, to ask whether the comparison task itself can *improve* children's subsequent ability to detect the higher-order commonalities.

Study 1 was a baseline study that varied the degree of concrete support for the higher-order relational match. The results showed that although 6- and 8-year-olds were able to recognize higher-order relational matches across different dimensions (e.g. size vs. saturation), 4-year-olds chose relationally only in the same-dimension condition; they were at chance on cross-dimensional matches. That is, they could match *little-big-little* with *little-big-little* (with different objects), but not with *light-dark-light*.[6] To test whether the comparison process could help the 4-year-olds learn to detect common higher-order structure along different dimensions, Study 2 utilized a *progressive alignment* technique in which children were given the same-dimension matches before the cross-dimensional matches. The rationale is that within-dimension comparisons, being strong overall matches, should be very easy for children to notice and align. By hypothesis, each time a pair of these concrete relational structures is aligned, their common structure is promoted. If so, then concentrated repeated experience on within-dimension pairs should help the child to notice the pattern of symmetry or monotonicity.

The manipulation in Study 2 was fairly minimal. Children received the same triads as in Study 1. The only difference was that this time the trials were blocked so that within-dimension matches preceded cross-dimensional matches (see Fig. 1). This small change in presentation had a large effect. The 4-year-olds in this study who scored above the median on the same-dimension triads showed significantly more relational responding on the cross-dimensional triads (80%) than those who scored at or below the median. In contrast, children in Study 1 (in which cross- and within-dimension triads were mixed) showed no such difference: They were at chance on the cross-dimensional triads regardless how they did on the within-dimension triads. It appears that receiving the 'easy' within-dimension triads did indeed help children to notice the higher-order patterns of symmetry and monotonicity. In a control study, we showed that alignment experience on both dimensions – size and saturation – was required in order to gain cross-dimensional insight.

In a further study, we used a more intensive training task (Study 4 in Kotovsky and Gentner, 1996). After a pre-test on the cross-dimensional triads, 4-year-olds received training with feedback on the same-dimension triads to a criterion of seven out of eight correct (relational) answers (roughly two runs-through). Then they were tested on the eight cross-dimensional triads, without feedback. Children chose relationally on 74% of the post-test items, significantly better than their pre-test performance of 41%. These findings again confirmed that experience with concrete similarity comparisons can improve children's ability to detect cross-dimensional similarity.

---

[6]Research by Smith and Sera (1992) indicates that *big* and *dark* both have positive polarity for young children.

4.2. Symbolic juxtaposition

It appears that experiential juxtaposition can make common relational structure more salient. We next asked whether the use of relational language could also promote such alignment and abstraction. As discussed above, such a demonstration would help explain how a child's internal learning processes can connect to cultural systems. There is precedent for supposing that words can act to guide children's attention, in the studies showing that noun labels can call attention to object categories, overriding competing associations (e.g. Markman and Hutchinson, 1984; Waxman and Gelman, 1986; Markman, 1989; Waxman and Markow, 1995). It seems reasonable that such semantic orienting effects should occur for relational terms as well as for object terms, although possibly at a later age (Gentner, 1982; Gentner and Boroditsky, 1998). Thus we conjectured that providing labels for the higher-order relations might increase the salience of the common relational structure.

We taught 4-year-olds labels for the relations of monotonic change ('more-and-more') and symmetry ('even'). On the symmetry-training trials, children were told that the 'picky penguin' (Waxman and Gelman, 1986) only liked 'even' patterns. Then they sorted the 12 individual patterns used in the same-dimension symmetry triads according to whether they were *even*. If they made an error, the correct answer was explained. The same method was used for monotonic-increase. After going through each sequence once, the children were given the cross-dimensional triads task with no feedback. Those 4-year-olds who scored above the median on the labeling task were significantly more likely to show relational responding on the cross-dimensional trials than those below the median. Learning to use relational labels appeared to increase children's attention to common relational structure.

4.3. Comparison and re-representation

Why should repeated within-dimension alignments facilitate subsequent cross-dimensional alignment? We have suggested that highlighting the higher-order structure was important, but this is not enough. In addition, some degree of re-representation seems to be required. Consider a typical 4-year-old in Study 4 (Kotovsky and Gentner, 1996) (the training study). At first she sees no likeness between *little-medium-big* and *light-shaded-dark*. Yet after experiencing training only on within-dimension triads, she is able to see the cross-dimensional match. We suggest that initially she represented the relations in dimension-specific fashion, so that difference in magnitude was conflated with the dimension of difference. In other words, her representations were expressed in terms of first-order relations such as *bigger* (x,y) and *darker* (a,b). These relations cannot be matched. We suggest that the within-dimension comparisons made the higher-order pattern of monotonicity more salient in her representations, so that it constituted a partial match in the subsequent cross-dimensional trials. As noted above, a partial match invites re-representation to improve the match. The relations were re-represented to separate the common pattern of magnitude change from the (non-common) specific dimension of change, resulting in partially matching relations, represented roughly as *greater* (*size*(x), *size*(y)) and *greater* (*shading*(a), *shading*(b)). Although this may seem like a trivial distinction, it allows for noticing that the *same* relation of magnitude change is occurring across different dimensions. The (unlike) dimensional values can then be put into correspondence by virtue of their like relational roles. In this way, the child can see that a higher-order commonality holds across different dimensions. Separating a higher-level constancy from the specific dimension over which it occurs is a critical learning step. (See Gentner et al., 1995 for a more detailed discussion and simulation.) The emerging appreciation can be seen in the comments of one 8-year-old in Study 1. On her first six trials, she responded correctly to three within-dimension trials and incorrectly to all three cross-dimension trials, on which she showed her frustration with comments like 'it can't be the size, because those two are the same size. It can't be color.' Finally, on her seventh trial, she exclaimed 'even though the smaller ones come first and the big one's in the middle, it's exactly the same – but different!' She went on to choose correctly for the remainder of the study.

We suggested earlier that children's initial representations are often highly conservative. Their knowledge is described as 'concrete', 'situated' or 'contextually embedded'. What we are suggesting here is that comparison processes can facilitate seeing that the same relational patterns may apply across different concrete situations. In this way comparison promotes the abstraction or disembedding of relations from their initial rich contexts. This research further suggests that this abstraction process can be promoted by learning relational labels. So the capacity to see consistent mappings between structures across different dimensions is promoted both by direct comparisons and by learning common language that invites later comparison – 'symbolic juxtaposition'. This proposal is consistent with research suggesting that dimensional structure develops gradually (Smith and Kemler, 1977; Smith, 1989) and that verbal cross-dimensional matches developmentally precede perceptual cross-dimensional matches (Smith and Sera, 1992).

Our notion of re-representation is in the same spirit as Karmiloff-Smith's (1992) *representational redescription*. Both address the change from concrete, situated representations to more abstract representations. However, in our account, re-representation occurs on a smaller scale. Whereas representational redescription involves metalevel insight and occurs only after considerable mastery has been attained, we envision re-representation as more like local tinkering (Burstein, 1983; Kass, 1989); and we assume that it can occur at any time during the course of learning. Many of the earliest early alignments and re-representations may be too simple to be noticed, but they nonetheless facilitate later juxtapositions.

4.4. Comparison and category abstraction

Comparison processes can contribute to children's learning of the deep commonalties that characterize a category. Such learning is important because although there is considerable evidence that even very young children believe that words name like kinds (Markman, 1989; Waxman and Markow, 1995), their initial sense of likeness may rely heavily on perceptual similarity, especially shape similarity (Landau et al.,

1988; Baldwin, 1992; Imai et al., 1994). In the first set of studies, following the basic Markman (1989) word versus no-word choice task, Imai et al. showed 3- and 5-year-old children a standard – e.g. a drum – along with three alternatives, e.g. a bucket (same shape), a flute (same category) and drumsticks (thematically related). When asked to choose the picture that had the same name as the standard (e.g. a *blicket* in dinosaur language), the children, especially the 3-year-olds, were highly likely to choose the same-shape item: 68% shape versus 10% taxonomic responses for 3-year-olds and 56% shape versus 28% taxonomic responses for 5-year-olds (chance, 33%). In fact, both age groups were significantly *more* likely to make shape choices in the word condition than in the no-word condition, in which they were simply asked to 'choose the one that goes with' the standard. However, there was a *shape-to-taxonomic* shift: 5-year-olds made significantly more taxonomic responses in the word condition (28%) than did 3-year-olds (10%).

This shape-to-taxonomic shift presumably reflects children's generally deepening conceptual knowledge. However, perhaps language itself, in combination with the learning mechanisms we have discussed, contributes to the shift. We hypothesize that learning common terms for same-shape items in basic-level categories might prompt comparisons among these items; this in turn would promote the discovery of deeper commonalities. Evidence for this conjecture comes from a further study by Gentner and Imai (1995) in which a fourth alternative (e.g. a tambourine) was added that shared *both* shape and taxonomic category with the standard. Children were allowed to make two choices. For their first choice, 3-year-olds in the word condition appeared to choose solely on the basis of shape: their responses were evenly split between the two shape alternatives, even though one shared taxonomic category with the standard and the other did not. So far, the results simply replicate the shape bias in word extension. When children were asked to choose a second *blicket*, however, with their first choice placed next to the standard to allow comparison, there was a dramatic change. Children who had chosen the same-shape/same-category alternative (the tambourine) chose the remaining categorical alternative (the flute) twice as often as the remaining shape alternative (the bucket) (60% vs. 33%). This contrasts strikingly with the behavior of children in the previous study (Imai et al.), who, given the same three alternatives (bucket, flute, drumsticks) overwhelmingly chose the shape alternative. Children who compared the drum and tambourine as blickets could perfectly well have settled for the conclusion that same-shape defined the meaning of *blicket*, but they did not. In fact, they were *six times* as likely to choose the alternative that shared category but not shape (the flute) (given the same three alternatives) as children who had seen the drum only as a *blicket* in the previous Imai et al. study. We suggest that comparing the two *blickets*– the drum and the tambourine – made commonalities such as 'playing music' more salient.[7]

One concern is that the results could reflect subject self-selection effects: the children who choose the same-shape same-category item on the first round may be just those who possess superior category knowledge. This seems unlikely given the magnitude of the difference. However, Gentner and Namy (unpublished data)

---

[7]This categorical bootstrapping effect of comparison occurred only in the word condition, not in the no-word condition.

have recently completed a study that clearly shows that juxtaposition of the two perceptually-similar exemplars, given a common label, can invite the child to notice further, more abstract commonalities. The materials, shown in Fig. 2, were designed so that each of two standards was perceptually similar to the same alternative, and conceptually similar to the other. When 4-year-olds were given the naming task with _either_ standard – e.g. the apple or the pear – and asked to 'find another dax', they tended to prefer the shape-similar item (the balloon) or to choose randomly. However, when a third group of children was given both standards at once and told 'these are both daxes. Can you see why they're both daxes?', the children showed a significant shift towards the category choice (the banana). These results show that comparisons among similar exemplars – even if initially prompted by common perceptual features – can and do serve to highlight deeper commonalities. Similarity processing is not a dead-end computation of a single product, as a behaviorist view might suggest, but a generative process.

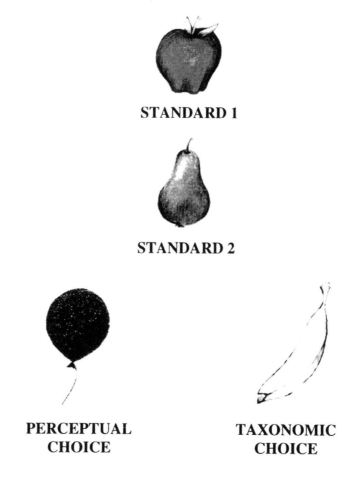

STANDARD 1

STANDARD 2

PERCEPTUAL
CHOICE

TAXONOMIC
CHOICE

Fig. 2. Sample materials used in the naming task (Gentner and Namy, unpublished).

4.5. Comparison and inference projection

A third way in which structural comparison can lead to learning is by the projection of inferences. Rattermann and Gentner (1990; and unpublished data) investigated children's ability to align two situations and to project a simple inference from one to the other. As in the prior study, the logic was, first, to investigate when this mapping ability naturally develops and, second, to investigate possible contributors to this development by asking whether the skill could be acquired earlier. Whereas the previous studies focused chiefly on progressive alignment, the Rattermann and Gentner studies focused on the effects of learning relational language. The task was a mapping task inspired by DeLoache's (1989, 1995) model-room search task. The child had to infer where a sticker was hidden in one space by mapping a corresponding location from an analogous space. As in Kotovsky and Gentner's studies, simple perceptual configurations were used so that an unambiguous higher-order relation – in this case, monotonic increase in size – was available (See Gentner and Rattermann, 1991; Rattermann et al., 1994).

Children aged 3, 4 and 5 years saw two triads of objects, the child's set and the experimenter's set, both arranged in monotonically-increasing order according to size. The child watched as the experimenter hid a sticker under an object in the experimenter's triad; she was told that she could find her sticker by looking 'in the same place' in her triad. The correct response was always based on relational similarity; the child was meant to choose the object of the same relative size and relative position, which were always correlated. In the high-similarity condition, the child's triad was identical to the experimenter's – e.g. E:123 → C:123. This is predicted to be an easy mapping, because object similarity and relational alignment converge on the same result: 2 → 2. In the cross-mapped condition, the object similarity matches were inconsistent with the best relational alignment – e.g. E:123 → C:234. This should be much harder; if the experimenter chooses her middle object (object 2), then to choose correctly (object 3), the child must resist the competing identity match (object 2). The child was always shown the correct answer, but was allowed to keep the sticker only if he had pointed to the correct object.

In Study 1, a developmental baseline was obtained by varying the match condition and the degree of object similarity between the two triads (see Fig. 3). As predicted, children were more accurate with literal similarity than with cross-mapped arrays. Also as predicted, there was an interaction between match type and object similarity. In literal similarity trials, for which the object matches agreed with the correct relational alignment, performance was better for rich objects than for sparse objects. For cross-mappings, in which the object matches conflicted with the correct relational alignment, the reverse was true: performance was better for sparse objects than for rich objects. Indeed, 3- and 4-year-olds performed at chance (33%) on the rich cross-mapped trials despite being shown the correct response on every trial.

Having thus established a challenging relational task, Rattermann and Gentner then investigated whether teaching children to apply relational language could help them perform the mapping. Children again received the cross-mapping task, but this time they were taught to use the labels *Daddy*, *Mommy* and *Baby* for both their own triad and for the experimenter's. (These family labels are often used spontaneously by preschool children to mark monotonic change (Smith, 1989).) The reasoning was that applying these labels would invite the child to map this monotonic pattern from families to the arrays in our study. Having this common higher-order relation of *monotonicity* should make it easier to align the two sets. The results of the labeling manipulation were striking. The 3-year-olds' performance in the cross-mapping task was far better on both the sparse and the rich stimuli (89% and 79% relational responding, respectively) than the baseline performance of same-age children in

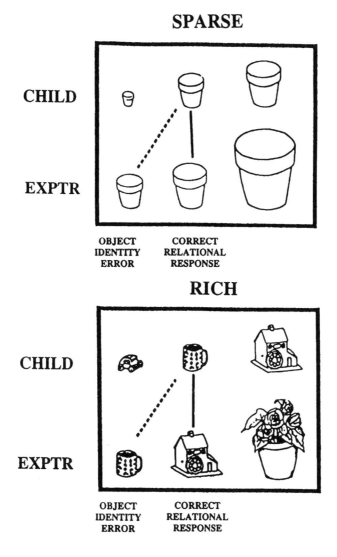

Fig. 3. Materials used in Rattermann and Gentner's mapping task.

Experiment 1 (54% and 32%, respectively). In fact, the 3-year-olds' performance with 'Daddy-Mommy-Baby' labels was comparable with that of 5-year-olds in the baseline study.

That a brief intervention could improve performance so strongly is evidence for a substantial role of knowledge change, as opposed to purely maturational change, in analogical development (Gentner, 1978a,b; Vosniadou, 1987; Brown, 1989; Goswami, 1992). Moreover, the gains are not specific to the initial materials; the children are able to transfer this learning to new triads even with no further use of the labels by the experimenters. Finally, in a recent follow-up, children were found to have preserved this learning over substantial periods. Children were brought back 4 weeks later and asked to play the game again (without the labels). Children initially taught relational labels performed far better (65%) than those in the no-label (31%, chance).

Our account of this improvement, as noted above, is that the relational labels invited higher-order representation (Gentner and Rattermann, 1991). Just as object labels appear to facilitate noticing object-level similarities, so relational labels may facilitate the noticing and matching of relational structures.[8] It appears that the use of relational labels can invite children's attention to common relational systems, thereby allowing even very young children to carry out a relational alignment. We speculate that the relational shift in children's similarity mapping may be promoted in part by the learning of relational language.

5. Comparison as a mechanism for the application and extension of knowledge

So far our case for comparison has focused on its role as a mechanism for new learning and progressive abstraction. However, structure-mapping processes can also function to apply available knowledge to new cases. Consider the phenomenon of property induction from categories. Although category-based induction and similarity-based inference are commonly said to involve different processes – the former consisting in the extrapolation of knowledge on the basis of category structure and the latter consisting in the projection of knowledge from one specific instance to another – we think it worth exploring some connections.

6. Inductive inference

Carey's (1985) studies of inductive inferences in biology revealed striking differences between adults and children. When asked questions of the form 'species X has property p. Do you think species Y has property P?' adults differentiated across both properties and ontological categories, e.g. they assumed that *breathing* was a reasonable inference about animals, whereas *having bones* was specific to vertebrates. In

---

[8]However, the present effects are not due to linguistic labels per se, but to learning labels that convey *relations*. A further control study showed that children taught *object* labels – such as 'Jiggy-Zimbo-Gimli' – did not improve in their performance.

contrast, regardless of the property, 4-year-olds ascribed it to other creatures on the basis of their overall similarity to humans. Carey suggested that young children may use humans – as their most central or typical biological creatures – to reason about less familiar species. Lacking knowledge, young children rely on a kind of analogizing, whereas adults and older children can use category-level conceptual knowledge.

Results like this have led to the statement that children's induction is comparison-based and adults' is category-based. However, adults continue to use comparison along with their category-based processes. Indeed, most models of adult category-based induction include a similarity component. For example, the similarity-coverage model of Osherson et al. (1990) postulates three underlying components – *similarity*, *category coverage* and *category generation* – that give rise to a large set of empirical phenomena in category-based induction. An example of the positive effects of similarity between the premise and conclusion categories is that people consider (1) a stronger argument than (2)

(1)	Foxes have property P.
	Deer have property P.
	Therefore weasels have property P.
(2)	Elephants have property P.
	Deer have property P.
	Therefore weasels have property P.

However, other findings suggest that adults generate and make use of categories in this task. For example, adults show effects of *premise diversity* – the more diverse the premises, the stronger the argument: e.g. *hippo, hamster → mammal* is stronger than *hippo, rhino → mammal* – and of *monotonicity* – i.e. that adding premises strengthens a conclusion.

To study the development of these effects, Lopez et al. (1992) gave children inductive inference problems similar to those of Osherson et al. As in Carey's studies, they found a developmental pattern of early reliance on similarity, with category-based reasoning entering later. Both kindergarteners and second-graders showed effects that follow from the similarity component – namely, similarity of premise to conclusion, typicality of premise and homogeneity of the premise items. However, only second-graders showed effects that follow from category coverage – namely, premise diversity and monotonicity. Adults showed all these effects plus others that also require *generating* an inclusive category. As in the Osherson et al. studies, adults seemed to use both comparison-based and category-based processes. We return to the characterization of adult processes below.

6.1. Symbolic juxtaposition in inductive inference

Language may play a facilitating effect in category induction, as in the phenomena discussed earlier. S. Gelman and her colleagues (Gelman and Markman, 1986, 1987; Gelman, 1989; Davidson and Gelman, 1990) have shown that common category labels can invite young children to make inductions. For example, Gelman and Markman (1986) found that the use of a familiar common category label (e.g. 'bird') increased 4-year-olds' propensity to import knowledge from one creature to another. This finding is consistent with Gelman's suggestion that words signal conceptual essences for the child, and with the idea that 'a word can function as a promissory note, signaling subtle commonalities that the child does not yet perceive' (Gentner and Rattermann, 1991).

Davidson and Gelman (1990) investigated interactions of category labeling with perceptual similarity in children's induction. Children of 4–5 years of age were shown a novel animal (e.g. a gnu-like animal, called a 'zav') and taught that it has an unfamiliar property (e.g. 'has four stomachs'). They were then asked whether the property would be present in another animal. The design neatly separated effects of perceptual similarity from those of a common label. Children saw four test items in a 2×2 design (similar/non-similar $\times$ same-label/different-label). In two studies, children drew more inferences to perceptually similar (about 75%) than to perceptually dissimilar pictures (about 45%). There was no effect of common labels, whether the labels were novel (Experiment 1) or familiar (Experiment 2). However, in the third study, the correlation between similarity and common label was improved by omitting one of the 'conflict' pictures in each set (reducing the design to 3 cells). In this case, having a common label did help children (65% for same label vs. 47% for different label). When there was a contradiction between labels and appearances, young children based their inferences on appearances. However, when a genuine – though imperfect – alignment was available, a common label could then be anchored and extended. This pattern of findings is consistent with our earlier findings: Common labels invite comparison, but perceptual similarity is crucial for achieving an initial alignment. Furthermore, as in progressive alignment, once an 'easy' alignment is made, children can notice further, more abstract commonalities. As Gelman and Markman (1986) and Davidson and Gelman (1990) suggest, children notice that the members of a named category have many observable features in common and eventually extend this belief to unobservable properties as well.

6.2. Analogical inference projection

It is instructive to compare children's spontaneous use of analogy in inductive problems from the same domain, biology (Inagaki and Hatano, 1987, 1991; Inagaki, 1989, 1990). Inagaki and Hatano (1987) asked 5–6-year-old children questions such as 'what would happen if a rabbit were continually given more water?' The children often made explicit analogies to humans: e.g. 'we can't keep it [the rabbit] forever in the same size. Because, like me, if I were a rabbit, I would be 5 years old and become bigger and bigger'. Inagaki and Hatano noted several interesting features of children's use of humans to reason about other creatures. First, the personification responses were likely to be reasonable (100% of the explicit personification responses for rabbit were correct, as opposed to 71.5% of the non-personification responses). Second, children were more likely to use the analogy to humans the more similar the target entity was to humans. Both explicit and implicit personification responses occurred far more often for rabbit and tulip than for stone. This is consistent with the findings, noted above, that high similarity facilitates the process of alignment and mapping of inferences. Third, when asked questions for which the analogy with humans would yield incorrect responses (in a second study), children were far less likely to use the analogy.

According to the analogical reasoning account, the person analogy has a special status in early biological reasoning not because of category centrality but because humans, as the most familiar species, provide the richest and most systematic base domain to reason with. Inagaki (1990) provided strong evidence for this analogy account by testing children who had a rich knowledge base about another species, namely, goldfish. On the analogy account, they should be able to use this knowledge as a source of analogical reasoning about other animals. Inagaki (1990) compared 5-year-olds who were raising goldfish with those who were not. Not surprisingly, the goldfish-raisers showed superior factual and conceptual knowledge about goldfish. More importantly for our purposes, when asked questions about unfamiliar aquatic animals such as frogs, children who had raised goldfish were more likely to draw analogies from goldfish than were other children. Interestingly, the goldfish-raisers not only used the *goldfish* analogy more often for frogs than the non-raisers, but they also tended to use the *person* analogy for frogs – and even for goldfish – more often than did the non-raisers (15 vs. 8 explicit person analogies for frogs, respectively; and 18 vs. 12 for goldfish). Inagaki suggests that the goldfish-raisers had derived some understanding of the underlying commonalities between goldfish and humans, and that this helped them see commonalities between humans and frogs. This is consistent with our proposal of progressive alignment and schema abstraction. An alignment and mapping between two species should promote further alignments with other species.

6.3. Induction in adults: weak methods versus strong methods

The evidence from Lopez et al.'s research and other developmental work suggests early similarity-based induction, with a developmental gain in the use of categories in induction. However, as noted above, adults continue to use direct analogies. Striking instances of similarity effects have been documented in adults, including some that seem to flaunt the rules of inductive logic. For example, Osherson et al. (1990) showed that an argument from *robins* → *birds* is judged stronger than one from *robins* → *ostriches*. According to inductive logic, however, it is the latter argument that is stronger, since its conclusion is contained in the conclusion of the former. This phenomenon has been termed the 'inclusion fallacy'. Intuitively, it seems to stem from the greater alignability of robin with bird than with ostrich. Sloman (1993) found an equally-surprising effect in deductive reasoning. People tend to project properties from a superordinate to a subordinate category on the basis of their similarity (the 'inclusion-similarity phenomenon'). For example, the inference 'all birds have an ulnar artery. Therefore, all robins have an ulnar artery' received a higher rating than 'all birds have an ulnar artery. Therefore, all penguins have an ulnar artery'. Even more strangely, the argument from *animals* → *mammals* was rated stronger than the argument from *animals* → *reptiles*. These findings cannot be predicted by a category-based model, since the second category is perfectly included within the first in both cases. Such cases are convincing evidence for at least some direct comparison-based reasoning in adults, even in standard categorical reasoning tasks. Indeed, Sloman (1993) has proposed a model of induction that uses direct featural overlap between the premise and conclusion categories (a measure rela-ted to instance similarity), rather than invoking category membership to draw inferences.

The issue of categories versus similarity in induction can be thought of in terms of Newell and Simon's (1972) distinction between weak and strong methods of reasoning. *Weak methods* are general strategies that can operate without special knowledge of a domain: methods such as means-ends analysis or modus ponens. *Strong methods* are those that make intensive use of specific represented knowledge, such as the facts that raccoons are nocturnal and squirrels diurnal. Weak methods are extremely valuable because of their generality; they provide an avenue wherever knowledge is insufficient. Perhaps because of their abstract character, they tend to be learned late; they qualify as sophisticated knowledge. The fact remains, though, that strong methods are often better when the appropriate knowledge is present. Although Newell and Simon did not discuss analogy explicitly, close analogies clearly qualify as a strong method because they rely on specific knowledge of the base (although the mapping *process* is domain-general).

For example, it seems intuitively clear that an inference from *elk* to *deer* can proceed without recourse to the mammal category.[9] (It could be argued that such an inference would implicitly rely on a common category of 'hoofed, antlered North American ungulates', but then the notion of 'common category' becomes extremely slippery.) Following this line, we speculate that some of the developmental gains in inductive accuracy may come about not through a shift from comparison to category application, but through increasingly sophisticated analogizing. The distinction here is between relatively blind analogy – in which overall similarity provides the metric for attribution of properties – and informed analogy – in which similarity with respect to specific causal or functional systems determines the common system and the projected inference.

Consistent with these claims, there is evidence that adults' property induction is

---

[9]The persistent non-monotonicity effect found in both the Osherson et al. studies and the Lopez et al. studies – in which inference strength goes *down* with the addition of premises, contrary to the mono-tonicity prediction that increasing the number of premises should increase inductive strength – may reflect structural alignment of the premise categories. For example, *crow, peacock* → *bird* is stronger than *crow, peacock, rabbit* → *bird*. In the first case, the premises are strongly alignable, yielding a rich 'premise schema' which can project inferences to the conclusion category. The addition of a difficult-to-align premise (rabbit) may force a retreat from alignment-based reasoning to category-based reasoning – from strong reasoning to weak reasoning, in the Newell and Simon sense. Osherson et al. speculate that the effect arises from coverage effects; by enlarging the size of the inferred covering category, the similarity to the premise and conclusion categories is diluted. However, Sloman's (1993) example that *crocodile* → *alligator* is stronger than *crocodile, king snake* → *alligator* cannot be explained in this way (but could be explained by premise alignment, because *crocodile* has a richer match with *alligator* than does the premise schema that results from aligning *crocodile* and *king snake*).

guided by structural similarity, not merely by featural overlap. Lassaline (1996) found that argument strength did not depend on the overall similarity between premise and conclusion, but on whether there was a causally-connected inference that could be carried over as a candidate inference (as in Clement and Gentner, 1991). Further evidence that people are sensitive to connected *systems* of relations in induction comes from a study by Heit and Rubinstein (1994), who demonstrated that people make stronger inferences when the kind of property to be inferred (anatomical or behavioral) matches the kind of similarity between the animals (anatomical or behavioral). For instance, people make stronger behavioral inferences from tuna to whales (because both swim) than from bears to whales, but stronger anatomical inferences from, whales to bears (because both are mammals). If we assume that anatomy and behavior are represented by different systems of relations, then these findings are consistent with the finding that adults are strongly influenced by causal systematicity in drawing inferences from an analogy (Clement and Gentner, 1991; Bowdle and Gentner, 1998; Markman, 1998).

Overall, the findings on inductive reasoning in children and adults offer no compelling evidence for the idea that comparison is merely a stand-in or fall-back strategy when theory fails. Inagaki (1990) found that children who raised goldfish were more likely than those who did not to draw analogies from people to goldfish, despite the fact that they demonstrably knew *more* about goldfish. Thus the interpretation that analogy is used only in default of deeper knowledge is not tenable. Indeed, deeper knowledge of the target domain – goldfish – made children better able to notice and use commonalities that license cross-species analogies. This pattern fits the claim that alignment and mapping are instrumental in theory development. However, we *could* say that overall similarity is a stand-in for structural similarity, when the child has inadequate relational knowledge. The results suggest a knowledge-driven shift from analogies based on perceptual similarity to (a) analogies based on causal and relational similarity, and (b) derived abstractions.

7. The problem of selection of prior instances: why experiential learning is not sufficient

We have presented a case that comparison can be illuminating. But as Smith et al. point out, the benefits of comparison are crucially dependent on *which* instances are compared. Analogies will play a beneficial role in learning and reasoning only to the extent that the pairs that are compared are legitimately structurally similar. At first glance, the data are not encouraging. There is abundant evidence that memory retrieval is highly responsive to surface similarity between the current item and the prior stored item (e.g. the similarity of objects and characters) and relatively insensitive to relational similarity (Holyoak and Koh, 1987; Reed, 1987; Ross, 1987, 1989; Keane, 1988; Gentner et al., 1993; Reeves and Weisberg, 1994). This is true even when, once both items are present, people judge the match's quality and inferential soundness on the basis of structural similarity, ignoring surface similarity. For example, Gentner and Schumacher gave subjects a continuous reminding task in which they saw about 100 proverbs and for each one wrote out any previous proverbs that they were reminded of. Subjects were reminded of prior identity pairs (not surprisingly) and of prior mere-appearance pairs sharing a single nominal concept – e.g. 'a hair from here, a hair from there, will make a beard' and 'it is not the beard that makes the philosopher'. They were far less often reminded of prior relational matches – e.g. 'remove the dirt from your own eye before you wipe the speck from mine' and 'he who laughs at a crooked man should walk very straight'. Yet, in a subsequent rating task, they rated the analogy pairs (whether or not they had recalled them) as both more sound and more similar than the surface matches. Strangely, the very matches that come to mind most easily are often judged by the same subjects to be least useful in reasoning (See also Gentner et al., 1993).

If memory retrieval is strongly driven by surface similarity, then spontaneous comparisons are problematic as a route to insight. Comparisons among merely surface-similar instances would not only fail to promote rule-abstraction, they would lead to false generalizations. However, there are some rays of hope. First, people are not at the mercy of their memories, as noted above, subjects tend to reject surface remindings as inferentially worthless. Second, the study above is a bit oversimplified in its total separation of surface similarity from structural similarity. In real life, the two are highly correlated. This consideration leads to the *kind world* hypothesis: most things that look alike are alike relationally as well (Gentner, 1989; Medin and Ortony, 1989) – what looks like a tiger generally is a tiger. Of course, children will sometimes try improper similarity matches, our point is that there are vast numbers of useful overall similarity matches to be had. However, this is still not enough. Even given a kind world, purely experiential juxtapositions are not sufficient to explain the observed sophistication of adult thought. A further crucial factor, as discussed throughout, is the guiding effects of language and culture. We return to this point below.

8. Summary and discussion

We have argued that there is a continuum between similarity-based and rule-based processes and, further, that the process of structural comparison acts as a bridge by which similarity-based processes can give rise to abstract rules. This view of gradual abstraction of initially-conservative, context-specific representations is consistent with the proposal that abstractions can arise from comparison across highly specific instances (Elio and Anderson, 1981; Gick and Holyoak, 1983; Cheng and Holyoak, 1985; Forbus and Gentner, 1986; Medin and Ross, 1989). There is a graceful learning continuum from a fully-concrete mapping, in which the objects transparently match their intended correspondents, to an analogical mapping in which a relational structure is imported to a new domain with no support (or even with conflict) from the object matches, to a fully-abstract mapping in which the base domain contains variables and the target contains objects. At this point the mapping could be described as unification or rule application.

Our case for comparison as a bridge to abstraction has three broad themes. First, comparison provides learning mechanisms that promote learning. The mechanisms of highlighting, inference projection and re-representation have been attested empirically. More directly, we provided evidence that comparison can foster children's learning in diverse tasks, including detecting abstract cross-dimensional relational matches, mapping between two arrays, and category learning. Second, we gave evidence that even among adults there is a mix of comparison-based and rule-based processing, as would be expected if rules are typically formed by gradual abstraction from instances. For example, in category-based induction,[10] young children rely almost exclusively on comparison, while adults appear to use both comparison and category-level knowledge (though see Sloman (1996) for counter-arguments to the latter point). Third, we argued that even after abstract knowledge is present, alignment processes are needed to extend this knowledge to new cases.

The research discussed here is consistent with our claim that children's early representations are conservative and context-specific, relying on massive overlap of perceptual features, and that children gradually develop relationally-articulated representations that enable them to appreciate partial similarity and analogy. We considered two related ways of fostering relational insight: first, the progressive alignment of a series of cases so as to reveal common relational structure and, second, the use of relational language to invite the perception of common relations. The first of these represents alignment through experiential juxtaposition, the second, alignment through symbolic juxtaposition.

9. Arguments against similarity

Defenders of comparison processes must deal with Goodman's (1972) influential arguments against similarity. He argues that the claim that two things are similar is uninformative until we specify in *what respect* they are similar, and that when we do so the similarity statement reduces to whatever specific respect categorizes the items compared. So, for instance, to say that the numbers 8 and 10 have something in common is ambiguous, because there are many properties these numbers can share, but the more specific claim that 8 and 10 are similar because both are divisible by 2 is just to say that they are both even numbers. Thus similarity is either vague or superfluous.

However, as Kripke (1982) has pointed out, Goodman's arguments against similarity were inspired by Wittgenstein's discussion of rule-following but left part of Wittgenstein's discussion behind. Wittgenstein (1953) argues that 'what counts as the same or similar' cannot be established independently of our rule-governed activities, for anything can be similar to anything else in some respect. For example, if someone is given the series '2,4,6,8...' and is asked to 'go on in the same way', it is

---

[10]Content effects in deductive reasoning provide another example in which adults often use analogies to prior knowledge in cases where purely formal methods could apply (as in Cheng and Holyoak's (1985) discussion of the Wason card task).

indeterminate what is to count as the correct continuation (Wittgenstein, 1953). Following the rule cannot consist simply in being guided by our sense of similarity, for anything can count as 'going on in the same way' under some interpretation of the relevant similarities underlying the sequence '2,4,6,8...'. What is needed is just a grasp of the rule governing this number sequence – e.g. '+2'.

So far Wittgenstein's argument is that *similarities without rules are empty*, just as Goodman later argued. However, Wittgenstein goes on to apply the same reasoning to rule-following. He argues that following a rule cannot consist simply in being guided by a representation of the rule (e.g. '+2'). Such a representation *by itself* does not determine unequivocally how to continue the number series, for it can be interpreted and applied in various ways (e.g. as 'x + 2 if x < 1000, otherwise x + 4'). Wittgenstein emphasizes that rules are not self-interpreting: a rule does not contain within itself what counts as a correct application to each new case. One might address this concern by postulating further rules that fix the application of the rule, but this would lead to a regress, for these rules would also stand in need of interpretation. Wittgenstein's point is that, in order to be cognitively useful, rules have to be supplemented with standards of similarity for their application. As some commentators have emphasized (Baker and Hacker, 1984; Williams, 1994), the upshot of Wittgenstein's discussion is that our capacity to follow a rule is crucially dependent on our grasp of 'normative similarities', i.e. to similarities that have been disciplined by norms in rule-governed practices. Gagné (1970) notes that 'one could perhaps think of a whole range of situations of potential applicability of a learned rule that displayed decreasing degrees of similarity to the situation in which the rule had originally been learned' – an idea that mirrors our notion of progressive abstraction. Wittgenstein's arguments underscore the strong interdependence of rules and similarity. Goodman exploited the first strand of Wittgenstein's arguments, thereby posing a challenge to similarity theorists. However, the second part of Wittgenstein's argument, although often overlooked, is equally important. In short, we could summarize Wittgenstein's rule-following discussion by rephrasing the Kantian dictum about concepts and intuitions: *similarities without rules are empty*, *rules without similarities are blind*.

10. Separate systems for similarity and rules?

Some cognitive researchers have proposed that similarity-based and rule-based processes are both important in human cognition, but that they function as different cognitive systems (Smolensky, 1988; Sloman, 1996). Smolensky (1988) has argued that reasoning involves two different mechanisms: a conscious rule interpreter that processes knowledge algorithmically and an intuitive processor that operates at the subconceptual level. A more specific proposal is Sloman's (1996) proposal of two independent but interacting systems of reasoning, one associative and similarity-based, the other symbolic and rule-based. In Sloman's account, the associative system encodes and processes the covariation of features in the environment and makes estimates based on statistical regularities. In contrast, the rule-based system

operates on structured symbolic representations and reasons on the basis of underlying causal or mechanical structure. As evidence for the existence of two independent systems of reasoning, Sloman cites strong dissociations between rules
and similarity seen in fallacies like the inclusion fallacy or the conjunction fallacy, where similarity and rules lead to contradictory conclusions (Tversky and
Kahneman, 1983; Smith and Osherson, 1989; Shafir et al., 1990). For instance,
in the celebrated 'Linda the bank teller' example of the conjunction fallacy
(Tversky and Kahneman, 1983) participants judged that Linda (who, as a student,
'was deeply concerned with issues of discrimination and social justice') was more
likely to be 'a bank teller and active in the feminist movement' (B and F) than 'a
bank teller' (B). One explanation of this phenomenon is that participants were
swayed by the greater similarity of the description of Linda to a 'feminist bank
teller' than to the typical bank teller (Smith and Osherson, 1989). Even people who
know that B and F cannot be more probable than B experience the lure of the
conjunctive solution. Sloman argues that this strong inclination to draw contradictory inferences is due to a conflict between the rule-based and the similarity-
associative reasoning systems.

Contradictory responses could be generated *within* a single comparison-based
reasoning system, however, in at least three ways. First the retrieval process may
produce more than one alternative for a given contextual probe. Second, once two
comparands are present in working memory, the local-to-global alignment process
discussed above often produces contradictory responses over time, since early
responses will be dominated by local object matches and later responses by the
relational alignment (Falkenhainer et al., 1989; Ratcliff and McKoon, 1989; Goldstone, 1994a; Goldstone and Medin, 1994). A third way is that the same comparison
can give rise to two alternative interpretations, even under the same correspondences. For example, the statement that a given battle 'is the mother of battles'
could mean that it is the biggest (as a parent is larger than her offspring) or that it will
engender a host of others (which may be larger than the parent).

Although we find much to agree with in Sloman's two-system proposal, we think
it incorrect to relegate comparison processes to an associative subsymbolic system.
First, the accumulated evidence that the comparison process is structure-sensitive
(Gentner and Clement, 1988; Gentner and Markman, 1993, 1994, 1997; Markman
and Gentner, 1993a, 1996; Medin et al., 1993; Goldstone and Medin, 1994) suggests
that similarity cannot be captured by merely associative processes. To capture
similarity processing requires representations that include structural dependencies
among their parts – the same kind of structural specificity that is necessary for the
representation of rules.[11] Second, the evidence reviewed here shows that the process
of structural alignment can promote the noticing of structural regularities (Gick and
Holyoak, 1983; Markman and Gentner, 1993a; Gentner and Imai, 1995; Kotovsky
and Gentner, 1996) and that rule-based reasoning is bootstrapped by comparisons
between symbolically-structured representations. Thus we argue that similarity – or,

---

[11]Gentner and Markman (1993) have laid out a set of benchmark phenomena that computational
models, including connectionist models, must demonstrate in order to be said to have captured the
phenomena of structural similarity and analogy.

more accurately, the comparison process – must have full citizenship in the same symbolic cognitive system that contains rules.[12]

11. Implications for cognitive development: is onward always upward?

Our assessment of the developmental evidence suggests that the abstractness and content-independence characteristic of abstract cognition (Smith et al., 1992; Rips, 1994) are the result of considerable experience. On the 'career of similarity' view, similarity comparisons are initially conservative – heavily perceptual and context-bound – and become increasingly abstract and structurally-articulated with domain experience and with enculturation. This framework also emphasizes the possibility of cognitive pluralism. Adult cognition includes knowledge-intensive reasoning processes – e.g. strong similarity-based inferences – as well as general-purpose weak reasoning methods such as *modus ponens*. As Quine (1969) puts it, people 'retain different similarity standards... for use in different contexts'. According to our framework, rule-governed processes are based on structural similarity, but they may coexist, in adult cognition, with processes governed by other forms of similarity.

As discussed above, there is a danger in overrating the cognitive centrality of weak methods. General, abstract processes such as deductive inference or category-based reasoning tend to strike us as particularly elegant forms of cognition. However, recent evidence from cross-cultural research suggests that we should be cautious about assuming that particular weak methods are either central or universal in cognition. For example, Lopez et al. (1997) found that inductive reasoning among the Itzaj-Mayans resembled that of American subjects in making heavy use of similarity and typicality, but differed in its lack of reliance on premise diversity. When premise variability was high, Mayans often drew on their ecological knowledge concerning relations among the creatures, whereas Americans tended to compute a more abstract category. One way of construing these results is that the Mayans, who possess far more detailed knowledge of their ecology than do the American subjects, could and did rely on strong methods, such as strong representational alignment and detailed causal knowledge of interactions. These results suggest that which weak methods are developed and how they are used may be culturally influenced to some degree.

11.1. The role of language

Children delight in experiential comparisons. From the circular reaction in infancy, to sand-castles built and rebuilt, to crib talk, children love to present themselves with examples and variations. Yet learning via experiential juxtaposition

---

[12]However, we concede that some kinds of similarity may indeed be part of an associative system. For example, a kind of associative similarity may arise from caching the results of repeated similarity computations. (We probably do not need to recompute the alignment between *horse* and *zebra* when we encounter them anew, for example.)

alone would be hopelessly unsatisfactory. As the history of science makes clear, if each of us learned from the world alone we would lack such intellectual amenities as rational numbers, a zero, Newton's laws and other tools of thought. For these reasons, we've emphasized the role of culture and language in learning: specifically, in inviting comparisons. Common language can invite symbolic juxtaposition and serve as a signal that there are important commonalities to be discovered. In this way, language and other cultural systems influence which comparisons get made. Language thus augments direct experiential learning in two ways. First, by giving two things the same name, we invite children to compare them, even if they do not occur together in experience. Second, learning words for relations may increase the likelihood that the learner will encode relations in the same way across different situations. Such representational uniformity would promote cross-situation remindings. Thus when relational concepts become part of our mental store, they may facilitate implicit application of the cultural theories they embody to new experience.

Vygotsky (1962) argued that with the advent of language children augment their repertoire of pre-linguistic cognitive capabilities – reactive attention, associative learning and sensorimotor intelligence – with post-linguistic capabilities of focused attention, deliberate memory and symbolic thought (see also Bruner et al., 1966; Dennett, 1993). We would amplify this proposal by noting that symbolic representations permit structural comparison processes. Once language is present, the child may continue to use her associative system, but also possesses a symbolic system that permits structural representations and structured comparison processes. There is recent intriguing evidence of new cognitive capabilities at around the time that language emerges. Mandler and McDonough (1993) and Mandler (1996) find that 14-month-olds and probably 11-month-olds, but not 7–9-month-olds, will imitate actions across basic level categories. Xu and Carey (1996) found evidence that 12-month-olds, but not 10-month-olds, individuate objects on the basis of object kind and, further, that this ability may be correlated with knowledge of the names of the objects.

11.2. Conclusions

Although similarity is often treated rather slightingly in current theories of cognitive development, we suggest that similarity – even mundane within-dimension similarity – can act as a positive force in learning and development. We propose that simply carrying out similarity and analogy comparisons plays a fundamental role in the development of abstract structural representations. Comparisons – even overall similarity comparisons – can lead the child to focus on relational commonalities that would otherwise pass unnoticed. These structures may then be mapped from well-understood situations to less-understood situations.

We have argued that the capacity to perceive structural similarity is crucial for the development of an abstract symbolic system. Our point is not that structural similarity can replace rules, nor that rules are inevitably acquired via progressive abstraction. (After all, sometimes we are simply told the rule.) What we do suggest is that comparison is very often the critical path in the development of rules, especially early in development when higher-order knowledge is sparse and requires the support of concrete commonalities. Furthermore, we argue that at any age, structural alignment provides the necessary bridge in applying rules and abstract knowledge to ongoing experience. Comparison is fundamental to the development and use of rules in cognition.

Acknowledgements

This research was supported by NSF grant SBR-95–11757 and ONR contract N00014–92-J-1098 to the first author and by a Northwestern Cognitive Science Fellowship to the second author. We thank Ken Forbus, Jeff Loewenstein, Art Markman, Meredith Williams, Mary Jo Rattermann and Phil Wolff for insightful discussions of these issues, and Jacques Mehler, Steve Sloman and two anonymous reviewers for invaluable comments on a previous version.

References

Baillargeon, R., 1987. Object permanence in 3.5- and 4.5-month-old infants. Developmental Psychology 23, 655–664.

Baker, G.P., Hacker, P.M.S., 1984. Skepticism, Rules and Language. Blackwell, Oxford.

Baldwin, D.A., 1992. Clarifying the role of shape in children's taxonomic assumption. Journal of Experimental Child Psychology 54, 392–416.

Bowdle, B., Gentner, D., 1998. Informativity and asymmetry in comparisons. Cognitive Psychology, in press.

Brown, A.L., 1989. Analogical learning and transfer: what develops? In: Vosniadou, S., Ortony, A. (Eds.), Similarity and Analogical Reasoning. Cambridge University Press, New York, pp. 369–412.

Brown, A.L., Kane, M.J., 1988. Preschool children can learn to transfer: learning to learn and learning from example. Cognitive Psychology 20, 493–523.

Bruner, J.S., Olver, R.R., Greenfield, P.M., 1966. Studies in Cognitive Growth. Wiley, New York.

Burstein, M.H., 1983. Concept formation by incremental analogical reasoning and debugging. Proceedings of the International Machine Learning Workshop. University of Illinois, Urbana, IL, pp. 19–25.

Carey, S., 1985. Conceptual Change in Childhood. MIT Press, Cambridge, MA.

Catrambone, R., Holyoak, K.J., 1989. Overcoming contextual limitations on problem-solving transfer. Journal of Experimental Psychology: Learning Memory and Cognition 15 (6), 1147–1156.

Cheng, P.W., Holyoak, K.J., 1985. Pragmatic reasoning schemas. Cognitive Psychology 17, 391–416.

Chen, Z., Daehler, M.W., 1989. Positive and negative transfer in analogical problem solving by 6-year-old children. Cognitive Development 4, 327–344.

Chen, Z., Sanchez, R.P., Campbell, T., 1998. From beyond to within their grasp: the rudiments of analogical problem solving in 10- and 13-month-olds. Developmental Psychology, in press.

Chipman, S.F., 1977. Complexity and structure in visual patterns. Journal of Experimental Psychology: General 106, 269–301.

Chipman, S.F., Mendelson, M.J., 1979. Influence of six types of visual structure on complexity judgments in children and adults. Journal of Experimental Psychology: Human Perception and Performance 5, 365–378.

Clement, C.A., Gentner, D., 1991. Systematicity as a selection constraint in analogical mapping. Cognitive Science 15, 89–132.

Daehler, M., Chen, Z., 1993. Protagonist, theme and goal object: effects of surface similarity on analogical transfer. Cognitive Development 8, 211–229.

Davidson, N.S., Gelman, S.A., 1990. Inductions from novel categories: the role of language and conceptual structure. Cognitive Development 5, 151–176.

DeLoache, J.S., 1989. The development of representation in young children. In: Reese, H.W. (Ed.), Advances in Child Development and Behavior, Vol. 22. Academic Press, New York, pp. 1–39.

DeLoache, J.S., 1995. Early symbol understanding and use. In: Medin, D. (Ed.), The Psychology of Learning and Motivation, Vol. 32. Academic Press, New York.

Dennett, D.C., 1993. Learning and labeling. Mind and Language, 8(4), 540–548.

Elio, R., Anderson, J.R., 1981. The effect of category generalizations and instance similarity on schema abstraction. Journal of Experimental Psychology: Human Learning and Memory 7, 397–417.

Falkenhainer, B., Forbus, K.D., Gentner, D., 1989. The structure-mapping engine: algorithm and examples. Artificial Intelligence 41, 1–63.

Foard, C.F., Kemler-Nelson, D.G., 1984. Holistic and analytic modes of processing: the multiple determinants of perceptual analysis. Journal of Experimental Psychology: General 113, 94–111.

Fodor, J.A., 1990. A Theory of Content and Other Essays. MIT Press, Cambridge, MA, pp. 201–202.

Fodor, J.A., 1994. Why we are so clever. In: The Elm and the Expert: Mentalese and its Semantics. MIT Press, Cambridge, MA, p. 91.

Forbus, K.D., Gentner, D., 1986. Learning physical domains: toward a theoretical framework. In: Michalski, R.S., Carbonell, J.G., Mitchell, T.M. (Eds.), Machine Learning: An Artificial Intelligence Approach, Vol. 2. Kaufmann, Los Altos, CA, pp. 311–348.

Forbus, K.D., Gentner, D., 1989. Structural evaluation of analogies: what counts?. Proceedings of the Eleventh Annual Conference of the Cognitive Science Society 34, 341–348.

Forbus, K.D., Gentner, D., Law, K., 1995. MAC/FAC: a model of similarity-based retrieval. Cognitive Science 19, 141–205.

Gagné, R.M., 1970. The conditions of learning. Holt, Rinehart and Winston, New York.

Gelman, R., 1990. First principles organize attention to and learning about relevant data: number and the animate-inanimate distinction as examples. Cognitive Science 14, 79–106.

Gelman, S.A., 1989. Children's use of categories to guide biological inferences. Human Development 32, 65–71.

Gelman, S.A., Markman, E.M., 1986. Categories and induction in young children. Cognition 23, 183–209.

Gelman, S.A., Markman, E.M., 1987. Young children's inductions from natural kinds: the role of categories and appearances. Child Development 58, 1532–1541.

Gentner, D., 1977a. Children's performance on a spatial analogies task. Child Development 48, 1034–1039.

Gentner, D., 1977b. If a tree had a knee, where would it be? Children's performance on simple spatial metaphors. Papers and Reports on Child Language Development 13, 157–164.

Gentner, D., 1978a. On relational meaning: the acquisition of verb meaning. Child Development 49, 988–998.

Gentner, D., 1978b. What looks like a jiggy but acts like a zimbo? A study of early word meaning using artificial objects. Papers and Reports on Child Language Development 15, 1–6.

Gentner, D., 1982. Are scientific analogies metaphors? In: Miall, D.S. (Ed.), Metaphor: Problems and Perspectives. Harvester, Brighton, UK, pp. 106–132.

Gentner, D., 1983. Structure-mapping: a theoretical framework for analogy. Cognitive Science 7, 155–170.

Gentner, D., 1988. Metaphor as structure mapping: the relational shift. Child Development 59, 47–59.

Gentner, D., 1989. Mechanisms of analogical learning. In: Vosniadou, S., Ortony, A. (Eds.), Similarity and Analogical Reasoning. Cambridge University Press, London, pp. 199–241.

Gentner, D., Brem, S., Ferguson, R.W., Markman, A.B., Levidow, B.B., Wolff, P., Forbus, K.D., 1997. Analogical reasoning and conceptual change: a case study of Johannes Kepler. The Journal of the Learning Sciences 6 (1), 3–40.

Gentner, D., Boroditsky, L., 1998. Individuation, relativity and early word learning. In: Bowerman, M.,

Levinson, S. (Eds.), Language Acquisition and Conceptual Development. Cambridge University Press, UK, in press.

Gentner, D., Clement, C., 1988. Evidence for relational selectivity in the interpretation of analogy and metaphor. In: Bower, G.H. (Ed.), The Psychology of Learning and Motivation, Vol. 22. Academic Press, New York, pp. 307–358.

Gentner, D., Imai, M., 1995. A further examination of the shape bias in early word learning. Proceedings of the Twenty-sixth Annual Child Language Research Forum. CSLI Publications, Stanford, CA, 167–176.

Gentner, D., Markman, A.B., 1993. Analogy – watershed or Waterloo? Structural alignment and the development of connectionist models of cognition. In: Hanson, S.J., Cowan, J.D., Giles, C.L. (Eds.), Advances in Neural Information Processing Systems 5. Kaufmann, San Mateo, CA, pp. 855–862.

Gentner, D., Markman, A.B., 1994. Structural alignment in comparison: no difference without similarity. Psychological Science 5 (3), 152–158.

Gentner, D., Markman, A.B., 1995. Similarity is like analogy: structural alignment in comparison. In: Cacciari, C. (Ed.), Similarity in Language, Thought and Perception. BREPOLS, Brussels, pp. 111–147.

Gentner, D., Markman, A.B., 1997. Structure-mapping in analogy and similarity. American Psychologist 52 (1), 45–56.

Gentner, D., Rattermann, M.J., 1991. Language and the career of similarity. In: Gelman, S.A., Byrnes, J.P. (Eds.), Perspectives on Language and Thought: Interrelations in Development. Cambridge University Press, London, pp. 225–277.

Gentner, D., Rattermann, M.J., Forbus, K.D., 1993. The roles of similarity in transfer: separating retrievability and inferential soundness. Cognitive Psychology 25, 524–575.

Gentner, D., Rattermann, M.J., Markman, A.B., Kotovsky, L., 1995. Two forces in the development of relational similarity. In: Simon, T.J., Halford, G.S. (Eds.), Developing Cognitive Competence: New Approaches to Process Modeling. Erlbaum, Hillsdale, NJ, pp. 263–313.

Gentner, D., Toupin, C., 1986. Systematicity and surface similarity in the development of analogy. Cognitive Science 10, 277–300.

Gentner, D., Wolff, P., 1998. Metaphor and knowledge change. In: Dietrich, E., Markman, A. (Eds.), Cognitive Dynamics: Conceptual Change in Humans and Machines. MIT Press, Cambridge, MA, in press.

Gick, M.L., Holyoak, K.J., 1983. Schema induction and analogical transfer. Cognitive Psychology 15, 1–38.

Goldstone, R.L., 1994a. Similarity, interactive activation, and mapping. Journal of Experimental Psychology: Learning, Memory and Cognition 20(1), 3–28.

Goldstone, R.L., 1994b. The role of similarity in categorization: providing a groundwork. Cognition 52, 125–157.

Goldstone, R.L., Medin, D.L., 1994. Time course of comparison. Journal of Experimental Psychology: Learning, Memory and Cognition 20 (1), 29–50.

Goldstone, R.L., Medin, D., Gentner, D., 1988. Relational similarity and the non-independence of features in similarity judgments. Paper presented at the meeting of the Midwestern Psychological Association, Chicago, IL.

Goodman, N., 1972. Seven strictures on similarity. In: Goodman, N. (Ed.), Problems and Projects. Bobbs-Merrill, New York.

Goswami, U., 1992. Analogical Reasoning in Children. Erlbaum, Hillsdale, NJ.

Halford, G.S., 1987. A structure-mapping approach to cognitive development. International Journal of Psychology 22, 609–642.

Halford, G.S., 1992. Analogical reasoning and conceptual complexity in cognitive development. Human Development 35 (4), 193–218.

Halford, G.S., 1993. Children's Understanding: The Development of Mental Models. Erlbaum, Hillsdale, NJ.

Heit, E., Rubinstein, J., 1994. Similarity and property effects in inductive reasoning. Journal of Experimental Psychology: Learning, Memory and Cognition 20, 411–422.

Holyoak, K.J., Koh, K., 1987. Surface and structural similarity in analogical transfer. Memory and Cognition 15, 332–340.

Holyoak, K.J., Thagard, P., 1989. Analogical mapping by constraint satisfaction. Cognitive Science 13, 295–355.

Holyoak, K.J., Junn, E.N., Billman, D.O., 1984. Development of analogical problem-solving skill. Child Development 55, 2042–2055.

Hummel, J.E., Holyoak, K.J., 1997. Distributed representations of structure: a theory of analogical access and mapping. Psychological Review 104 (3), 427–466.

Imai, M., Gentner, D., Uchida, N., 1994. Children's theories of word meaning: the role of shape similarity in early acquisition. Cognitive Development 9, 45–75.

Inagaki, K., 1989. Developmental shift in biological inference processes: from similarity-based to category-based attribution. Human Development 32, 79–87.

Inagaki, K., 1990. The effects of raising animals on children's biological knowledge. British Journal of Developmental Psychology 8, 119–129.

Inagaki, K., Hatano, G., 1987. Young children's spontaneous personification as analogy. Child Development 58, 1013–1020.

Inagaki, K., Hatano, G., 1991. Constrained person analogy in young children's biological inference. Cognitive Development 6, 219–231.

Karmiloff-Smith, A., 1992. Beyond Modularity: A Developmental Perspective on Cognitive Science. MIT Press, Cambridge, MA.

Kass, A., 1989. Strategies for adapting explanations. Proceedings: Cased-Based Reasoning Workshop. Kaufmann, San Mateo, CA. pp. 119–123.

Keane, M.T., 1988. Analogical Problem Solving. Ellis Horwood, Chichester (Wiley, New York).

Keane, M.T., Brayshaw, M., 1988. The incremental analogical machine: a computational model of analogy. In: Sleeman, D. (Ed.), Third European Working Session on Machine Learning. Kaufmann, San Mateo, CA, pp. 53–62.

Keil, F.C., 1989. Concepts, Kinds, and Cognitive Development. MIT Press, Cambridge, MA.

Klahr, D., 1984. Transition processes in cognitive development. In: Sternberg, R.J. (Ed.), Mechanisms of Cognitive Development. Freeman, New York.

Kotovsky, L., Gentner, D., 1996. Comparison and categorization in the development of relational similarity. Child Development 67, 2797–2822.

Kripke, S., 1982. Wittgenstein on rules and private language. Harvard University Press, Cambridge, MA, p. 59.

Landau, B., Smith, L.B., Jones, S.S., 1988. The importance of shape in early lexical learning. Cognitive Development 3, 299–321.

Lassaline, M.E., 1996. Structural alignment in induction and similarity. Journal of Experimental Psychology: Learning, Memory and Cognition 22, 754–770.

Lopez, A., Atran, S., Coley, J.D., Medin, D.L., Smith, E.E., 1997. The tree of life: universal and cultural features of folkbiological taxonomies and inductions. Cognitive Psychology 32, 251–295.

Lopez, A., Gelman, S.A., Gutheil, G., Smith, E.E., 1992. The development of category-based induction. Child Development 63, 1070–1090.

Mandler, J.M., 1996. Preverbal reppresentation and language. In: Bloom, P., Peterson, M.A., Nadel, L., Garrett, M.F. (Eds.), Language and Space. MIT Press, Cambridge, MA, pp. 365–384.

Mandler, J.M., McDonough, L., 1993. Concept formation in infancy. Cognitive Development 8, 291–318.

Markman, A.B., 1998. Constraints on analogical inference. Cognitive Science, in press.

Markman, A.B., Gentner, D., 1993a. Structural alignment during similarity comparisons. Cognitive Psychology 25, 431–467.

Markman, A.B., Gentner, D., 1993b. Splitting the differences: a structural alignment view of similarity. Journal of Memory and Language 32, 517–535.

Markman, A.B., Gentner, D., 1996. Commonalities and differences in similarity comparisons. Memory and Cognition 24 (2), 235–249.

Markman, E.M., 1989. Categorization in Children: Problems of Induction. MIT Press, Cambridge, MA.

Markman, E.M., Hutchinson, J.E., 1984. Children's sensitivity to constraints on word meaning: taxonomic versus thematic relations. Cognitive Psychology 16, 1–27.

Medin, D.L., Ortony, A., 1989. Psychological essentialism. In: Vosniadou, S., Ortony, A. (Eds.), Similarity and Analogical Reasoning. Cambridge University Press, New York, pp. 179–195.

Medin, D.L., Ross, B.H., 1989. The specific character of abstract thought: categorization, problem-solving, and induction. In: Sternberg, R.J. (Ed.), Advances in the Psychology of Human Intelligence, Vol. 5. Erlbaum, Hillsdale, NJ, pp. 189–223.

Medin, D.L., Goldstone, R.L., Gentner, D., 1993. Respects for similarity. Psychological Review 100 (2), 254–278.

Murphy, G.L., Medin, D.L., 1985. The role of theories in conceptual coherence. Psychological Review 92, 289–316.

Newell, A., Simon, H.A., 1972. Human Problem Solving. Prentice-Hall, Englewood Cliffs, NJ.

Ortony, A., Reynolds, R., Arter, J., 1978. Metaphor: theoretical and empirical research. Psychological Bulletin 85, 919–943.

Osherson, D.N., Smith, E.E., Wilkie, O., Lopez, A., Shafir, E., 1990. Category-based induction. Psychological Review 101, 185–200.

Quine, W.V.O., 1969. Ontological Relativity and Other Essays. Columbia University Press, New York, pp. 167–172.

Piaget, J., 1951. The Child's Conception of Physical Causality. Routledge and Kegan Paul, London.

Ratcliff, R., McKoon, G., 1989. Similarity information versus relational information: differences in the time course of retrieval. Cognitive Psychology 21, 139–155.

Rattermann, M.J., Gentner, D., 1990. The development of similarity use: it's what you know, not how you know it. In: Dinsmore, J., Koschmann, T. (Eds.), Proceedings of the Second Midwest Artificial Intelligence and Cognitive Science Society Conference. MAICSS, Carbondale, IL, pp. 54–59.

Rattermann, M.J., Gentner, D., 1998. More evidence for a relational shift in the development of analogy: Children's performance on a causal-mapping task. Cognitive Development, in press.

Rattermann, M.J., Gentner, D., DeLoache, J., 1987. Young children's use of relational similarity in a transfer task. Poster presented at the biennial meeting of the Society for Research in Child Development, Baltimore, MD.

Reed, S.K., 1987. A structure-mapping model for word problems. Journal of Experimental Psychology: Learning, Memory and Cognition 13, 124–139.

Reeves, L.M., Weisberg, R.W., 1994. The role of content and abstract information in analogical transfer. Psychological Bulletin 115 (3), 381–400.

Rips, L.J., 1989. Similarity, typicality, and categorization. In: Vosniadou, S., Ortony, A. (Eds.), Similarity and Analogical Reasoning. Cambridge University Press, New York, pp. 21–59.

Rips, L.J., 1994. The Psychology of Proof. MIT Press, Cambridge, MA, p. 254.

Ross, B.H., 1987. This is like that: the use of earlier problems and the separation of similarity effects. Journal of Experimental Psychology: Learning, Memory and Cognition 13 (4), 629–639.

Ross, B.H., 1989. Remindings in learning and instruction. In: Vosniadou, S. Ortony, A. (Eds.), Similarity and Analogical Reasoning. Cambridge University Press, New York, pp. 438–469.

Ross, B.H., Kilbane, M.C., 1997. Effects of principle explanation and superficial similarity on analogical mapping in problem solving. Journal of Experimental Psychology: Learning, Memory and Cognition 23, 427–440.

Ross, B.H., Perkins, S.J., Tenpenny, P.L., 1990. Reminding-based category learning. Cognitive Psychology 22, 460–492.

Rovee-Collier, C.K., Fagen, J.W., 1981. The retrieval of memory in early infancy. In: Lipsett, L.P. (Ed.), Advances in Infancy Research, 1. Ablex, Norwood, NJ, pp. 225–254.

Shafir, E.B., Osherson, D.N., Smith, E.E., 1990. Typicality and reasoning fallacies. Memory and Cognition 18 (3), 229–239.

Siegler, R.S., 1989. Mechanisms of cognitive development. Annual Review of Psychology 40, 353–379.

Skorstad, J., Gentner, D., Medin, D., 1988. Abstraction processes during concept learning: a structural view. Proceedings of the Tenth Annual Conference of the Cognitive Science Society, Montreal, Canada. Erlbaum, Hillsdale, NJ, pp. 419–425.

Sloman, S.A., 1993. Feature-based induction. Cognitive Psychology 25, 231–280.

Sloman, S.A., 1996. The empirical case for two systems of reasoning. Psychological Bulletin 119 (1), 3–22.

Smith, E.E., Langston, C., Nisbett, R.E., 1992. The case for rules in reasoning. Cognitive Science 16, 1–40.

Smith, E.E., Sloman, S.A., 1994. Similarity- versus rule-based categorization. Memory and Cognition 22, 337–386.

Smith, E.E., Osherson, D.N., 1989. Similarity and decision making. In: Vosniadou, S., Ortony, A. (Eds.), Similarity and Analogical Reasoning. Cambridge University Press, New York, pp. 60–75.

Smith, L.B., 1984. Young children's understanding of attributes and dimensions: a comparison of conceptual and linguistic measures. Child Development 55, 363–380.

Smith, L.B., 1989. From global similarities to kinds of similarities: the construction of dimensions in development. In: Vosniadou, S., Ortony, A. (Eds.), Similarity and Analogical Reasoning. Cambridge University Press, New York, pp. 146–178.

Smith, L.B., 1993. The concept of same. In: Reese, H.W. (Ed.), Advances in Child Development and Behavior, Vol. 24. Academic Press, San Diego, CA, pp. 215–252.

Smith, L.B., Kemler, D.G., 1977. Developmental trends in free classification: evidence for a new conceptualization of perceptual development. Journal of Experimental Child Psychology 24, 279–298.

Smith, L.B., Sera, M.D., 1992. A developmental analysis of the polar structure of dimensions. Cognitive Psychology 24, 99–142.

Smolensky, P., 1988. On the proper treatment of connectionism. Behavioral and Brain Sciences 11 (1), 1–74.

Spelke, E.S., 1988. Where perceiving ends and thinking begins: the apprehension of objects in infancy. In: Yonas, A. (Ed.), Perceptual Development in Infancy: Minnesota Symposia on Child Psychology 20. Erlbaum, Hillsdale, NJ, pp. 197–234.

Spelke, E.S., 1990. Principles of object perception. Cognitive Science 14, 29–56.

Tversky, A., Kahneman, D., 1983. Extensional versus intuitive reasoning: the conjunction fallacy in probability judgment. Psychological Review 90 (4), 293–315.

Vosniadou, S., 1987. Children and metaphors. Child Development 58, 870–885.

Vygotsky, L., 1962. Thought and Language. MIT Press, Cambridge, MA. (Original work published 1934.).

Vygotsky, L.S., 1987. Thinking and speech. In: Riever, R.W. Carton, A.S. (Eds.), The Collected Works of L.S. Vygotsky. Plenum, New York.

Waxman, S.R., Gelman, R., 1986. Preschoolers' use of superordinate relations in classification and language. Cognitive Development 1, 139–156.

Waxman, S.R., Markow, D.B., 1995. Words as invitations to form categories: evidence from 12- to 13-month-old infants. Cognitive Psychology 29, 257–302.

Williams, M., 1994. The significance of learning in Wittgenstein's later philosophy. Canadian Journal of Philosophy 14 (2), 173–204.

Winston, P.H., 1982. Learning new principles from precedents and exercises. Artificial Intelligence 19, 321–350.

Wittgenstein, L., 1953. Philosophical Investigations. Blackwell, Oxford, UK, pp. 85ff, 185ff.

Xu, F., Carey, S., 1996. Infants' metaphysics: the case of numerical identity. Cognitive Psychology 30, 111–153.

Index

Abstractions
  applications, 158
  blurring, 163
  filtering, 163
  matching, 121–123
  perception, 157–159
  plausible, 132
  relative, 116
  representation, 121–123
  similarity, 158, 179
Adaptive resonance theory, 28
Additive rule, representation matching, 122
Agnosia. *See also* Brain damage, selective
  deficits
  visual, 164
Alignment, progressive, 186
Alzheimer's disease, lexical processing, 99
Amodal symbols, 148, 170
Analogical systems
  abstract properties, 152
  freeloading, 151–153
  inference projection, 196
Analogy, 180
  alignment, 12
  children, 196
  comparison, 12
  metaphor, 11
Animal story, causal potency, 36
Argumentation, rule-based, 12
Artifacts
  adult concepts, 54
  categories, 69, 71
  terminology, 54
Artificial categories
  Allen-Brooks experiment, 86–88
  basic mechanisms, 86
  cognitive studies, 86–91
  exemplar similarity, 86

neuroimaging, 105
  rule application, 86–91
  triggering conditions, 89
Artificial grammar learning, 131
Artificial intelligence (AI)
  hybrid systems, 138
  rule-based processing, 135
  rules vs. similarity, 7, 112
Associated property, 66
Associations
  children, 29–32
  developmental trends, 33
  empiricist model, 44
  non-categorical, 65
Associative learning, 22
Attention. *See* Selective attention
Attributes
  categorization, 52
  weighting, 84–86
Availability heuristic, 9

Back-propagation networks, 114, 119
Barsalou, Lawrence W., 145
Behavior, rule-following, 117
Binding, perceptual, 164
Biological categories
  differences, 69, 71
  perception, 157
Biology, inductive inference, 194
Blurring, perception and conception, 163
Brain, activation areas, 102–105
Brain damage, selective deficits, 97, 106
Breakdown patterns, neuropsychology, 133

Candidate inferences, structure-mapping,
  182
Categorization
  alternative strategies, 81–83

analysis, 60–65
artificial, 86–91
bimodal distributions, 58
children, 93
coverage and generation, 195
developmental, 55
discourse context, 73
explicit and implicit, 107
fixed and variable, 56
fuzziness, 51–59
judgments, 67
mechanisms, 92–96
metamorphosis study, 57, 59
metaphor, 12
monotonicity, 58, 73
multiple procedures, 56, 82
neuroimaging data, 11
overlapping, 59
PET studies, 99–106
predicted probability, 64
probabilistic, 18
procedures, 83
prototype theory, 52
psychology, 81
regression model, 67
residual variance, 63–65
rule-based, 53, 99–105
rules vs. similarity, 19, 23–29
scatterplots, 60, 78
semantic, 69
similarity-based, 10, 23, 51, 99
task vagueness, 73
theories and prototypes, 72
threshold function, 61
types, 11
unitary views, 82
Causality
  covariation models, 23
  differential knowledge, 42
  domain-specific, 25–28
  theories, 20
Causal potency
  case study, 35–40
  children, 34
  properties, 34
  response patterns, 39

Cerebellum, rules and memory, 103–105
Child development
  common systems, 185–187
  comparison process, 188–194
  learning, 184–194
  trends, 33
Children
  associative learning, 29–32
  case study, 35–40
  conceptual theory, 29–32
Classification. *See also* Categorization
  context theory, 10, 24
  distinguishability, 126
  gradedness, 125
  procedures, 83
  rigidity, 125
  rule-based, 58, 72
  similarity, 53, 58
Cognition. *See also* Knowledge; Perception
  abstract, 204
  artificial categories, 86–91
  development, 204
  inference rules, 118
  modus ponens, 118
  processing, 5
  property-based, 5
  rule complexity, 130
  rules vs. similarity, 111–113
Cognitive science, empiricism, 44
Common systems, highlighting, 185–187
Comparison. *See also* Similarity
  category abstraction, 189–191
  child development, 188–194
  inference projection, 192–194
  interrelated knowledge, 184, 194
  learning, 184–194
  representation, 188
  structure-sensitive, 179
  two-system, 202
Compositionality, rule-based systems, 6
Conception
  agnostic view, 150
  blurring, 163
  cross-modal matching, 166
  differentiation, 165
  dimensions, 165

eliminative view, 148–150
empiricist dogmas, 17
filtering, 163
perception, 145–147
productivity, 167
rules vs. similarity, 147
selectivity, 161–163
subcategories, 165
theories, 146
Concepts
adult learning, 24
central components, 17
children, 29–32
fuzziness, 51–59
hybrid models, 20–23
kinship terms, 54
natural kinds, 20–23
Roschean view, 18
similarity, 18, 57
theories and prototypes, 55, 72
Conditional probability, 8
Conditional sentences, rule priming, 130
Connectionist networks, 114, 122
Constructivism, Piagetian, 178
Continuum, perception and conception, 168
Contrasting categories, 66–68
differences, 70
membership, 64
Corrected typicality, 61
Critical instances, classification, 129
Cross-mapping, difficulty, 183
Cross-modal matching, 166

Decision-making models, 12
Deductive inference, rule-based, 8
Deductive reasoning, 125
Democritus, 147
Diagnosticity, Tversky principle, 74
Differential knowledge, 42
Differentiation, child development, 166
Dimensionalization, 166
Discriminative stimulus, 28
Distinguishability, class and specific, 126
Dogmas, conceptual empiricism, 17
Domain-specific causality, 25–28
Dynamical similarity, 7

Dyslexia, phonological, 133

Empiricism, cognitive science, 44
Error patterns, neuropsychology, 133
Exemplar similarity
artificial categories, 86–91
basic mechanisms, 86–88
brain damage, 97
cognitive studies, 86–96
component distinctions, 84–86
dissociations, 90
implications, 91
neuroimaging data, 97–105
PET studies, 99–105
rule application, 83–86
schematic model, 93
triggering conditions, 89
Experience, knowledge revision, 137
Experiential learning, 199
Experimental psychology, 2
Explanation
categorization, 23–29
children, 34
concepts, 18
Explicit concepts, kinship terms, 54
Extensional reasoning, 58
Extrapolation, generalization patterns, 131

Familiarity, 64
Feature frequencies, 30
Feeble similarity, 5
Field dependence, 163
Filtering, perception and conception, 163
Fixed categorization, 56
Framework theories, 20
Freeloading, analogical systems, 151–153
Free sorting, 90
Frontal lobes, rule application, 98
Function learning, 131
Fuzziness, natural categories, 51–59

Generalization
extrapolation, 131
patterns, 131–133
rules vs. similarity, 112
transfer and reversal, 131

Generalized context model (GCM), 24
Gentner, Dedre, 177
Goldstone, Robert L., 145
Graded classification, 125

Hampton, James A., 51
Heuristics, reasoning, 9
Hybrid models, concepts, 20–23

Imaginary animals experiment, 86–88
Inclusion fallacy, 197
Inductive inference
  adults, 197–199
  children, 194, 196
  symbolic juxtaposition, 195
  theories, 9
  weak vs. strong, 197–199
Infants
  causal relations, 30
  feature patterns, 32
Inference. *See also* Inductive inference
  analogical projection, 196
  comparison process, 192–194
  deductive, 8
  mental models, 6
  reasoning, 73
  rule-based, 1–3
Instances, effects, 128
Instance-space, manipulations, 129
Instructions, rule application, 91
Intensional categorization, 52
Intuitive reasoning, 59
Isotropy, common-sense knowledge, 135

Jonides, John, 81
Judgments
  analytic vs. holistic, 154
  similarity, 4, 12

Kant, Immanuel, 148
Keil, Frank C., 17
Kind world hypothesis, 200
Kinship terms, explicit concepts, 54
Knowledge. *See also* Learning
  application, 194
  common-sense, 135

comparison, 194
developmental, 33
differential, 42
extension, 194
hybrid models, 17
instance-based, 30
partial theories, 136
perception and conception, 148–150
revision, 137
structure, 17

Language
  cognitive development, 204
  processing, 112
Learned response, reversal, 132
Learning. *See also* Knowledge
  associative, 22, 25
  behaviorist theories, 112
  categorization, 189–191
  child development, 184–194
  common systems, 185–187
  comparison, 184–194
  domain system, 45
  experiential, 199
  explanation, 25
  function, 131
  Mandler schema, 45
  perception, 18, 155, 188
  representation, 188
  similarity-based, 18, 178
  structure-mapping, 184
  symbolic juxtaposition, 188
  theory, 28
Levin, Daniel T., 17
Lexical processing, 98
Linguistics. *See also* Language
  rule-based, 6
  rules vs. similarity, 112
Literal similarity, 180, 183
Literal statements, 11
Locke, John, 149
Logical rules, 6

McNemar test, causal potency, 38
Mapping tasks, 192. *See also* Structure-
  mapping

Medicine, causal theories, 25
Medina, José, 177
Membership, contrasting categories, 64, 66
Memory
  automatic retrieval, 89
  cerebellum, 103–105
  dissociations, 90
  failure, 133
  familiarity, 89
  hippocampus, 97
  PET studies, 99–105
Metaphor. *See also* Structure-mapping
  analogy, 11
  categorization, 12
  salience imbalance, 11
Monotonicity, 58
  categorization, 73–75
  child development, 193
  developmental, 185
Motherhood, prototype concept, 54n
Motion, perception, 157
Multiple procedures, categorization, 82

Naming tasks, 191
Natural categories
  cognitive studies, 92–97
  exemplar similarity, 92–97
  fuzziness, 51–59
  prototype theory, 53
  rule application, 92–97
  structure, 71
Natural kinds
  adult concepts, 20, 54
  categorization, 22
  child concepts, 30
  hybrid models, 20–23
  Quinean model, 10
Natural science, 20
Negative priming, 163
Neural networks
  behavior models, 28
  differentiation, 166
  rule application, 98
Neuroimaging, rules vs. similarity, 97–105
Neuropsychology
  dissociations, 90

error and breakdown, 133
  rules vs. similarity, 97–105
Newborns, imitative ability, 44
No-similarity concept, 5
Notions, child responses, 41

Objects
  attributes, 52
  recognition, 165
  similarity, 180, 183
Old-new recognition, 128
Outliers, residual variance, 62, 71
Overall similarity, 183
  categorization, 154
  perceptual systems, 154
  primitive appeal, 153–155
Over-regularization, 134

Parallel connectivity, structure-mapping,
  181
Parkinson's disease, lexical processing, 99
Patalano, Andrea L., 81
Perception. *See also* Conception
  abstractions, 157–159
  agnostic view, 150
  analogical systems, 151–153
  associative learning, 157
  blurring, 163
  children, 32
  cross-modal matching, 166
  differentiation, 165
  dimensions, 165
  eliminative view, 148–150
  filtering, 163
  freeloading, 151–153
  Gibsonian view, 44
  knowledge, 148–150
  learning, 155–157
  many roles, 150
  productivity, 167
  rules vs. similarity, 147
  selectivity, 161–163
  similarity, 13, 32, 147, 153, 180
  stimulation, 159
  structure and binding, 164
  subcategories, 165

symbol systems, 149
theories, 146
Wu's experiments, 159
Philosophy, 20
  perception and conception, 147
  rules vs. similarity, 112, 113n
Phonological dyslexia, 133
Physics, causal theories, 26
Piaget, Jean, 178
Pictures, rapid identification, 29
Positron emission tomography (PET), 99–105
Prefrontal cortex, rules and memory, 104
Premise diversity, 195
Preschool children, conceptual theory, 30
Priming
  negative, 163
  rule, 129
Primitive features, associative learning, 22
Prior instances, selectivity, 199
Problem-solving, causal theory, 26
Procedures
  categorization, 83
  multiple, 82
  vs. strategies, 82n
  types, 83
Processing
  analytic vs. holistic, 84, 107
  blurring, 163
  cognitive, 161
  cross-modal matching, 166
  differentiation, 165
  dimensions, 165
  filtering, 163
  perceptual, 160
  productivity, 167
  rule-based, 111, 180
  selectivity, 161–163
  serial vs. parallel, 84–86
  similarity-based, 111, 179
  strategic vs. automatic, 85
  structure and binding, 164
  subcategories, 165
Production rules, 7
Productivity
  perception and conception, 167

rule-based systems, 6
Progressive alignment, 186
Projecting inferences, 184
Properties
  causal potency, 34–40
  part or associated, 66
Prototype similarity, categorization, 106
Psychological disorders, 29
Psychology
  categorization, 81
  experimental, 2
  perception and conception, 147
  rules vs. similarity, 112

Reading rules, 133
Real world concepts, categorization, 24–29
Reasoning. *See also* Inference
  associative, 202
  categorization, 88
  comparison-based, 203
  deductive, 125
  extensional, 58
  heuristics, 9
  inductive, 9
  inferential, 73
  instance-based, 123, 128
  intuitive, 59
  rules vs. similarity, 8, 112
  similarity-based, 58, 123, 136
  symbolic, 202
Recognition, old-new, 128
Relational language, 192
Relations, connected systems, 181
Reminding tasks, 200
Representation matching
  abstraction, 121–123
  ideal abstraction, 122n
  partial and strict, 120–123
  rules vs. similarity, 117–121
  space of possibilities, 117
Representations
  abstract vs. concrete, 125
  learning, 188
  perception, 151
  redescription, 189
  rules vs. similarity, 117, 119

structured, 124
types, 115
Representativeness, decision-making, 12
Residual variance, categorization, 63–65
Response
  child, 39
  learned, 132
  patterns, 39
Reversal, generalization, 132
Rigid classification, 125
Rips, Lance J., 1, 56
Rule application
  artificial studies, 86–91
  basic mechanisms, 86–88
  cognitive studies, 86–96
  component distinctions, 84–86
  dissociations, 90
  exemplar similarity, 83–86
  implications, 91
  natural categories, 92–97
  neural circuits, 98
  neuroimaging data, 97–105
  PET studies, 99–105
  schematic model, 84, 92
  triggering conditions, 89
  verbal materials, 97
Rule-based systems
  categorization, 99–105
  compositionality, 8
  inference, 1–3
  productivity, 6
  systematicity, 6
Rules
  active interplay, 138
  categorization, 23–25
  cerebellar memory, 103–105
  cognitive process, 111–113
  compositionality, 6
  computational studies, 7, 124, 134
  development, 177–181
  distinguishability, 126
  dual route, 133
  empirical research, 111–113, 126–136
  error and breakdown, 133
  explanations, 23–29
  explicit, 13

following, 118
forms and types, 5
generalization, 131–133
integrating, 137
logical, 6
over-regularization, 134
plausibility, 135
possible theories, 135
priming and complexity, 129
problem, 113
psychology, 4
qualifying, 5
reasoning, 8
representation matching, 117–121
separate systems, 202
serial vs. parallel, 124
Shanks definition, 132
similarity alternative, 5–7
symbolic vs. connectionist, 124
terminology, 179–181
thinking, 3
universal, 115n
verbal protocols, 130
Russell, Bertrand, 148

Salience imbalance, metaphor, 11
Scenes, encoding steps, 29
Schizophrenia, attention deficits, 162
Scholastic Aptitude Test (SAT), 26
Science, philosophy, 20
Selective attention, 24, 149, 162
Selectivity, perceptual and conceptual, 161–
  163
Set theory, Frege's formalization, 135n
Shift, characteristic to defining, 33
Similarity. *See also* Exemplar similarity
  analysis, 60–65
  animal sense, 11
  arguments against, 201
  behaviorist theories, 178
  categorization, 10, 23, 51, 99
  child development, 183
  choice, 12
  classes, 180
  cognitive process, 111–113
  computational considerations, 7, 124, 134

databases, 21
developmental theories, 183
distinguishability, 126
dynamical systems, 7
empirical research, 111–113, 126–136
existential, 115n
explanation, 1–3
feeble, 5
inductive inference, 195
inner product, 119n
instances, 128
integrating, 137
judgments, 4, 12
literal and object, 180
mimicry argument, 114
monotonicity, 58
neuroimaging data, 97–105
overall, 153–155
perception, 13, 32, 55, 147, 153, 180
plausibility, 135
possible theories, 135
primitive appeal, 153–155
problems, 2, 113
prototype, 106
psychology, 4
reasoning, 8, 136
representation matching, 117–121
rule development, 177–181
rules alternative, 6
separate systems, 202
serial vs. parallel, 124
superficial, 64, 72
terminology, 179–181
theory-neutral, 21
thinking, 1–3
types, 4
weak vs. strong, 4
Wittgenstein's argument, 202
Simons, Daniel J., 17
Sloman, Steven A., 1
Smith, Edward E., 81
Smith, W. Carter, 17
Social formation, Vygotsky's theory, 178
Species, childhood concepts, 55n
Strategy vs. procedure, 82n
Strong similarity, 4, 197

Structure-mapping, 181–183
candidate inference, 182
engine model, 182
metaphor, 11
one-to-one correspondence, 181
parallel connectivity, 181, 182
psychology, 182
terminology, 180
Subjective probability, 12
Superficial similarity, 64, 72
Surface features, problem-solving, 27
Surface similarity, 180
Symbol systems
amodal, 148, 170
conception, 170
inference, 151, 195
Lenat's project, 151
perception, 149
Symmetry, developmental, 185
Synesthesia, 167
Syntactic priming, 130
Systematicity
analogy and similarity, 181
developmental, 184
rule-based systems, 6

Tabulation space, knowledge models, 22
Thalamus, rules and memory, 104
Theory-neutral similarity, 21
Thinking. *See also* Cognition; Perception
rules, 2–4
similarity, 1–3
studies, 8–12
Thought. *See also* Conception
abstract, 178
conception, 145
hybrid models, 17
patterns, 29
perception, 145
processes, 18
Tienson's experiment, 3
Threshold function, categorization, 60–63
Tienson's thought experiment, 3
Topic, metaphor, 11
Transfer, generalization, 131
Tversky diagnosticity principle, 74

Typicality
  boosting ratings, 64, 74
  categorization, 53, 62, 73
  causal mechanisms, 43
  corrected, 61
  familiarity, 64
  feature, 21
  threshold function, 61

Variable categorization, 56
Vehicle, metaphor, 11
Verbal rules, 97, 130
Visual cortex, rules and memory, 103–105
Vygotsky's theory, social formation, 178

Weak inference, 197–199
Weak similarity, 4
Wisconsin Card Sort Test, 98
Wittgenstein's similarity argument, 202
Words
  concepts, 33
  Stroop effects, 29
Working memory, 84–86